Advanced programming in
VBA-Excel
for beginners

With examples of DLL libraries
and Add-Ins in Visual Basic **.NET**

Dorian Oria San Martín

Proofreader: Andrés Felipe Rojas Nariño

Design and layout:
Dorian Oria San Martín
dorian.oria@gmail.com

Contents

Dedication

I dedicate this book to all those who every day go to sleep with a clear conscience for having given of themselves the best possible.

OM NAMAHA SHIVAYA

Thanks

This book was in plans for more than a year and could have taken longer.

I owe my friend **Andrés Felipe Rojas Nariño** that the book is ready.

A lot of gratitude to him.

Some time ago, a friend told me that there is no work that is original to us.

We are only co-authors. The author of all work is the **Great Creator** and we only have the fortune of having been chosen to manifest the unmanifest.

So: Thank you **Father** for trusting me.

Chapter 1. What is VBA?

1.1 Introduction

VBA stands for Visual Basic for Applications and it is a language developed by Microsoft to program applications for Word, Access, Excel or Powerpoint. Even though it is based on Visual Basic, it is not capable of making executable programs independent of the Office application in which the program is being made. It's like a more simplified version of Visual Basic, but no less powerful.

In this book we are going to work with VBA for Excel. In this case, VBA allows controlling all the objects that make up Excel, its properties, methods and events. This in turn allows these objects to be used to make powerful applications.

All the code and subroutines in this book can be found at: http://infiniterand.com/es/ and https://goo.gl/dhBpDW

1.2 Programming environment

To do this, Excel provides us with an IDE (Integrated Development Environment) with all the tools we need to make an application. In figure 1.1 we can see what the VBA Excel IDE looks like.

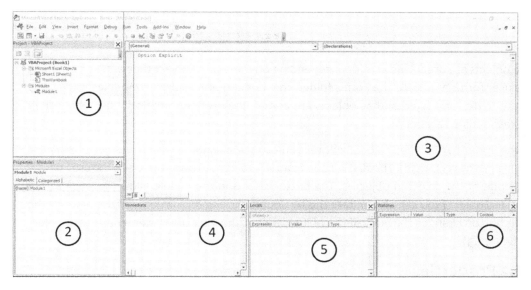

Figure 1.1. Integrated development environment.

Next, we will give a description of each one of the windows.

1.2.1 Project Explorer

Window 1 (shown in figure 1.2) is the Project Explorer and shows the open projects (in this case VBAExcel.xlsm) and the objects it contains. These objects can be spreadsheets (worksheets), the book itself (workbook), modules and user forms.

Figure 1.2. Project Explorer window.

The objects are organized in folders depending on the type of object they are. For example, the user forms are inside the Forms folder, the modules are inside the Modules folder, etc. These folders are fixed and as objects are added, they will automatically fall within their corresponding category.

In the upper part of the Project Explorer you can see a window with three buttons (figure 1.2, inside the rectangle). The first button from left to right allows you to see the area where the code of the selected object is. The button that is in the middle allows you to see the selected object (you can also imitate this by double clicking on the name of the object). The right button changes the view of the objects by not showing the folder where each object is (figure 1.3).

1.2.2 Properties

Window 2 (figure 1.4) shows the properties of the object that has been selected in the

Project Explorer window. In the case of figure 1.4, the properties of the spreadsheet selected in figure 1.2 are being shown.

Figure 1.3. Project Explorer window without showing folders.

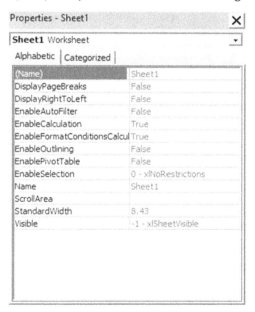

Figure 1.4. Properties Window.

1.2.3 Window Code

Window 3 (figure 1.5) allows you to write code for each one of the objects contained in the Project Explorer (figure 1.2). You can have as many windows open as you want, so that you can see the code of several objects at the same time. You can copy and paste code between different windows.

To see the code window, just double click on the object shown in the Project Explorer. For example, figure 1.5 shows the code window of the worksheet object selected in figure 1.2.

Figure 1.5. Code window.

At the top of the window there are two drop-down lists. The one on the left corresponds to the box of the objects, that is, where the object associated with the selection made is displayed. On the right side, a list of events and procedures related to the selected object is displayed.

In the case of having selected the worksheet object, the method that is inserted by default in the code window is Worksheet_SelectionChange. You can display the list to see the other available events, as shown in figure 1.6.

Imagine for a moment that in the Module 1 object (figure 1.2) we have two subroutines called modulo1 and modulo2.

If we have more than one subroutine, these can be seen in the upper list on the right, as shown in figure 1.7. In figure 1.7 we only can see one subroutine because we have the option "Procedure View" selected (indicated by the arrow).

Figure 1.6. Code window showing available events for the Worksheet object.

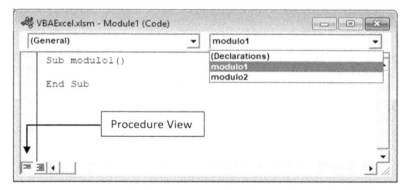

Figure 1.7. Code window with the option "Procedure View" activated.

If we press the button "Full Module View", then the code window will look like its shown in figure 1.8.

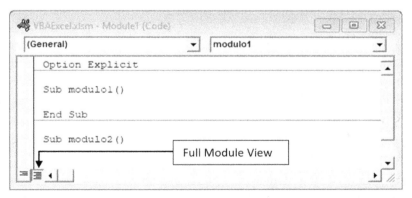

Figure 1.8. Code window with the option "Full Module View" activated.

1.2.4 Window Immediate

Window 4 (figure 1.1) is called Immediate. In this window you can write or paste a line of code to be executed after pressing Enter. The reverse operation can also be done, but what is written in the Immediate window is not saved there. Let's see an example of how it works. Insert the code shown in figure 1.9, into the Module 1 object.

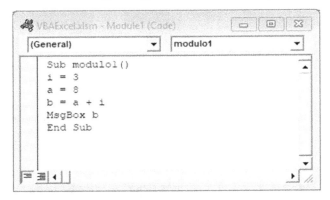

Figure 1.9. Sample code for Immediate window.

Copy lines 3 and 4 to the Immediate window, as shown in figure 1.10.

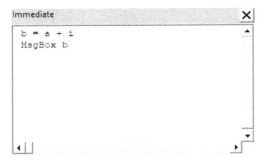

Figure 1.10. Excerpt from the code shown in figure 1.9.

Now, let's go back to the code window and execute the subroutine, step by step, using the F8 key. When you press this key while the cursor is in the space of a subroutine, it is executed, and its name is highlighted in yellow as shown in figure 1.11. As we press the F8 key, the subroutine is executed line by line.

Press the F8 key until the fourth line is highlighted (b = a + i). When we stop there, the instructions for assigning values to the variables i (i = 3) and a (a = 8) have already been executed. Let's stop here for a moment and go to the Immediate window. Put the cursor somewhere on the first line and press Enter. By doing this, the instruction of that line is executed. Pressing Enter again executes the instruction of the second line. After this, the window shown in figure 1.12, product of the *MsgBox* instruction, will appear.

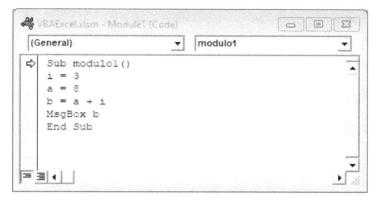

Figure 1.11. Step-by-step execution of a subroutine.

Figure 1.12. MsgBox window, shown from the Immediate window.

The idea of the Immediate window is to test code before it runs in the code window or just try other operations. For example, it is possible, when the line is highlighted or before being highlighted, to put it as a comment so that it does not run (this is done by placing the character '(single quote) at the beginning of the line, as shown in figure 1.13.

While a line is highlighted in yellow, it has not been executed. Note that in this case, with the yellow line highlighted, we added the character (') and the line was no longer highlighted. As the line is now commented, it will not be executed, moving to the next line that is not commented.

Now, after the commented line, let's experiment adding the line:

b=i-a

Figure 1.14 shows what the code looks like now.

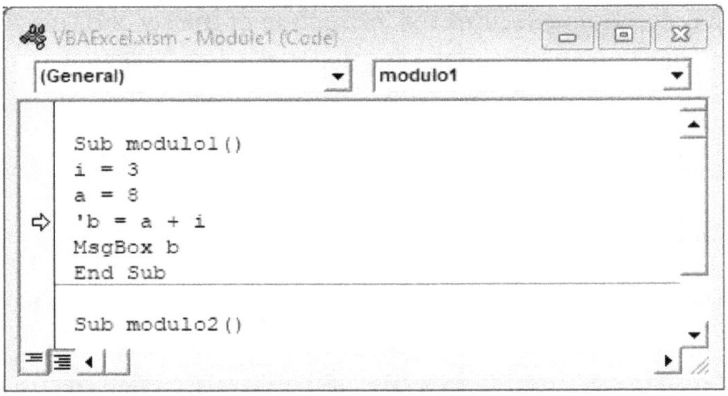

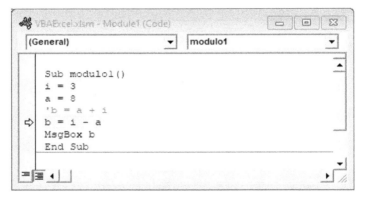

Figure 1.13. Commenting on a line of code.

Figure 1.14. Code after adding the new instruction.

Note that we now have a different expression than the one in the Immediate window (figure 1.10). If we continue executing the code when pressing F8, the result of course will now be different.

Then, we see how with the Immediate window we can execute several lines, not necessarily contained in the code window. What is important in this case is to take into account that if the instructions that are in the Immediate window are executed first, then the window that will be seen as a message will be the one shown in figure 1.15.

Figure 1.15. Result of the execution of the instructions of the Immediate window.

This happens because at no time, neither executing the code of the code window nor in the Immediate window, values have been assigned to the variables "i" and "a". If you want to give values to the variables "i" and "a" in the Immediate window, you must add those lines to the beginning of the Immediate window or you must have executed the subroutine step by step until you assign values to the variables "a" and " i ". To do this, you must place the cursor at the beginning of the line you want to scroll down and press *Ctrl + Enter*. This must be done as many times as how many lines you wish to add. Figure 1.16 shows how the Immediate window looks after adding the two instructions to assign values to "i" and "a".

```
Immediate                                              X
    i=3
    a=8
    b = a + i
    MsgBox b
```

Figure 1.16. Immediate Window after adding value assignment to the variables "a" and "i".

The code in the Immediate window will be executed from the line where the cursor is located. In our case, we must place the cursor on the first line and press Enter so that the instruction of each line can be executed.

The Immediate window can also be used to display information resulting from the execution of code, as if it were a Command Prompt window. For this, the **Debug.Print** instruction is used. Observe and execute on your own the code shown below.

Subroutine 1.1.

1	Sub UsoInmediato()
2	Debug.Print " Example about how information can be sent to the Immediate window "
3	End Sub

1.2.5 Window Locals

Let's look at window 5 (figure 1.1). This window is called Locals (figure 1.17). In this window, all the variables of the subroutine that is being executed and their values are automatically displayed.

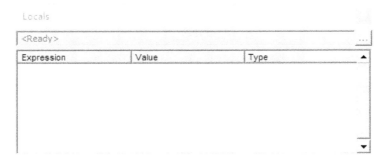

Figure 1.17. Window Locals.

In order to see the variables and their values, it is necessary to execute the instructions one by one (step by step by instructions or F8) or by adding a breakpoint in some line of the code, so that the execution stops there. Adding a breakpoint can be done in four ways:

1. Right clicking on the line where you want the execution to stop. By doing this you will see a window like the one shown in figure 1.18.

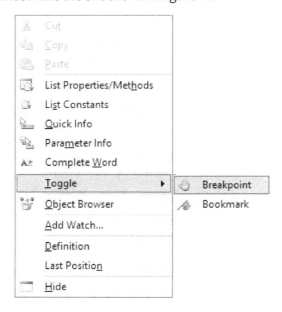

Figure 1.18. Option 1 to add breakpoint.

2. Clicking with the left mouse button on the bar to the left of the code (enclosed in rectangle, figure 1.19) next to the line where you want to stop the execution.

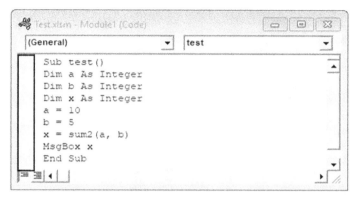

Figure 1.19. Option 2 to add interruption point.

3. Go to Debug and select the corresponding option, as can be seen in figure 1.20.

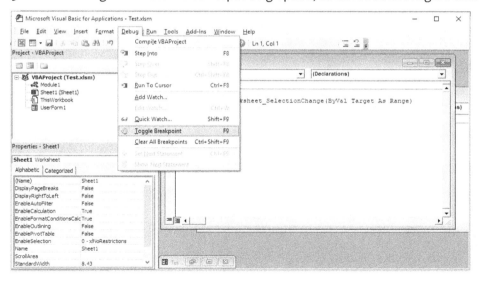

Figure 1.20. Option 3 to add breakpoint.

4. Positioning the cursor on the line where you want to add the breakpoint and pressing the F9 key.

For all of the above ways explained, the point of interruption will be seen as shown in figure 1.21.

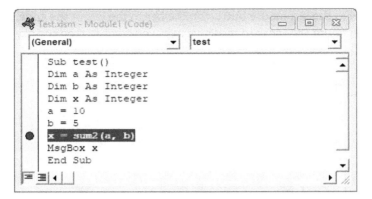

Figure 1.21. View of the breakpoint.

If the code of the test subroutine is then executed (by pressing F5), the code will be executed up to the line where the breakpoint has been entered (figure 1.22).

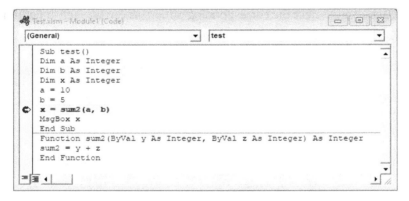

Figure 1.22. Execution of subroutine test to the breakpoint.

In the example shown in figure 1.22, note how the breakpoint has been placed on a line where a function is invoked. For now, we will not go into detail about this.

Now, going back to the window Locals, it will look as shown in figure 1.23.

As you can see, the program will run to the last line just before the breakpoint. That is why, as shown in figure 1.23, the variable "x" still has no value since that instruction has not yet been executed. If you continue from now on with the execution of the program step-by-step (F8), you can see how the instructions that are inside the function being invoked will be executed, in this case, the sum function (figure 1.24).

Locals

VBAProject.Module1.test			...
Expression	**Value**	**Type**	▲
⊞ Module1		Module1/Module1	
a	10	Integer	
b	5	Integer	
x	0	Integer	
			▼

Figure 1.23. Window Local showing the values of the variables used in the subroutine test.

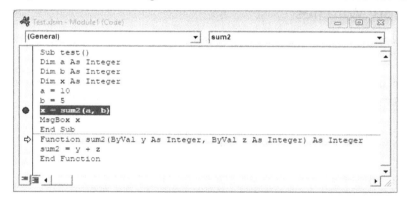

Figure 1.24. Execution of the function sum2.

Now that the instructions of the function sum2 are going to be executed, let's go back to the window Locals for a moment. If you press the button shown enclosed in a black square in figure 1.23, it will bring up the window shown in figure 1.25. This window is called Call Stack and it is useful to see all the functions or subroutines that are being executed. The function shown in the top is called by the one below (in this case by the test subroutine).

Another way to execute code up to a certain point is the "Run to cursor" function, which can be activated with the key combination Ctrl + F8. As the function name implies, it executes the program up to the line where the cursor is. A difference with respect to interruptions is that they can be added as many as desired, while the execution to the cursor can be added only once and if you want to use it again, you must place the cursor on each line where you want to stop the execution.

If several breakpoints have been added and you want to delete all of them, you can do it by pressing the key combination Ctrl + Shift + F9.

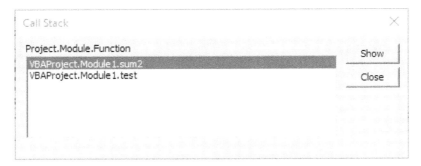

Figure 1.25. Call Stack.

1.2.6 Window Watches

Let's now look at the window Watches (window 6 in figure 1.1). This window can be seen in figure 1.26.

This window allows us to evaluate an expression that is not necessarily declared or is part of the code that is running. For example, let's look at the code in figure 1.27.

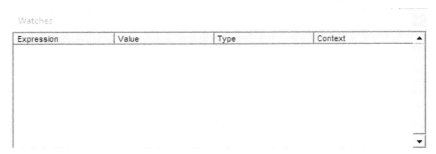

Figure 1.26. Window Watches.

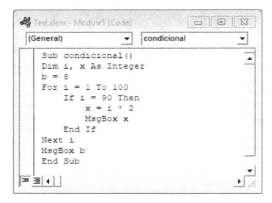

Figure 1.27. Subroutine conditional.

Now, let's add a watch that will be displayed in the window Watches (figure 1.26). To do this, you can click with the right mouse button inside the window and a menu of options like the one shown in figure 1.28 appears. Another way to achieve this is by doing a similar process with the mouse, but this time in the line where we want to add the watch (inside the code window). When doing so in this space, the options menu shown in figure 1.29 appear.

Figure 1.28. Adding a watch from the window Watches.

With any of the options explained above, a window like the one shown in figure 1.30 will appear. In this window we have added the expression sqr(i), which means square root of "i".

Once this expression is accepted, the window Watches will look as shown in figure 1.31.

To see how the value of the variable "i" changes in the window Watches, try running the code step by step (F8).

After several runs, the window Watches will look similar to the one shown in figure 1.32.

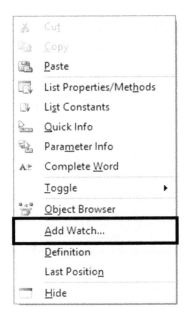

Figure 1.29. Adding a watch from the code window.

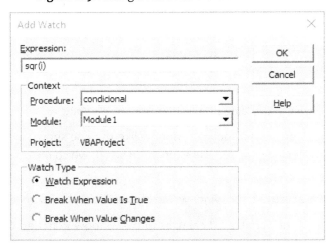

Figure 1.30. Window to add watch.

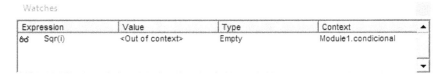

Figure 1.31. Window Watches after adding a watch.

Watches

Expression	Value	Type	Context
66 Sqr(i)	2.23606797749979	Double	Module1.condicional

Figure 1.32. Window Watches showing the value of "i" after several iterations.

While the execution is being done in this way (step by step or with interruption point) you have the opportunity to make changes in the value of variables in the code. For example, at this time let's try changing the value of the variable "b" to 7. This can be done by dragging the variable "b" of the code to the Inspections window. By doing this, the last value assigned to that variable will appear in the window, which for the purposes of our code it was made on line 3 (b = 8). When doing so, the Inspections window will look as shown in figure 1.33.

Watches

Expression	Value	Type	Context
66 Sqr(i)	2.23606797749979	Double	Module1.condicional
66 b	8	Variant/Integer	Module1.condicional

Figure 1.33. Window Watches showing the value of "b".

At this time, you can decide to change the value of the variable "b", let's suppose to 7. For that, click on the number 8 and edit the value. If we now execute the rest of the complete code (F5), it will be shown that now the value of the variable "b" is the new value that we gave it, as shown in figure 1.34.

Microsoft Excel   X

7

Aceptar

Figure 1.34. Value of the variable "b" after having been changed.

If you want to modify the watch, click with the right mouse button inside the window

Watches and a menu like the one shown in figure 1.35 will appear.

Cut
Copy
Paste
Edit Watch...
Add Watch...
Delete Watch
Collapse Parent
Run Macro
Reset
Definition
Dockable
Hide

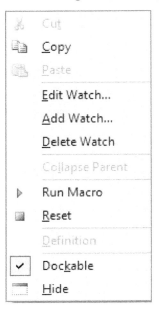

Figure 1.35. Window where the option to modify the watch (Edit Watch) is offered, add a new one or delete one.

Something worth noting is that in the code window while the instructions are executed, it is possible to see the values that the variables are taking just by putting the mouse over the variable. For this, the execution of the code has to be stopped, either by running step by step or by an interruption. For example, when placing the mouse over the variable "i", a very small window appears, showing the value that it currently has (figure 1.36).

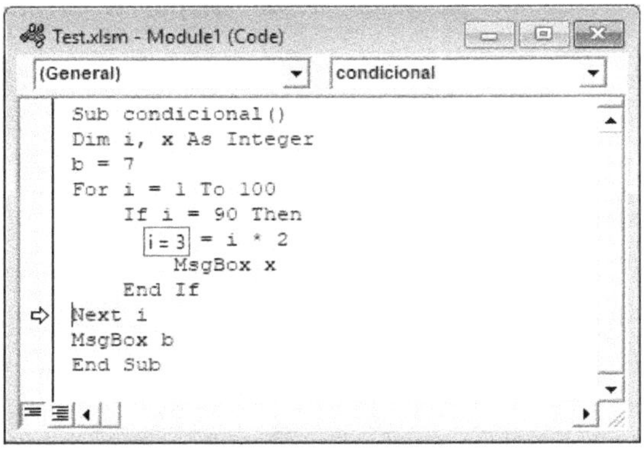

Test.xlsm - Module1 (Code)
(General)
condicional
Sub condicional()
Dim i, x As Integer
b = 7
For i = 1 To 100
If i = 90 Then
i = 3
= i * 2
MsgBox x
End If
Next i
MsgBox b
End Sub

Figure 1.36. Showing the value of a variable during the execution of the subroutine.

Another interesting aspect of the VBA-Excel editor is that it has the possibility to add more toolbars. For example, when you click with the right button on the toolbar, a menu of options like the one shown in figure 1.37 is displayed.

Figure 1.37. Toolbar options.

By default, the toolbar displayed is the Standard. If other bars are selected, these will be shown in the menu shown in figure 1.37. If a toolbar is added, it will usually appear floating. This can be moved and anchored under the menu bar.

There are many more options available in the VBA-Excel editor, but for now, the ones shown so far are sufficient. You can explore other options on your own and as you progress through the book, more will be shown.

1.3 Object Browser

The object browser (figure 1.38) shows the classes, properties, methods, events and constants that are available in VBA-Excel from any object library and also shows the procedures of the project in which you are working. It can also be used to find and use custom objects created by the user.

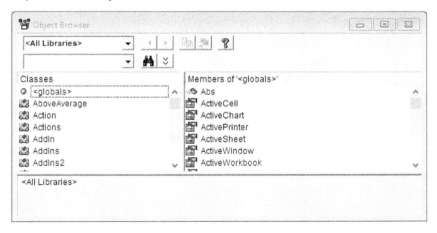

Figure 1.38. Object Browser.

This window is accessed from the VBA environment and can be done in several ways:

1. From the toolbar Standard, using the button ⌨ .
2. Pressing the key F2.
3. From the submenu "View" of the menu bar.

In the window Object Browser there are several elements that allow the search of a method or property that apply to a library of objects and obtain information about the selected method or property.

Let's see what are considered the most important elements. You can experiment with the other buttons.

1. Combo-Box Project/Library `<All Libraries>      ▼`
   When you click on this element (widget), the window shown in figure 1.39 is displayed.

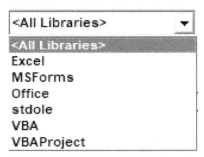

Figure 1.39. Menu that shows the main groupings of the VBA-Excel objects, including those that have been created in the active project.

This list shows the libraries currently referenced for the active project with which you are working on. If the option "All" is selected, then all the classes of all the libraries of the active project will be shown. If the option "VBAProject" is selected, all project objects and all their members will be displayed, that is, the functions and subroutines of all active classes listed (figure 1.40). It is suggested to select other options to become familiar with the classes of each library. By default, each time a library is selected in the menu in figure 1.39, all the members of that library are displayed (<global>). If you want to look only at the members of a particular class, it should be selected in the area where the classes are, for example, if "Module1" is selected, all the functions and subroutines that are there will be listed in the Members area (figure 1.41).

2. Search Text

    In this control, which is below the control explained above, a search word can be placed. This word can be a class, method, property or event for which you want information. Imagine for a moment that we want to obtain information about the "worksheet" object. This object is a member of the Worksheets collection. If we select the object (class) Worksheet in the Classes area of the Object Browser, we will see in the area next to it the members that compose it. These members are all the methods, properties and events that comprise it (figure 1.42).

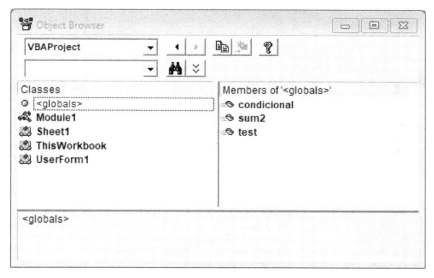

Figure 1.40. Object Browser showing the objects created in the active project (Excel workbook).

3. Details area

    In this area (enclosed in a rectangle in figure 1.43), the definition of the member of the class is shown. In that area, there is a hypertext that links it to the class or library to which it belongs.

Figure 1.41. Object Browser showing the members of the class Module1. On the left is the code window in which the members (subroutines) indicated are.

Figure 1.42. Components of the Worksheet object.

Figure 1.43. Details area of the selected member in the Object Browser.

Chapter 2. Macros, modules and user forms

2.1 Introduction

A macro is a set of instructions translated into VBA code done by Excel as we execute a task. Macros are useful because they allow, among other things, to automate repetitive tasks. They are also useful because they write code for us which we can then modify to fit our purposes. Many times, we do not remember the name of some objects and how to work with them, so macros allow us to access that information. Virtually any operation that is done in Excel is likely to generate VBA code. The product of a macro is a subroutine.

2.2 Recording a macro

Let's see the following example. We have some information about my family members, as shown in figure 2.1.

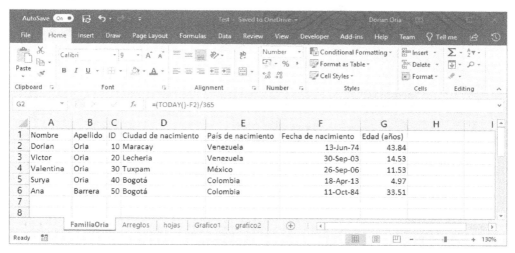

Figure 2.1. Information about my family group.

It is required to sort this data by age, from youngest to oldest. This operation is going to be done with Excel, but while we are executing the task, we will be recording a macro, which will contain all the necessary code to repeat the task as many times as we need with a single click and without having to manually re-execute all the steps to get the information sorted.

Before beginning the task, the recording process must be started. For this we go to the "Developer" tab. Excel should look like it is shown in figure 2.2. Once there, press the "Record Macro" button, which in figure 2.2 is enclosed in a rectangle. When you do this, the window shown in figure 2.3 appears.

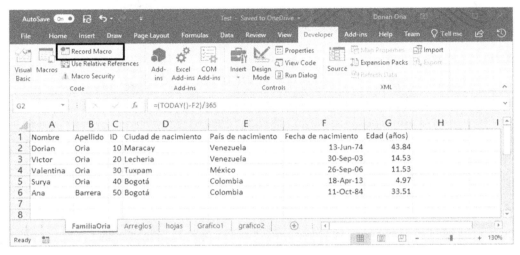

Figure 2.2. Excel interface showing the "Developer" tab.

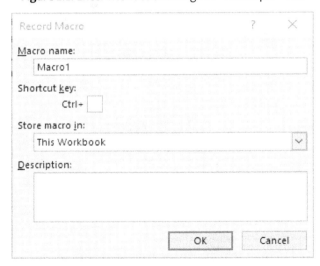

Figure 2.3. Window "Record Macro".

Once the operation is finished, press the button again to stop recording. In the window of figure 2.3 you can customize the name of the macro. Figure 2.4 shows how the now customized window in figure 2.3 looks like. Note that at this time it is possible to add shortcuts to the macro, that is, a combination of keys to invoke the macro directly. In our example, to activate the macro we have assigned the key combination Ctrl + Shift + O.

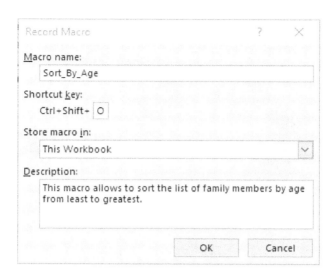

Figure 2.4. Window "Record Macro" with custom name and shortcut options.

Once the OK button is pressed, everything that is done from now on will be recorded as VBA code until the operation is manually stopped. Figure 2.5 shows how the button to stop recording the macro now looks (enclosed in a rectangle).

Figure 2.5. Excel toolbar showing the button to stop recording the macro.

The data, in addition to have been sorted age, has been enclosed in a table and this has been given some tweaks, such as color to the headings, bold for the titles of the columns, a white color for the content of the table and a lighter background color than the header. The table now looks as shown in figure 2.6.

Once the macro is finished, we go to the Visual Basic environment (Alt + F11) and look for the module where the macro is contained. It is possible for VBA to add a new module to place the created macro there. Macros are created as subroutines (they start with the keyword Sub). Our macro will look like it is shown in the subroutine 2.1. The numbers in the left column correspond to the line number and are added only for quick reference. They are not part of the code.

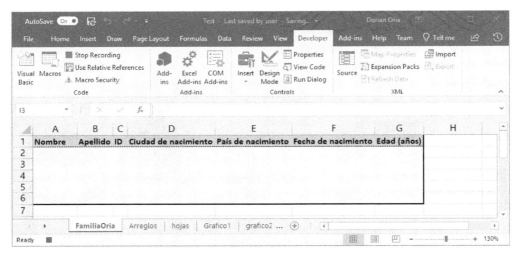

Figure 2.6. Data of my family ordered by age.

Subroutine 2.1.

```
1     Sub Sort_By_Age()
2     '
3     ' Sort_By_Age Macro
4     ' This macro allows to sort the list of family members by age from least to greatest
5     '
6     ' Shorcut: Ctrl+Shift+O
7     '
8         Columns("A:G").Select
9         Workbooks("test.xlsm").Worksheets("FamiliaOria").Sort.SortFields.Clear
10        ActiveWorkbook.Worksheets("FamiliaOria").Sort.SortFields.Add Key:=Range( _
11            "G2:G30"), SortOn:=xlSortOnValues, Order:=xlAscending, DataOption:= _
12            xlSortNormal
13        With ActiveWorkbook.Worksheets("FamiliaOria").Sort
14            .SetRange Range("A1:G6")
15            .Header = xlYes
16            .MatchCase = False
17            .Orientation = xlTopToBottom
18            .SortMethod = xlPinYin
19            .Apply
20        End With
21        Range("A1:G6").Select
22        Selection.Borders(xlDiagonalDown).LineStyle = xlNone
23        Selection.Borders(xlDiagonalUp).LineStyle = xlNone
24        With Selection.Borders(xlEdgeLeft)
25            .LineStyle = xlContinuous
```

```
26    .ColorIndex = 0
27    .TintAndShade = 0
28    .Weight = xlMedium
29  End With
30  With Selection.Borders(xlEdgeTop)
31    .LineStyle = xlContinuous
32    .ColorIndex = 0
33    .TintAndShade = 0
34    .Weight = xlMedium
35  End With
36  With Selection.Borders(xlEdgeBottom)
37    .LineStyle = xlContinuous
38    .ColorIndex = 0
39    .TintAndShade = 0
40    .Weight = xlMedium
41  End With
42  With Selection.Borders(xlEdgeRight)
43    .LineStyle = xlContinuous
44    .ColorIndex = 0
45    .TintAndShade = 0
46    .Weight = xlMedium
47  End With
48  Selection.Borders(xlInsideVertical).LineStyle = xlNone
49  Selection.Borders(xlInsideHorizontal).LineStyle = xlNone
50  Range("A1:G1").Select
51
52  Range("A1:G1").Borders(xlDiagonalDown).LineStyle = xlNone
53  Selection.Borders(xlDiagonalUp).LineStyle = xlNone
54  With Selection.Borders(xlEdgeLeft)
55    .LineStyle = xlContinuous
56    .ColorIndex = 0
57    .TintAndShade = 0
58    .Weight = xlMedium
59  End With
60  With Selection.Borders(xlEdgeTop)
61    .LineStyle = xlContinuous
62    .ColorIndex = 0
63    .TintAndShade = 0
64    .Weight = xlHairline
65  End With
66  With Selection.Borders(xlEdgeBottom)
67    .LineStyle = xlDash
```

```
68          .ColorIndex = 0
69          .TintAndShade = 0
70          .Weight = xlThin
71      End With
72      With Selection.Borders(xlEdgeRight)
73          .LineStyle = xlContinuous
74          .ColorIndex = 0
75          .TintAndShade = 0
76          .Weight = xlMedium
77      End With
78      Selection.Borders(xlInsideVertical).LineStyle = xlNone
79      Selection.Borders(xlInsideHorizontal).LineStyle = xlNone
80      Selection.Font.Bold = True
81      With Selection.Interior
82          .Pattern = xlSolid
83          .PatternColorIndex = xlAutomatic
84          .Color = 49407
85          .TintAndShade = 0
86          .PatternTintAndShade = 0
87      End With
88      Range("A2:G6").Select
89      With Selection.Interior
90          .Pattern = xlSolid
91          .PatternColorIndex = xlAutomatic
92          .Color = RGB(255, 255, 0)
93          .TintAndShade = 0
94          .PatternTintAndShade = 0
95      End With
96      With Selection.Font
97          .ThemeColor = xlThemeColorDark1
98          .TintAndShade = 0
99      End With
100  End Sub
```

For now we are not going to worry about analyzing the content of the macro. It is only intended at this time so you familiarize yourself with the use of the macro recorder and know how to do it and then access its content. Later we will see how we can, once the macro is recorded, modify it to fit our purposes. You will see that this allows you to add incredible power to Excel.

Just to get an idea about the power and practicality of a macro, copy the contents of the

"FamiliaOria" spreadsheet and paste it into another spreadsheet. Change the name. For the purposes of the exercise, I changed it to "FamiliaOria2". Once this is done, go to the code of the newly recorded macro, which we call Sort_By_Age (Subroutine 2.1). Once there, change the name of the "FamiliaOria" sheet to "FamiliaOria2" (lines 9, 10 and 13). However, for the execution of the macro or subroutine you can do it in several ways. From the VBA environment, you can place the cursor on any line inside the subroutine and press F5. It can also be done by pressing the "Run Sub/UserForm (F5) button on the toolbar Standard (enclosed in a square in figure 2.7).

Figure 2.7. Toolbar Standard in VBA environment.

Also from the VBA environment you can execute the subroutine from submenu Run of the Menu Bar.

Another way to run the macro is from the Excel environment. In order to do this, go to the tab Developer and press the button Macros (enclosed in a rectangle in figure 2.8).

Figure 2.8. Toolbar of the tab Developer in the Excel environment.

When you try to run the macro from the Excel environment, the window shown in figure 2.9 appears. On the window we select the subroutine we want to execute and press the button "Run". In our case, we will run the subroutine Sort_By_Age. Another way to run the macro from the Excel environment is by pressing the keys that we set as a shortcut when we start recording the macro. In our case it was **Ctrl + Shift + O**. If you do not remember the keys combination, the Excel macro recorder graciously recorded the key combination for us and wrote it as a comment at the beginning of our subroutine.

Once the macro is executed, the table that is now in the "FamilyOria2" worksheet should look exactly like the one in the "FamilyOria" worksheet. As you may have noticed, saying that it took a second to do what we wanted would probably be exaggerated. Already with this example you could experience your first edition of a macro. With each new exercise, you will understand the Excel object model, as well as its methods and properties.

In the version of Excel that we are using, there is a special format for saving Excel spreadsheets that contain macros. The format must have *.xlsm* (Excel Macro-Enabled Workbook) extension. Otherwise, Excel will not run the code into the file.

Figure 2.9. Windows Macro.

2.3 Modules

A module can contain procedures (in the form of functions or subroutines), types, declaration of data and definitions. All the declarations and definitions that are made in a module are public by default. This means that they can be invoked from the code window of any object listed in the Project Explorer.

Let's do the following experiment. Let's move the code shown in figure 1.19 to the code window of the object Sheet1. To access this window, find the object in the Project Explorer and double-click on it. A window like the one shown in figure 2.10 will appear (when the code window is opened for the first time it is empty, but as shown in figure 2.10 I have already added the code). In the code window Module1 we have left the function sum2. When executing from the window shown in figure 2.10, you will see that the same result occurs as when the subroutine was executed from Module1.

To insert a module in the active project, you can click with the right mouse button on any object shown in the Project Explorer and the menu shown in figure 2.11 will appear.

Another way to do it is through the "Insert" menu of the Menu Bar.

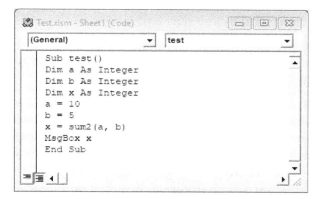

Figure 2.10. Code in figure 1.19 now on the Sheet1 object.

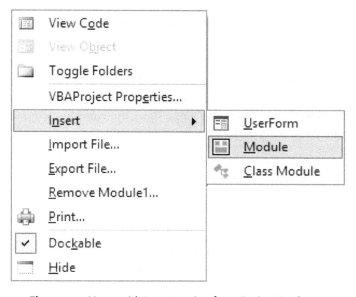

Figure 2.11. Menu with Insert option from Project Explorer.

2.3.1 Subroutines

Subroutines are procedures that execute a task within a program and do not return a value. The subroutines start with the reserved word **Sub** and end with the **End Sub** statement. Subroutines can receive input arguments from the procedures from which they are invoked. An example of a subroutine is shown in figure 2.10. A macro, such as Sort_By_Age is a subroutine (subroutine 2.1). If there are no inserted modules when a macro is created, VBA inserts them automatically.

2.3.2 Functions

A function is a procedure that executes a task within a program and returns a value. The functions start with the keyword **Function** and end with the **End Function** statement. Functions, like procedures, can also receive input arguments from the procedures from which they are invoked. For example, in figure 1.22 the function sum2 is shown, it is invoked from the test subroutine (line 7). The function sum2 returns the result of adding two numbers. When arguments are passed to a function, the order in which the arguments appear in the declaration of the function is important. Let's see the same example that was depicted in figure 1.22, now in figure 2.12. In line 7 of the test subroutine the function sum2 is invoked. Two arguments are passed: the values that have the variables "a" and "b". So that the function can give a fair treatment to the values that it will receive from the beginning, they must be in the same order. In our example, the variable "y" in the function sum2 receives the value of the variable "a" and the variable "z" receives the value of the variable "b". It's as if the function said: I receive the values you want to send me, but in my domain they have these names. As it can be noted, in line 2 of the function, sum2 is equal to y + z. The variable that will have the value to be returned must be called the same as the name of the function. For those who have had the opportunity to program in Visual Basic, they will see a difference in this, because in Visual Basic the word **Return** is used to return an operation, without necessarily generating another variable.

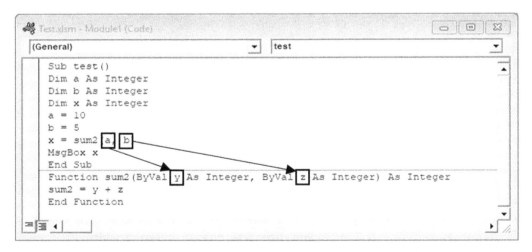

Figure 2.12. Subroutine test showing the process of passing values to the function sum2.

Another aspect to keep in mind is that the variable types in the function that will receive the values from the invocation must be of the same type as the variables that are sent to it. However, the function does not necessarily have to return the same type of variable.

It is important to note that functions in VBA can also be used in a cell in a spreadsheet, so it is advisable not to use names for functions that already exist in Excel. In our case we used sum2 as a name for our function, because there already is a function called **sum** in Excel.

There may be functions that do not return anything, so in this case they would behave like a subroutine. Moreover, in these cases, the reserved word **Function** or **Sub** can be used indiscriminately. The keyword **Call** is used to call or invoke a subroutine or to call a function that does not return anything,. In chapter 13 we will see an example of this.

2.3.3 References

In programming languages, a reference is a library that performs a task that our program does not do and that is included as part of it. It's like a function with greater complexity. Parameters are also sent to it so that it executes a task. References can be inserted in our application, through the menu tool in the menu bar of the VBA environment and can be dynamic libraries (.dll files), executable files or Activex controls. Figure 2.13 shows an example of a window that opens when you want to insert a reference. To search for the reference, press the "Browse" button. In doing so, a window like the one in figure 2.14 is displayed. The file that must be selected is the one with the extension .tlb. Once this is done, we are ready to use the library (figure 2.15).

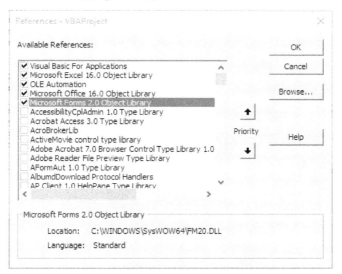

Figure 2.13. Window listing active and possible references to activate.

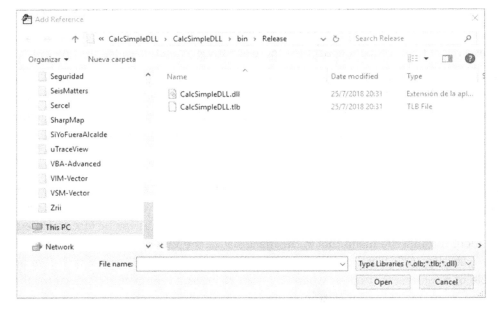

Figure 2.14. Window to select the reference.

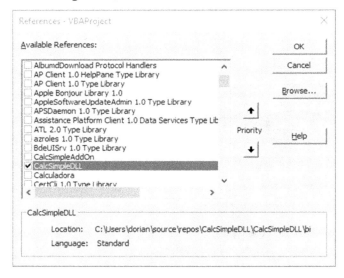

Figure 2.15. Window showing a selected reference.

In chapter 14, the process of making a library in Visual Basic will be completely shown.

Below is the example code that was programmed in VBA to illustrate how to use a library.

Subroutine 2.2.

1	Sub calculator()
2	Dim i, j As Double
3	i = 4.4
4	j = 7.3
5	Dim classCalc As New calc.calc
6	MsgBox "The result of " & i & " + " & j & " = " & classCalc.add(i, j) & vbNewLine & _
7	" The result of " & i & " - " & j & " = " & classCalc.subs(i, j) & vbNewLine & _
8	" The result of " & i & " * " & j & " = " & classCalc.mul(i, j) & vbNewLine & _
9	" The result of " & i & " / " & j & " = " & classCalc.div(i, j)
10	End Sub

To be able to use the library we must create a new object based on the library that we have just referenced. This is done on line 5 of the code shown. classCalc will be the name that we will assign to that object (you may use the name you prefer). The first word calc corresponds to the name of the library and the second word calc (in the expression New calc.calc) corresponds to the name of the object (class), inside which are the functions of the calculator. Later, in chapter 14 we will see the code of the library in Visual Basic. To refer to each function, we will use the name of the newly declared class followed by a period and then the name of the function. Thus, if we want to refer to the sum function, we write classCalc.add (line 6 of the subroutine code). The sum function receives two numbers. Thus, when the function is invoked from our VBA code, we must also pass the same number of parameters to it. When the code is executed, the window of figure 2.16 is displayed.

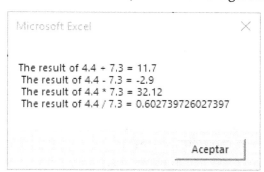

Figure 2.16. Result of the execution of the subroutine 2.2.

2.3.4 Type statements

Type statements are used within a module to define a type of data defined by the user and may contain one or more elements. Next, the SEGY data type (http://en.wikipedia.org/wiki/SEG_Y) will be displayed and then used in a subroutine in which values will be assigned and then displayed.

1	Type SEGY
2	RN As Integer 'Reel Number
3	DT As Integer 'Data traces per record
4	SR As Integer 'Sample rate (microseconds)
5	NS As Integer 'Number of samples per data trace
6	Format As Integer 'Data sample format code
7	End Type

Subroutine 2.3.

1	Sub ShowSEGYInfo()
2	Dim InfoSEGY As SEGY
3	InfoSEGY.RN = 5430
4	InfoSEGY.DT = 2600
5	InfoSEGY.SR = 2000
6	InfoSEGY.NS = 3401
7	InfoSEGY.Formato = 1
8	MsgBox "The file, which Reel Number is " & InfoSEGY.RN & " has " & InfoSEGY.DT & _
9	" traces" & vbNewLine & _
10	"sample rate (microseconds): " & InfoSEGY.SR & vbNewLine & _
11	"Number of samples per trace: " & InfoSEGY.NS & vbNewLine & _
12	"Format: " & InfoSEGY.Format
13	End Sub

2.4 Class Modules

A class is a type. Classes can be used like any other type (string, integer), in such a way as to declare variables, parameters, properties. Classes do not consume memory. They start doing it at the moment when, through a process called "instantiating", we have a variable of that type and an instance of that class is created with the keyword New. A class is defined by its properties which describe the attributes of the class and its methods (Sub and Function procedures), which carry out actions on the object. To enter a class, you can repeat the same procedure explained in numeral 2.3, only in this case the option that is highlighted in the menu shown in figure 2.17 will be chosen.

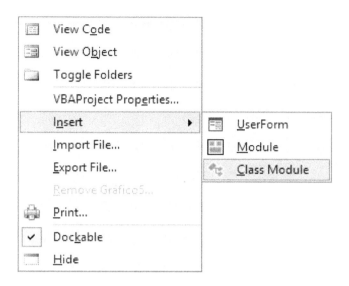

Figure 2.17. Inserting a class module.

By default, the class that will be inserted is called Class1 (if it is clear from the first one that is added). In the Properties window (window 2, explained in the introduction, figure 1.4) you can change the name of the class. In this case we have changed the name to RSEGYF, as you can see in figure 2.18.

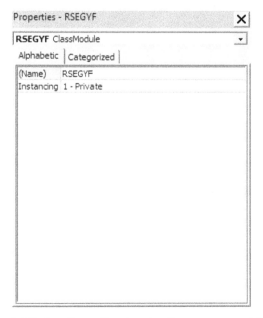

Figure 2.18. Window Properties showing the new name of the class.

Now let's go to the example. The code shown below is the one of the class that we want to create.

Subroutine 2.4.

1	Option Explicit
2	Public RN As Integer
3	Public DT As Integer
4	Public SR As Integer
5	Public NS As Integer
6	Public Function TextString(ByVal RN As Integer, ByVal DT As Integer, ByVal SR As Integer, ByVal NS As Integer) As String
7	TextString = "The SEGY file" & " has Reel Number: " & RN & vbNewLine & _
8	"has: " & DT & " traces" & vbNewLine & _
9	"sample rate: " & SR & " microseconds" & vbNewLine & _
10	"samples per trace: " & NS & " samples"
11	End Function

Now, in a code window of any object that is not a class, you can write the code of the 2.5 subroutine, which will be the one that will use the class that we have created (RSEGYF).

Subroutine 2.5.

1	Sub ShowSEGYInfo()
2	Dim myText As String
3	Dim myClass As New RSEGYF
4	Dim InfoSEGY As SEGY
5	InfoSEGY.RN = 5430
6	InfoSEGY.DT = 2600
7	InfoSEGY.SR = 2000
8	InfoSEGY.NS = 3401
9	InfoSEGY.Formato = 1
10	myText = myClass.TextString (InfoSEGY.RN, InfoSEGY.DT, InfoSEGY.SR, InfoSEGY.NS)
11	MsgBox myText
12	End Sub

Figure 2.19 shows the result of the execution of the 2.5 subroutine.

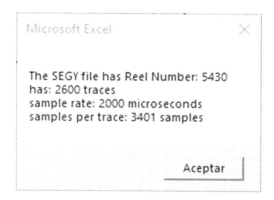

Figure 2.19. Result of the execution of the sub-routine 2.5.

2.5 Userforms

Userforms provide us with an interface that allows us to capture and display information. Both the userforms and the controls have properties, methods and events against which code can be written. As we are adding userforms (as in the case of classes, modules and Excel objects), Excel will call them according to a consecutive number: UserForm1, UserForm2 and so on. However, these names can be changed and it is suggested that they are changed since this facilitates the understanding of the code. The name that is placed to refer to the userform (Name property) does not necessarily have to correspond to the name with which you want the form to display (Caption property).

Userforms can be added using a procedure similar to adding modules and classes (figure 2.17). When a userform is added, the Toolbox appears, as shown in figure 2.20.

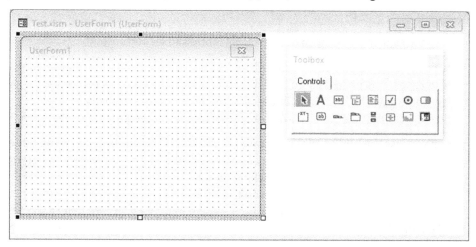

Figure 2.20. New userform and toolbox.

The window Toolbox can be customized. Among the different customization options are:

1. Add tabs. To add tabs and other options related to tabs, such as moving, changing or deleting the name and adding informative text on the tab, the right mouse button is pressed at the height of the Controls tab and the menu shown in figure 2.21 appears.

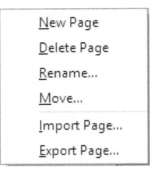

Figure 2.21. Toolbox configuration options menu.

2. Add other available controls, both in VBA-Excel and other Activex controls from other applications. To do this, click with the right mouse button in the area where the other controls are. Once this is done, the menu shown in figure 2.22 appears. When you click on Additional Controls, the window shown in figure 2.23 appears.

Figure 2.22. Menu to add additional controls to the toolbox.

We may have Activex controls not listed in the window shown in figure 2.23. In these cases, it is necessary to add the control beforehand as a reference (2.3.3). After that, it will appear listed in the window of additional controls.

3. Add controls that we have customized. For example, adding a label to the form. To do this, press the button that has drawn a letter "A" **A** . This button can be added by dragging and dropping it on the userform or by doing a simple click on it (with the left mouse button) and then clicking on the userform.

Let's change the text that is shown on the label, by clicking on the area where the text is. In edit mode, the control looks as shown in figure 2.24. We delete the text and change it to one of our preference. We click outside the text area and end the edit mode of the label.

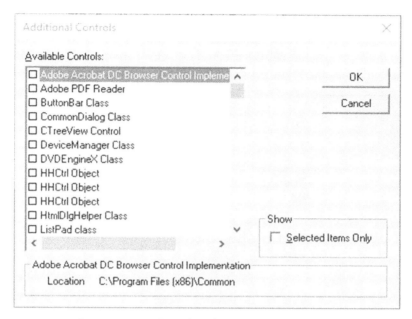

Figure 2.23. Window of available Additional Controls.

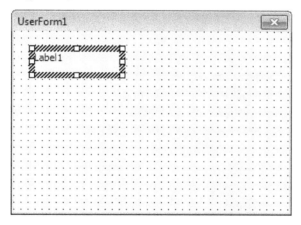

Figure 2.24. Userform with an added label.

4. Drag the control to the Toolbox. The button will look like the button where it came from, but the difference is that it is personalized. If you wish, drag the control back to the form and you will see that now instead of saying Label1 as it happened with the first label that was added, now it will show the text that you edited. Figure 2.25 shows what the label looks like with the changed text and what the Toolbox looks like with this custom control. As you can see, both controls (the original and the custom) look the same. You can change the image that is displayed and the label

that shows information when the mouse is over the control (tooltip). To do this, click on the control with the right button, this brings up the same window that is shown in figure 2.22, but with all the options active. The option Customize Item is selected and this causes the window shown in figure 2.26 to appear.

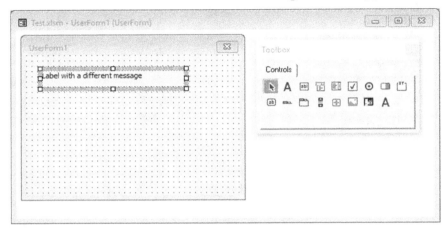

Figure 2.25. Form showing the label with the customized text and toolbox showing the new custom label control.

Figure 2.26. Window to customize control.

In later chapters, when we begin to work with more practical examples, the various elements of the Toolbox will be introduced and their operation explained.

Chapter 3. Variables, constants, operators and arrays

3.1 Introduction

The true power of Excel is achieved by combining the handling of the different objects it has with some basic knowledge of programming in Visual Basic for Applications (VBA). In general, VBA-Excel language is very similar to Visual Basic. It is a slightly lighter version than Visual Basic (although not less powerful). This means that if you have programming knowledge in Visual Basic, this chapter will be a piece of cake. Same applies if you know how to program in another language, since It is said that the hardest to learn is the first programming language and the others are learned easier.

In this part we will talk a little about variables, constants, arrays, operators, instructions to control repetition flows and other concepts necessary to fully exploit the full power of Excel and VBA.

3.2 Scope of declaration

VBA, as well as VB and any other programming language, uses variables to store values. A variable has a name and also has a type. A variable can also represent an array if it stores an indexed set of closely related elements.

Unlike other languages such as C, C ++, C #, Java, among others, in VBA Excel it is not strictly necessary for the user to declare the variables so that the program can be executed. However, in practice it is quite useful to do so, since this increases the readability of the programs, without counting on the fact that this makes a more optimal use of memory. In the case of VBA, if the variable type is not declared, it does it for us, assuming that the variable that we do not declare is of the Variant type.

Another advantage of declaring the variables is that VBA-Excel allows you to use the autocompletion feature to complete the name of the variables. An example of that is shown in figure 3.1. We have two variables that start with the word name. By typing in the line 5: result = var and pressing Ctrl + Space (space bar), VBA-Excel suggests expressions to complete the rest of the expression. As it can be seen in the next example, VBA shows us first those that match with the expression "var", which in this case are the variables that are declared in line 2 of the subroutine.

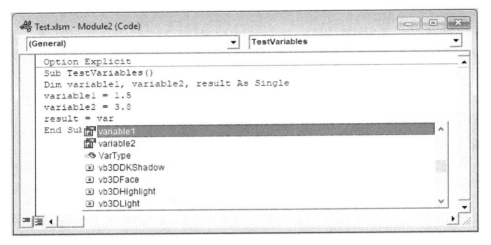

Figure 3.1. VBA-Excel showing the auto-complete feature.

Some restrictions to name variables are:

1. The first character must be a letter.

2. The names of variables are not case sensitive. It is the same to write var than Var.

3. Spaces, periods, exclamation marks or the characters @, &, $ or # cannot be used.

4. Names that are already being used in subroutines, functions, methods, or declarations, cannot be used. Nor can reserved words be used, such as Integer, Single, Dim, Sub, End, With, etc.

5. Variable names cannot be repeated in the same context.

If you want VBA to remind you that you must always declare the variables you are going to use, you can use the expression *Option Explicit* at the beginning of a module, as shown in figure 3.1.

If we try to run the following code and we are using *Option Explicit*, the error shown in figure 3.2 will occur.

Subroutine 3.1.

1	Sub Explicit()
2	t = 5
3	MsgBox t
4	End Sub

Figure 3.2. Error that occurs when a subroutine is run without declaring the type of variables using *Option Explicit*.

This error occurred because the variable "t" was not declared in that routine. Thus, the instruction should be added before line 2:

Dim t As Integer

The statement *Option Explicit* only works in the module where it was declared. One way to ensure that it is part of all the modules is by activating it through Options in the Tools menu of the Menu Bar (rectangle in figure 3.3). This only works for the modules that are to be added after having made this change. It does not apply to modules that have already been added. In these it must be done manually by writing the instruction.

Other considerations to take into account when working with variables depend on the scope in which you want the variable to be present. For example, at the subroutine level, you can declare a variable using the reserved word **Dim** and the variable will only be available for that context. A variable declared with **Dim** or **Private** at the beginning of a module will be public in that module, that is, it can be invoked from any subroutine. However, it will not be available in the rest of the application. These statements must be at the beginning of the object's code window, above any subroutine or function of that object.

If it is necessary for the variable to be available for all procedures of all objects (modules, userforms, Excel objects), then, the word **Public** must be used at the beginning of any module and before any subroutine or function. It is only admitted in modules. It does not work for the purpose described if it is used in other objects. If the word **Public** is used in another object that is not a module, the variable will behave in the same way as if it had been declared with **Dim** or with **Private**.

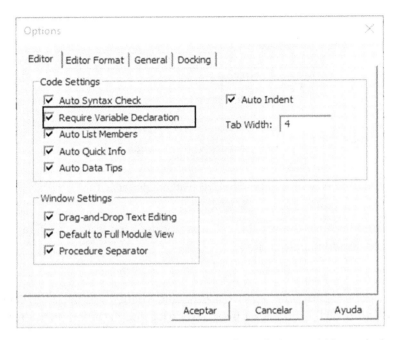

Figure 3.3. Options window, highlighting the option to force declare variables at the beginning of any module.

Let's see the example shown in figure 3.4. The variable "x" has been declared as **Public** in a module (Module5). Then, in another object (Sheet1), a subroutine has been written, which is shown in figure 3.5. In this subroutine, two numbers are added and the result is stored in the variable "x". Proceed to execute the subroutine SumX. Once executed, let's return to the code window of the module shown in figure 3.4 and execute the ShowX subroutine. When doing so, the window shown in figure 3.6 will appear.

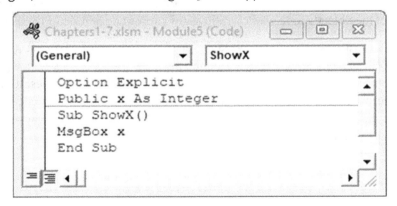

Figure 3.4. Module showing a public declaration of a variable ("x").

The objective with this example is to show the following:

1. Since the variable was declared **Public** in a module, it becomes global for all objects in the active application. Then, notice how a subroutine could be executed in another object where the variable "x" is used without having been declared inside the procedure (figure 3.5) or within the object itself (code window of the object Sheet1). Once the subroutine is executed, a different subroutine is executed to show the value of "x" (figure 3.4), which is in the code window of another object (in this case within a module).

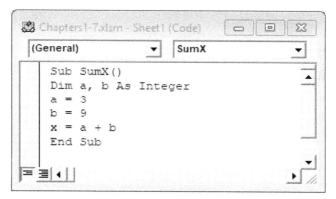

Figure 3.5. Subroutine that calculates the sum of two numbers and store the result in the variable "x".

2. While the application is still open, this value of "x" will remain in memory until we change it in another procedure (or in the same procedure where the assignment instruction was executed) or until the application is closed.

Figure 3.6. Result of the execution of the subroutine ShowX shown in figure 3.4.

Another special way to define a scope for a variable is by using the reserved word **Static**. **Static** variables are a special case because they retain their value, even after completing the execution of the subroutine or function. However, they only work within the scope where they are declared. The stored value of these variables cannot be used outside the scope in which they were declared. For example, let's see the following code.

Subroutine 3.2.

1	Sub test()
2	Dim b As Integer
3	Dim a As Integer
4	a = 4
5	b = 5
6	x = sum3(a, b)
7	MsgBox x
8	End Sub

In this subroutine a function called **sum3** is invoked.

Subroutine 3.3.

1	Function sum3(ByVal y As Integer, ByVal z As Integer) As Integer
2	Static v As Integer
3	suma = y + z
4	v = v + 1
5	MsgBox "The subroutine has been run: " & v & " times"
6	End Function

Within the function we have a variable declared as **Static,** which is where we want to keep track of the times the function **sum3** is run. This value will be displayed when line 5 of the function is executed (figure 3.7). Each time the function is invoked, it will increase the value of the variable "v". This value will disappear from the memory only when the application is closed or the button ▪ is pressed (located in the toolbar Standard). If you have questions about using **Static,** change it to **Dim** and see what happens.

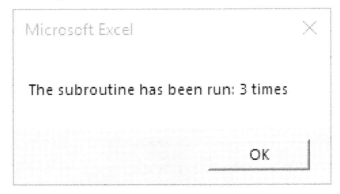

Figure 3.7. Window showing the times the function sum3 has been run.

Now, if we tried to show the value of the variable "v" in another subroutine, as it was done in the case of the variable "x" shown in figure 3.4, we would see that it does not show any value. For example, after having executed the 3.2 subroutine, try executing the subroutine 3.4 and see what happens.

Subroutine 3.4.

```
1  Sub ShowV()
2  MsgBox v
3  End Sub
```

3.3 Types of variables

3.3.1 Variant

This type of variable stores numeric and non-numeric values. It is quite useful when you are not sure of the type of variable and can only be known at runtime. A variable Variant can also be explicitly declared. For example:

Dim X

Dim X As Variant

With a variable type *Variant*, other types of data such as integers, floats, doubles, etc can be represented.

Because this variable can contain almost any type of data, it is necessary that 16 bytes of memory storage be separated, even if the data type requires less than that. This could be an inconvenience due to the large memory consumption in case no variable is declared in our code according to its true nature. In the case of containing a string of characters, 22 bytes plus the length of the string are needed.

3.3.2 Boolean

This type of variable only has two states: True or False (True or False). It is used as a flag (flags) or conditional.

3.3.3 Byte

Corresponds to an 8-bit variable and can store values between 0 and 255.

3.3.4 Integer

A variable Integer needs 16 bits and the values it can represent vary from -32768 to 32767.

3.3.5 Long

It is also a variable to store whole numbers, but very large, between the range -2147483648 and 2147483647.

3.3.6 Single

It is a type of data of 32 bits that is used to store fractional values and its rank goes from

-3.402823×10^{38} a $-1.401298 \times 10^{-45}$ for negative values and from 1.401298×10^{-45} to 3.402823×10^{38} for positive values.

3.3.7 Double

The difference between this variable and the single type is that this is a 64-bit data type. The range of possible values to represent with this type of variables ranges from

$-1.79769313486232 \times 10^{308}$ to $-4,94065645841247 \times 10^{-324}$ for negative values and from $4,94065645841247 \times 10^{-324}$ to $1.79769313486232 \times 10^{308}$ for positive values.

3.3.8 Currency

In a strict sense, it is a whole type variable. It is scaled by a factor of 10,000 to add four digits to the right of the decimal point. It allows for up to 15 digits to the left of the decimal point, resulting in a range of approximately -922337000000000 to +922337000000000.

3.3.9 Date

This type of variable has a range of 64 bits and can be used to store dates and/or hours. In case you want to represent dates, it must be enclosed between two numeral signs (#) and must be of the form mm/dd/yyyy. For example: #6/13/1974#. This format is independent of the local data format on your computer. This ensures that the code has an equal behavior regardless of the country in which the code is executed or the local configuration of the system in which the application is executed.

In the case of time, this can be specified in 12 or 24 hour format. For example: #2:28:45 PM# or #14:28:45#. In case minutes or seconds are not specified, then the time must contain AM or PM.

Additionally, a variable **Date** can support that both the date and the time are stored, as shown in the following example

Dim dateAndTime As Date = #6/13/1974 07:30 AM#

3.3.10 String

This variable is used to store strings of characters and needs 10 bytes more in memory than the length of the string (for cases in which variable length strings are involved). A single string can contain up to 2 billion characters. Strings of characters must be enclosed in double quotes. If you want quotation marks to appear as part of the character string, they must be enclosed in double quotes. For example:

Subroutine 3.5.

```
1   Sub quotes1()
2   Dim string1 As String
3   string1 = """Hello"""
4   MsgBox string1
5   End Sub
```

The result of the execution of this subroutine is shown in figure 3.8. Notice how in this example the word Hello is enclosed in double quotes.

Figure 3.8. Result of the execution of the subroutine 3.5.

For the cases in which the strings are fixed length, the variable only occupies in memory the length of the string.

3.3.11 Object

This type of variable stores memory addresses referring to objects. You can assign any type of reference to a variable Object (string, array, class, interface). A variable **Object** can also refer to any type of data (numeric, **Boolean**, Char, **Date**, structure or enumeration).

This variable can be used when it is not known, at compile time, what kind of data the variable could point to.

Regardless of what type of data the variable **Object** refers to, it does not contain the value of the data as such, but a pointer to that value.

Although **Object** is a type of reference (reference type), Visual Basic treats it as a type of value (value type) when it refers to a data of type value. The variable uses 4 bytes of memory in the system.

The following code shows an example of the use of the variable **Object**.

Subroutine 3.6.

```
1  Sub getType()
2  Dim Object1 As Object
3  Set Object1 = UserForm1
4  With Object1
5     .Caption = "Test"
6     .Show
7  End With
8  MsgBox TypeName(Object1)
9  End Sub
```

Assuming we have a userform called UserForm1, the previous code generates the windows shown in figures 3.9 and 3.10.

Figure 3.9. Object UserForm1.

Figure 3.9 shows that the userform has the title that we added with the code in line 5. With the instruction in line 6 we will show the userform. In line 8, using the MsgBox function, the name of the type of object for which the reference was created is shown, in this case, it is an object of type *UserForm* (form).

Figure 3.10. MsgBox showing the type of object referenced.

3.4 Constants

As the name implies, constants are values that do not change during program execution. It is useful when working with scientific constants, for example, when you need to use these values several times. In addition, they help in the readability of the algorithms. To declare a constant the reserved word **Const** is used and to name them the same rules apply as for the variables.

In VBA Excel, constants can be declared within subroutines or functions, regardless of where they are. However, if you want to use global scope constants (available through all modules, classes and VBA objects), then you can define them only in the modules, although they can be invoked from any VBA object (userforms, windows of code of classes, spreadsheets and other modules), provided that they are declared with the reserved word **Public** and at the beginning of each module, before the beginning of any subroutine or function. If they are declared **Private** then they will be public only in the scope of the module where the declaration is made. You can also use **Private** to make a constant available or public for any procedure within the scope of the object (userform, class or Excel spreadsheet code window). Remember that according to the latter, those constants will not be available outside of those objects using **Private**.

Let's see how it works. In module Chapter3 we have declared the constant *e* as **Public** (figure 3.11). Now, to show what happens when this is done, let's write the code shown in figure 3.12 in the code window of a spreadsheet (Sheet1).

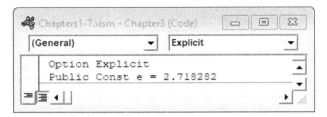

Figure 3.11. Declaring a constant.

Figure 3.12. Code to show the value of the constant declared in the previous figure.

When executing the code shown in figure 3.12, the window shown in figure 3.13 appears.

Figure 3.13. Window showing the value of the constant declared in figure 3.11.

If you try to make a statement like the one shown in figure 3.14 (code window of a spreadsheet), it will generate the error shown in figure 3.15.

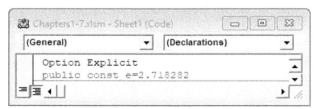

Figure 3.14. Declaration of a constant in an object other than a module.

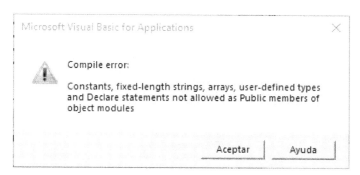

Figure 3.15. Compile error generated when trying to declare a constant outside the scope of a module.

I invite you to do the exercise of changing the word **Public** by **Private** in the code shown in figure 3.11 and execute the code shown in figure 3.12 to see what happens.

3.5 Adding Comments

Comments are very important in programming. It is usual that while we are writing code, we have clear ideas about the operations that are done in each line. However, sometimes it happens that after finishing and wanting to return we have to make an effort to remember, especially when using variable names that may not give an easy idea about what they do. A comment allows the code to be more readable, add information that explains what each code section does or each line or any other information that you want to make the code can be understood later when it is revised again. In addition, it is usual that not all programmers think the same way or even agree on how to name the variables. This is why comments should be made in such a way that if another person has access to the code, he/she can understand it.

In VBA, comments can be added in a line or after a sentence, adding them before starting an apostrophe ('). An example of comments can be seen in Subroutine 2.1. When a line is commented, VBA shows it in green.

Unlike languages such as C or C ++, if in VBA we want to make comments that occupy several lines, there is no way to enclose them with a symbol or two. Each line must be commented individually and therefore carry an apostrophe. Fortunately, VBA offers a quick way to do it. Just follow these steps:

1. Click with the right mouse button on the area where the VBA environment toolbars are. When doing this, a menu appears offering the possibility to activate/deactivate toolbars (figure 3.16).

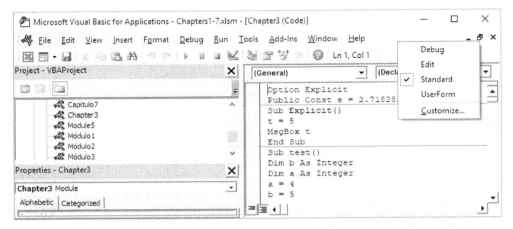

Figure 3.16. VBA environment where the menu is shown with options to enable toolbars or customize them.

2.   Choose the option "Edit". This brings up the toolbar that is highlighted in figure 3.17.

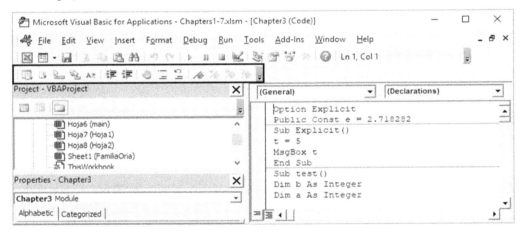

Figure 3.17. VBA environment showing the toolbar "Edit".

3.   In the code window where the lines you wish to comment are located, select them and then press the button that is shown enclosed in a square in figure 3.18. If you want to "uncomment" them later, select them and press the button next to them.

3.6 Use of labels

I remember when I started programming, the first language I learned was BASIC. At that time, I was in college and owed a CASIO FX-880P scientific calculator. This calculator could be programmed in BASIC. Each line of code required a number. Usually the first line was 10 and it started with the CLS instruction. Then the next lines were numbered from 10 to 10. After the number of each line a space was left and the instruction was written. VBA allows this way of programming to be used. Note that in a strict sense, each line can be labeled differently from a number (line 10 of the code shown). However, the common way was numbers. Below is an example code.

Figure 3.18. Toolbar "Edit" where the button for commenting line blocks is highlighted.

Subroutine 3.7.

1	Sub BASIC()
2	10: Dim name As String
3	20: Dim age As Integer
4	30: name = InputBox("Tell me your name:")
5	40: age = InputBox("How old are you:")
6	50: If age < 40 Then
7	55: Debug.Print name & " you are a little chicken, possibly you did not know BASIC"
8	56: GoTo goodBye
9	60: End If
10	goodBye: Debug.Print "See you"
11	End Sub

The instruction Debug.Print in line 10, shows a message in the window Immediate.

It is not necessary to put labels on all the lines. It can be only in one. Even today, it is sometimes useful to use labels when a program is required to stop performing an operation and jump to another part of the code (instruction **GoTo**, line 8). Although there are some who think that this is not elegant, it does not stop being useful.

3.7 Operators

VBA already comes with several built-in operators, among them there are the mathematical operators used to work with chains, comparison or logic. All operators work in VBA in the same way they work in a cell of a spreadsheet, with the exception of the MOD operator, which we'll discuss later.

Next, we are going to review the operators that we are going to use throughout this book.

3.7.1 Assignment operator

In VBA, the "equal" sign (=) is used as the assignment operator. Be careful not to confuse the way an assignment operator works in programming as it is used in mathematics. For example, let's look at the following expression:

i = i + 1

In mathematics, the previous expression would not make sense. However, in programming, this expression indicates that 1 is added to the value that the variable "i" had and that the result stores it in the same variable "i". Later we will see examples of the utility of this type of assignments.

3.7.2 Mathematical operators

The mathematical operators available in VBA are shown in Table 3.1.

Table 3.1. Mathematical operators.

Function	Operator symbol	Precedence
Sum	+	5
Substraction	-	5
Multiplication	*	2
Division	/	2
Exponentiation	^	1
Integer division (returns the integer part of a division)	\	3
Arithmetic module	Mod	4

The operators of all the functions mentioned in Table 3.1 are the same as those that can be used in a spreadsheet. In the case of **Mod**, this operator returns the remainder of the division. Let's see it with an example. If we divide 78 by 7, we will realize that it is not an exact division. The whole part of the division gives us 11. So, if we multiply 7 x 11, the result is 77, so to get to 78 we must add 1. This 1 that must be added is what would be the remainder of the division.

It is important to be clear about the precedence with which the operators are applied in the absence of parentheses (although I recommend using parentheses for better readability). Subroutine 3.8 is a sample code to see how the issue of precedence works. Try to execute each of the operations manually and verify that they match the results of the execution of the code.

Subroutine 3.8.

```
1   Sub precedence()
2   Dim w, x, y, z1, z2, z3 As Integer
3   w = 3
4   y = 2
5   x = 4
6   z1 = w ^ 3 - 1 * y - x 'this is a comment
7   z2 = w ^ (3 - 1) * y - x
8   z3 = w ^ 3 - 1 * (y - x)
9   MsgBox "z1= " & z1 & vbNewLine & _
10              "z2= " & z2 & vbNewLine & _
11              "z3= " & z3 & vbNewLine
12  End Sub
```

When executing the previous code, the window shown in figure 3.19 appears.

Figure 3.19. Result of the execution of the subroutine 3.8.

3.7.3 Concatenation operator.

The symbol of this operator is the *ampersand* (&) and is used to join two strings of characters. This operator can also be used for the same purpose as within a cell in a spreadsheet. Let's see the following example, interestingly enough about how both VBA and Excel can implicitly make conversions between variable types.

Subroutine 3.9.

```
1   Sub Concatenate()
2   Dim x As Integer
3   Dim y As Integer
4   Dim z As String
5   x = 78
6   y = 7
7   z = x & y
```

8	z = z + 1
9	MsgBox z
10	End Sub

When executing this code, the result shown in the window is 788. How is this possible? Why didn't we get an error if "x" and "y" are Integer variables and "z" is declared as variable **String**? In this case, the first value that the variable "z" took (line 7) was the result of concatenating 78 with 7 (values of "x" and "y" respectively). Then, in line 8 we give the order to increase the value of "z" by 1. At that time, VBA converts **String** to **Integer**. In a cell in Excel, try the same experiment and you can verify that Excel also does the conversion implicitly.

3.7.4 Comparison operators

These operators compare two numbers or two chains (strings) and the result of that comparison is a logical result (True or False). Table 3.2 shows the comparison operators used in VBA. Further ahead we will have the opportunity to see how they all work.

Table 3.2. Comparison operators.

Operator	Action
=	Equal to
<>	Different from
<	Smaller than
>	Greater than
<=	Smaller than or equal to
>=	Greater than or equal to

3.7.5 Logical operators

These operators compare Boolean expressions and return a Boolean result. In other words, they compare true or false expressions whose result can be true or false. Table 3.3 shows the logical operators available in VBA. However, later we will give examples of the most used, which for our purposes are the first three of the table.

Table 3.3. Logical operators.

Operator	Action
Not	Executes a logical negation on an expression.
And	Execute a logical conjunction between two expressions.
Or	Execute a logical dilemma between two expressions.
XoR	Execute a logical exclusion between two expressions.

| Eqv | Execute a logical equivalence between two expressions. |
| Imp | Execute a logical implication (inference) between two expressions. |

3.7.6 Line-continuation operator (_)

This operator allows that if an instruction is very long, it can be continued on the next line. An example of this can be seen in the subroutine 3.8 (lines 9 and 10).

3.7.7 Coma Operator (,)

This operator can be used in the declaration process of several variables of the same type, without the need to write a declaration for each one. An example of this can be seen in the subroutine 3.8 (line 2).

3.7.8 Colon operator (:)

It allows two instructions to be together in the same line. It is useful for cases in which instructions are short. For example:

t = 5: v = v + 1

3.8 Arrays

An array is a set of data that is related to each other. That is, the data can be age (integers), names (chains), etc. It is mandatory that the arrangements are declared before being used unlike with normal variables. The declaration of an array is similar to that of a variable, but the value of the largest index that the array will contain must be specified. It is important for this to be clear since in VBA you can change the lowest index between 0 and 1, so the number of elements in the array will depend on this.

VBA by default assumes that the lowest index value is 0 (*Option Base 0*). Thus, we declare an arrangement as follows:

 Dim A(100) As Integer

The number of elements contained in arrangement "A" is 101. VBA offers the possibility to change the value of the lowest index to 1. This is done with the *Option Base 1* instruction.

In the case of our arrangement "A" and after the previous instruction, we can conclude that the size of the array is 100 items since the value of the lowest index is now 1.

Another way to declare an arrangement and that provides more flexibility to handle the lower index is as follows:

Dim A(0 To 100) As Integer

which would be equivalent to

Dim A(100) As Integer, in the case of *Option Base 0*.

Dim A(1 to 100) As Integer

It would equal

Dim A(100) As Integer, in the case of *Option Base 1*.

However, any value can also be used for the smallest index, as long as it is less than the value of the higher index. That is, a statement like the one that follows can not be possible, because it will give an error in compilation time (figure 3.20).

Dim A(6 To 3) As Integer

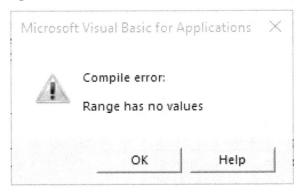

Figure 3.20. Compilation error when declaring an array with a lower index greater than the top index.

A possible statement would be:

Dim A(3 To 6) As Integer

In this case, the value of the lowest index would be 3, that is, it could not have elements A (1) or A (2) or any whose index is outside of that established in that declaration.

There is no other way to declare such an arrangement with Option Base, that is, the *Option Base 3* instruction cannot not be used, since it would give an error like the one shown in figure 3.21.

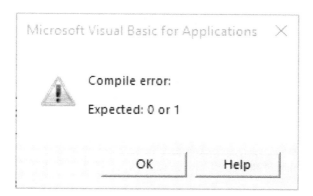

Figure 3.21. Compilation error when trying to use Option Base with an option other than 0 or 1.

The instruction *Option Base* (with any of its options 0 or 1) must be at the beginning of a module, before any subroutine or function. It can only appear once per module and must be before any settlement statement that includes dimensions. If you try to use it within a procedure, the compile-time error shown in figure 3.22 will be generated. The statement *Option Base* will cause all arrays that are declared to have the lowest index value as specified.

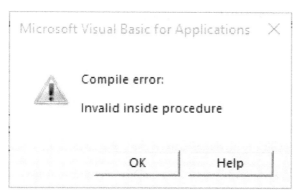

Figure 3.22. Compilation error when trying to use the instruction *Option Base* inside a subroutine.

3.8.1 Size of an array

The number of elements of an array can be determined by knowing the value of the highest index, subtracting the value of the lowest index and adding it 1. Let's see the example shown in the subroutine 3.10.

Subroutine 3.10.

1	Sub workingArrays()
2	Dim A(2 To 8) As Integer
3	Dim n, ISup, IInf As Integer

4	A(3) = 5
5	A(2) = 8
6	A(3) = 9
7	A(4) = 10
8	A(6) = 25
9	A(8) = 32
10	ISup = UBound(A)
11	IInf = LBound(A)
12	n = ISup - IInf + 1
13	MsgBox " The amount of elements in the array is: " & n
14	End Sub

The arrangement "A" is declared in line 2 which contains elements whose lowest index is 2 and the highest index is 8. The arrangement has been declared in such a way that all the elements it contains will be of the *Integer* type.

Between lines 4 and 9 values are assigned to various elements that make up the array. Note that no values have been assigned to elements A (5) and A (7). VBA automatically assigns them zero.

In line 10, the value of the upper index of the array "A" is determined by using the **UBound** instruction. In our case, as stated in line 2 it should be 8.

In line 11, the value of the lower index of the array "A" is determined by using the **LBound** instruction. In our case, as stated in line 2 it should be 6.

In line 12, the number of elements of the arrangement is calculated by subtracting the values calculated in the two previous lines and in the end, 1 is added.

Figure 3.23 shows the result of the execution of the subroutine 3.10.

If an attempt is made to assign a value to an element whose index is not in the range declared in line 2 of the previous code, when executing the code, the error message shown in figure 3.24 will be displayed.

3.8.2 Dynamic arrays

In case you do not know the number of elements that a priori will have an arrangement, then this can be declared as shown below:

Dim A() As Integer

This is what is known as a dynamic array. It is an arrangement whose size can be adjusted during the execution of the program.

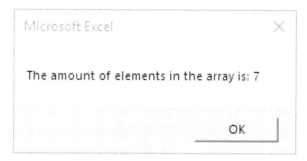

Figure 3.23. Result of the execution of the subroutine 3.10.

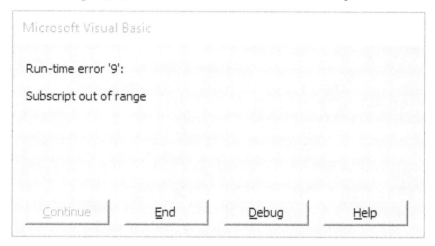

Figure 3.24. Error occurred when trying to assign a value to an array element whose index is outside of that declared on line 2 of subroutine 3.10.

To adjust the size of the array, you can use the following instruction:

ReDim A(100) As Integer

Where 100 is the value of the highest index of the array. **ReDim** can only appear in a subroutine or function, since it is an instruction for runtime. The instruction **ReDim** also allows the same syntax as for fixed-size arrays. Each **ReDim** can change the number of elements, as well as the values of the lower and upper indexes of the array. For example:

ReDim A(50 To 250) As Integer

The instruction **ReDim** not only resizes the array, but also deletes the contents of each of the elements that were formerly in it. It assigns empty for arrays that contain *Variant* type values, zero for numerical arrays, zero-length strings for string arrays, and nothing for object arrays. This may be convenient if you want the arrangement to have new data, but it can be an inconvenience because if what you want is that the array grows as you generate information for new elements, without losing the information of the existing elements. This can be avoided by using the reserved word **Preserve**, as shown in the following example:

ReDim Preserve A(o To 250) As Integer

Preserve only works to preserve the array information, as long as only the value of the largest dimension is changed. Let's see the following example.

Subroutine 3.11.

1	Sub ExamplePreserveUse()
2	Dim family() As String
3	ReDim family(3) As String
4	family(0) = "Surya"
5	family(1) = "Valentina"
6	family(2) = "Victor"
7	family(3) = "Anama"
8	ReDim Preserve family(0 To 5) As String
9	MsgBox family(2) & "-" & family(5)
10	End Sub

In line 2, the arrangement "family" has been declared as dynamic. Before starting to add elements to the array, it is necessary to resize it, which is done in line 3.

Between lines 4 and 7, elements are added to the array.

The array is resized again in line 8, but we use the reserved word **Preserve** so that it retains the information of the elements already entered.

Line 9 shows the values contained in the elements whose indexes are 2 and 5.

Figure 3.25 shows the result of the execution of the subroutine 3.11

Figure 3.25. Result of the execution of the subroutine 3.11.

Notice in the previous figure that after the script there is nothing. This is because we try to show information about an element that has not yet been assigned something other than an empty string ("").

Redim cannot change the number of dimensions of an array.

3.8.3 Populate arrays from the code

This can be done in many ways. Let's say for example that we want to populate the array "M" and that it will contain 4 strings of names:

1. Entering the names for each element.

    ```
    Dim M(3) As String
    M(0) = "Anama"
    M(1) = "Surya"
    M(2) = "Valentina"
    M(3) = "Victor"
    ```

2. Declaring the array as **Variant** and using the reserved word **Array**:

    ```
    Dim M or Dim M(), with this instruction the array is declared as Variant.
    M= Array("Anama", "Surya", "Valentina", "Victor")
    ```

3. If you have a text string then use the function **Split**. This function divides the text string according to the character that separates the elements we want to divide. In our example is the comma (,).

    ```
    Dim TextString As String
    TextString = "Anama,Surya,Valentina,Victor"
    Dim M() As String
    M = Split(TextString, ",")
    ```

3.8.4 Sort arrays

VBA Excel does not have support for sorting stored values in an array. However, Excel has functionalities that allow it to do so taking advantage of the power of the object Range that belongs to the Worksheets object (spreadsheet).

Even when we are going to work with slightly more advanced topics (such as the introduction of Excel objects), it is convenient to show here how we can order an array.

Let's see the following example. We have a list of names (array "M") that you want to sort alphabetically.

Subroutine 3.12.

```
1   Sub SortExample()
2   Dim h As Worksheet
3   Dim i As Integer
4   Dim M
5   Dim TextString As String
6   M = Array("Surya", "Anama", "Valentina", "Victor")
7   Set h = Sheets("Arrays")
8   TextString = ""
9   For i = 0 To 3
10      h.Range("A" & i + 1) = M(i)
11  Next i
12  With h.Sort
13     .SortFields.Clear
14     .SortFields.Add Key:=h.Range("A1:A4"), SortOn:=xlSortOnValues, _
15        Order:=xlAscending, DataOption:=xlSortNormal
16     .SetRange h.Range("A1:A4")
17     .Header = xlGuess
18     .SortMethod = xlStroke
19     .Apply
20  End With
21  For i = 0 To 3
22      M(i) = h.Range("A" & i + 1)
23      TextString = TextString & M(i) & ","
24  Next i
25  MsgBox "The sorted names are: " & TextString
26  End Sub
```

In line 2, the variable *h* is declared as a Worksheet object. We will see this in detail later when we see the various objects that Excel has.

In line 6 the array of names is built.

In line 7 we make the variable *h* equal to the spreadsheet that we call "Arrays".

In line 8 we assign an empty string ("") to the variable TextString . It is the equivalent of assigning zero to a numeric variable to start it.

Between lines 9 and 11 we have a **For-Next** control structure that allows you to write the array of names (M) in the "Arrays" spreadsheet. This is done to take advantage of the functions that Excel has to sort data.

Between lines 12 and 20 the sorting of the information in the spreadsheet is done. I in particular do not know all the details with which VBA - Excel counts, so I often record a macro that does something I want to do (or similar) and then I take from the code what interests me.

In line 13 Excel is prepared so that it can receive the field that will be used as the key to sort the information. This instruction is essential.

Between lines 14 and 15, the field that will be used as the key to sort the information is added. In our exercise, the names (**SortOn: = xlSortOnValues**) will be sorted alphabetically from A to Z (**Order: = xlAscending**).

In line 16, the range of information to be sorted is established. In our case, it coincides with the set of data that will be used as the key to sort the information.

In line 17 the subroutine is indicated if the data list has a header or not. In our case, the data column has no header (**Header = xlGuess**). If the data has a header, then the instruction would have been **Header = xlYes**.

Line 18 indicates the method to use to sort the data.

In line 19, the procedure of sorting the data (**.Apply**) is finally applied.

Between lines 21 and 24, new values are assigned to the "M" array that contains the names and the text string is built. This text string will then be displayed by using the **MsgBox** instruction in line 25.

Figure 3.26 shows the result of the execution of the subroutine 3.12.

Figure 3.26. Result of the execution of the subroutine 3.12.

3.8.5 Using the function Erase in arrays

The function Erase used in arrays performs differently depending on the types of arrays and the variables defined in them. For example, in the case of arrays whose dimension is static or fixed, the values are restored to their default values. If the array contains integers, these values are all zeroed. In the case of an array of strings, all elements are carried to empty strings (""). Subroutine 3.13. is an example of the use of **Erase**.

Subroutine 3.13.

1	Public Sub EraseStatic()
2	Dim family(3) As String
3	Dim i As Integer
4	family(0) = "Surya"
5	family(1) = "Valentina"
6	family(2) = "Victor"
7	family(3) = "Anama"
8	Debug.Print "Name"
9	For i = LBound(family) To UBound(family)
10	Debug.Print family(i)
11	Next i
12	Erase family
13	Debug.Print "Nombre"
14	For i = LBound(family) To UBound(family)
15	Debug.Print family(i)
16	Next i
17	End Sub

Between lines 4 and 7 names are assigned to the elements of the array "family".

etween lines 9 and 11, the contents of the array "family" are sent to the window Immediate.

In line 12, the contents of each of the elements of the "family" array are deleted.

Between lines 14 and 15, the contents of the array are again sent to the window Immediate.

When executing this code, the window "Immediate" will be seen as shown in figure 3.27. Remember that you have access to this window through the instruction **Debug**. As you can see in the figure below, now it only sends empty strings to the window.

In the case of dynamic arrays, the function **Erase** clears the entire array. If you want to use the array again, then you must use **ReDim**. If after having deleted an array, we try to access an element of that array, we will get an error like the one shown in figure 3.24. Let's see the following sample code.

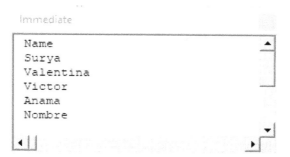

Figure 3.27. Window Immediate showing information sent by the subroutine 3.13.

Subroutine 3.14.

1	Public Sub EraseDynamic()
2	Dim family()
3	ReDim family(3)
4	Dim i As Integer
5	family(0) = "Surya"
6	family(1) = "Valentina"
7	family(2) = "Victor"
8	family(3) = "Anama"
9	Debug.Print "Name"
10	For i = LBound(family) To UBound(family)
11	Debug.Print family(i)
12	Next i
13	Erase family
14	Debug.Print "Name"
15	For i = LBound(family) To UBound(family)
16	Debug.Print family(i)
17	Next i
18	End Sub

When executing the code, the window "Immediate" will look as shown in figure 3.27, after executing the first **For** loop (between lines 10 and 12). Then, when trying to execute the second **For** loop (between lines 15 and 17) and after having deleted the array (line 13), an error appears as shown in figure 3.24.

3.8.6 Multidimensional arrays

So far we have worked with one-dimensional arrays. Multidimensional arrays have more than one dimension, as if they were several overlapping single-dimension arrays. An example of a multidimensional array is as shown below:

Dim A(5,4) As Long

With *Option Base 0*, then our matrix will have 6x5 = 30 elements, distributed in 6 rows by 5 columns.

The same definition rules apply for single-dimension arrays as well as to multidimensional arrays.

With *Option Base 0*, then our matrix will have 6x5 = 30 elements, distributed in 6 rows by 5 columns. The same definition rules for single-dimension arrays apply to multidimensional arrays. VBA only allows arrays of up to 60 dimensions (hopefully they reach for your purposes)

3.8.7 Passing an array to a subroutine or function

Arrays are passed to a function or to other subroutine using **ByRef**, this means that a reference to the array is actually being passed. Let's see the following example.

Subroutine 3.15.

1	Public Sub PassingArrays()
2	Dim family(3) As String
3	family(0) = "Surya"
4	family(1) = "Valentina"
5	family(2) = "Victor"
6	family(3) = "Anama"
7	ShowNames family
8	End Sub

Subroutine 3.16.

1	Function ShowNames(ByRef arrayf() As String)
2	Dim i As Integer
3	Debug.Print "Name"
4	For i = LBound(arrayf) To UBound(arrayf)
5	Debug.Print arrayf(i)
6	Next i
7	End Function

This subroutine calls the function ShowNames (subroutine 3.16) in line 7. This function will write in the window Immediate each of the elements that make up the array, as shown in figure 3.27. Note that the expression **ByRef** will cause the function ShowNames to receive a reference to the array family. Another aspect that is worth noticing is that this particular function does not return anything.

3.8.8 Returning an array from a function

Based on the previous example, let's imagine now that we want the array of names to be built in the function then return it to the subroutine and show it in the window Immediate.

Subroutine 3.17.

```
1   Sub ReceivingArrays()
2   Dim family() As String
3   Dim i As Integer
4   family = PopulateNames
5   Debug.Print "Name"
6   For i = LBound(family) To UBound(family)
7       Debug.Print family(i)
8   Next i
9   End Sub
```

Subroutine 3.18.

```
1   Public Function PopulateNames() As String()
2   Dim arrayf(3) As String
3   arrayf(0) = "Surya"
4   arrayf(1) = "Valentina"
5   arrayf(2) = "Victor"
6   arrayf(3) = "Anama"
7   PopulateNames = arrayf
8   End Function
```

The result of the execution of this program will be the same as the one obtained with the code shown in the previous point.

In line 4 (subroutine 3.17) we make the array "family" equal the output of the function PopulateNames. Note that in this case the function has been invoked without passing any arguments to it.

The function does not receive anything, so there is nothing between the parentheses, but notice that the function does return something. That something is an array, which contains elements of type String. The parentheses after the word String at the end of the function name indicate this.

Chapter 4. Control structures

4.1 Introduction

The control structures allow to regulate the way in which the execution of a program flows. They are used to tell the algorithm to repeat a task a predetermined number of times or as long as a condition is met. The control structures can be:

1. Decision structures.
2. Loop structures.
3. Other structures (With – End With, nested structures).

Let's see in detail each one of them. All the programs shown here can be written in the code windows of the modules.

4.2 Decision structures

4.2.1 If – Then – Else

This structure allows to evaluate one or more conditions and execute one or more instructions depending on the result of the evaluation.

This structure can be as complex as necessary. For example, it is possible to add an **Elsif** condition, in case the result of a condition is False and you want to ask again. It is also possible to add **Else** if after having evaluated a condition, you want to do something more without asking for new conditions. This came out tangled up, I think that I did not understand what I said. It seems to me that the most practical way is going through several examples from simple to more complex.

Subroutine 4.1.

```
1   Sub TestIf()
2   Dim age As Integer
3   age = InputBox("How old are you?", _
4   "Testing the structure If-Then-Else")
5   If age >= 18 Then
6       MsgBox "Congratulations, you can go to bed late", vbOKOnly, _
7       "Permission to go to bed late"
8   End If
9   End Sub
```

The previous example shows the simplest form of an **If** structure. The user is asked to enter his age and depending on it, the person may or may not be late to bed. However, there is no message for those who enter an age under 18 years. In the next subroutine, we will add an **Else** instruction to give a message for those under 18.

Subroutine 4.2.

```
1   Sub TestIfElse()
2   Dim age As Integer
3   Dim message As String
4   age = InputBox("How old are you?", _
5   "Testing the structure If-Then-Else")
6   If age >= 18 Then
7       message = "Congratulations, you can go to bed late"
8       Else
9       message = "What a pity, you have to sleep early"
10  End If
11  MsgBox message, vbOKOnly, "Permission to go to bed late"
12  End Sub
```

Before moving on to the next code, notice how we have added custom titles to the windows where information is requested (line 4) and where information is displayed (line 7).

Now, in the following example, we will see that according to the age, there are films that according to the Motion Picture Association of America's Film-rating System a person can or cannot watch.

Subroutine 4.3.

```
1   Sub TestIfElseElsif()
2   Dim age As Integer
3   Dim message As String
4   age = InputBox("How old are you?", _
5   "Testing the structure If-Then-Else")
6   If age < 10 Then
7       message = "You can watch movies classified G"
8       ElseIf age > 9 And age < 14 Then
9       message = "You can watch films classified G and PG"
10      ElseIf age > 13 And age < 18 Then
11      message = "You can watch films classified G, PG and PG-13"
12      Else
13      message = "You can watch the movie you want"
14  End If
15  MsgBox message, vbOKOnly, "Movies you can watch"
16  End Sub
```

When executing the previous code, the user is invited to enter his/her age through the window shown in figure 4.1.

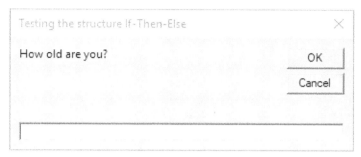

Figure 4.1. Window that invites the user to enter their age.

Then, depending on the age, a corresponding message will appear. For example, I am lucky because I am over 18 years old. Thus, when entering my age, the program indicates what is shown in figure 4.2.

Figure 4.2. Authorization message to watch any movie, thanks to being over 18 years old.

4.2.2 Select – Case

This type of structure allows the evaluation to be done only once and depending on the possible values resulting from the evaluation, a certain set of instructions are executed. We are going to rewrite the previous code with this structure to see how it looks.

Subroutine 4.4.

```
1   Sub SelectCase()
2   Dim age As Integer
3   Dim message As String
4   age = InputBox("Que edad tienes?", _
5   "Testing the structure Select-Case")
6   Select Case age
7       Case Is < 10
```

8	message = "You can watch movies classified G"
9	GoTo EndS
10	Case Is < 14
11	message = "You can watch films classified G and PG"
12	Case Is < 18
13	message = "You can watch films classified G, PG and PG-13"
14	Case Else
15	message = "You can watch the movie you want"
16	End Select
17	EndS: MsgBox message, vbOKOnly, "Movies you can watch"

4.3 Loop structures

4.3.1 While – Wend

It allows the execution of a series of instructions, once one (or several) condition(s) established at the beginning of the flow has been met. Let's see the following example.

Subroutine 4.5.

```
1   Sub testWhile()
2   Dim i As Integer
3   i = 0
4   Debug.Print "Number"
5   While i < 10
6       Debug.Print i
7       i = i + 1
8   Wend
9   End Sub
```

This program will show the numbers from 0 to 9 in the Immediate window. As we can see in line 5, the condition is that it shows the numbers until the variable "i" is less than 10. Another important aspect to note is that a **While** stream in VBA ends with the word **Wend** (line 8) and not in **End While** as it happens in Visual Basic.

4.3.2 Do – Loop Until

This structure, unlike the previous one, executes the instructions at least once and the evaluation of whether or not it continues at the end of the structure. The following example will show you how to obtain the same result of the previous program, but with this structure.

Subroutine 4.6.

```
1   Sub TestDo()
2   Dim i As Integer
```

```
3   i = 0
4   Debug.Print "Number"
5   Do
6      Debug.Print i
7      i = i + 1
8   Loop Until i > 9
9   End Sub
```

Once the previous subroutine has been executed, it will show an output similar to that obtained with the subroutine of the previous numeral.

4.3.3 For – Next

This structure allows a series of instructions to be repeated a known number of times. You can put controls to the execution through nested decision structures. Continuing with our problem of showing the numbers from 0 to 9, let's see what the program looks like with this structure.

Subroutine 4.7.

```
1   Sub TestFor()
2   Dim i As Integer
3   Debug.Print "Number"
4   For i = 0 To 9
5      Debug.Print i
6   Next i
7   End Sub
```

This subroutine will show the same result as the previous two subroutines.

4.3.4 For – Each – Next

This structure can be used when you want to repeat a series of instructions for each element of an array or collection. It is not necessary to know in advance how many elements the array has.

Subroutine 4.8.

```
1   Sub testForEach()
2   Dim A(4) As String
3   Dim name As Variant
4   A(0) = "Surya"
5   A(1) = "Valentina"
6   A(2) = "Victor"
7   A(3) = "Anama"
8   A(4) = "Dorian"
9   Debug.Print "The members of my family are: "
```

10	For Each name In A
11	Debug.Print name
12	Next
13	End Sub

In this example we have created an array "A" with the names of my family members (including myself). The output of this program is shown in figure 4.3. Look at something interesting in this program: the array containing the names is declared as a **String** type. However, the control variable "name" (line 10) must be **Variant** (line 3). If it is declared otherwise, an error will occur, such as the one shown in figure 4.4.

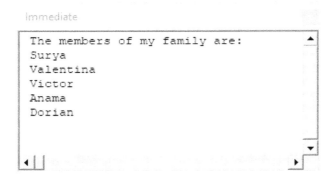

Figure 4.3. Result of the execution of the subroutine 4.8.

Figure 4.4. Error that occurs when declaring a control variable as a different type to Variant in a For - Each - Next loop.

In case it is necessary to quit the **For - Each - Next structure**, it is possible to use the **Exit For** instruction. Imagine for a moment that we want to stop the loop when the condition *name = Victor* is fulfilled. The code would look as shown in subroutine 4.9.

Subroutine 4.9.

1	Sub testForEach2()
2	Dim A(4) As String

```
 3  Dim name As Variant
 4  A(0) = "Surya"
 5  A(1) = "Valentina"
 6  A(2) = "Victor"
 7  A(3) = "Anama"
 8  A(4) = "Dorian"
 9  Debug.Print "The members of my family are: "
10  For Each name In A
11     If name = "Victor" Then
12        Exit For
13     End If
14     Debug.Print name
15  Next
16  End Sub
```

The execution of the program will only show the names Surya and Valentina.

4.4 Other structures

4.4.1 With – End With

This structure allows you to specify a reference to an object only once and then execute a series of instructions to access its members. This allows, among other things, to simplify the code and improve performance because VBA does not have to reset the reference for each statement that accesses the object. An example of the use of this structure is shown in subroutine 3.12.

4.4.2 Nested structures

This means that control structures can be placed within other control structures. Then, when one control structure is placed inside another, it is said to be nested. Let's see the following example.

Subroutine 4.10.

```
 1  Sub NestedStructure()
 2  Dim i, age As Integer
 3  For i = 1 To 3
 4  age = InputBox("How old are you?", _
 5  "Testing Nested Structures")
 6     If age > 30 Then
 7        Debug.Print "You must take care of your health"
 8     Else
 9        Debug.Print "Have you enjoyed your life?"
10     End If
```

| 11 | Next i |
| 12 | End Sub |

When executing this code, the messages shown in figure 4.5 will be displayed. These messages do not have to be the same when you execute them, since the ages you enter may be different.

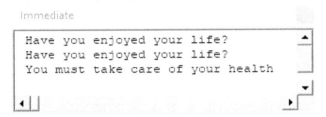

Immediate

```
Have you enjoyed your life?
Have you enjoyed your life?
You must take care of your health
```

Figure 4.5. Result of the execution of the subroutine 4.10.

Nested structures can also be useful when working with arrays. Imagine for a moment that we want to find the matrix transpose from the matrix shown below:

$$A = \begin{matrix} 1 & 2 & 3 \\ 4 & 5 & 6 \\ 7 & 8 & 9 \end{matrix}$$

The transpose matrix will be:

$$A^t = \begin{matrix} 1 & 4 & 7 \\ 2 & 5 & 8 \\ 3 & 6 & 9 \end{matrix}$$

In this example, we will work again with objects belonging to Excel. For now, practice with this exercise as it will be given and later the Excel object model will be explained in detail.

In a spreadsheet, within an Excel file, we will place the values of the matrix that we want to transpose. Something similar to what is shown in figure 4.6.

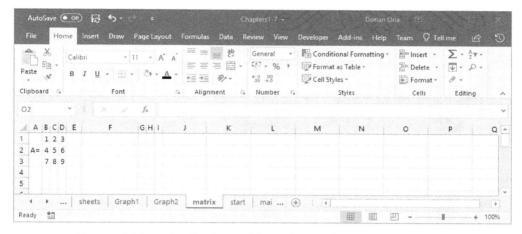

Figure 4.6. View of an Excel spreadsheet showing the input matrix values.

Now, in a VBA module type the code shown below.

Subroutine 4.11.

```
1   Sub TransposeMatrix()
2   Dim r, c As Integer 'r: rows, c: columns
3   With Worksheets("matrix")
4   For r = 0 To 2
5     For c = 0 To 2
6       .Cells(r + 1, c + 7) = .Cells(c + 1, r + 2)
7     Next c
8   Next r
9   End With
10  End Sub
```

As you can see in the code, there are two structures nested inside a **With - End With** structure.

Line 3 begins with the **With - End With** structure, in which a reference is made to the Worksheets object, which in our case we have called "matrix". Once the reference to that object is made, we refer to the Cells object (which is another way to refer to a cell or Range object), which allows access to each of the cells of a spreadsheet. This can be imagined as if each spreadsheet were a gigantic matrix. The parameters of the Cells object indicate the coordinates of that cell. The first parameter corresponds to the row and the second to the column. The rows grow down and the columns to the right. So the first cell (the one in the upper left corner) corresponds to the cell (1,1).

In our algorithm, the letter r is used as an index to refer to the rows and the letter c to refer to the columns.

Once you execute this code, the Excel sheet shown in the previous figure will look like in figure 4.7.

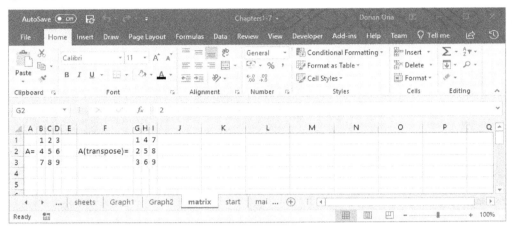

Figure 4.7. Result of the execution of the subroutine 4.11.

Chapter 5. Objects and their hierarchy

5.1 Introduction

In terms of programming languages, an object is an entity that has specific properties and operations that can be done with them (methods). In our case, Excel can be seen as an object, which at the same time has other objects within it, so the Excel object is at the top of the object hierarchy.

Figure 5.1 shows graphically Excel objects and their relationships. These objects constitute in a certain way the backbone of VBA - Excel.

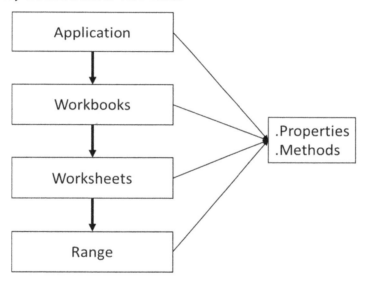

Figure 5.1. VBA-Excel object model.

The *Application* object represents the Excel program itself.

Workbooks is an object that represents the collection of all open books in an Excel session.

Worksheets represent each of the spreadsheets present in a book or Excel file.

Range represents each of the cells that are part of a spreadsheet.

5.2 Objects within Excel

The name of the Excel object within the VBA language is *Application*. This object in turn contains other objects:

- Addins
- Windows
- Workbooks
- WorksheetFunctions

Each of the objects mentioned above contain other objects. For example, the following objects are contained within the *Workbook* object:

- Charts
- VBproject
- Window
- Worksheet

In turn, each of the above objects also has objects within it. Take the *Worksheet* object as an example:

- Comment
- Hyperlink
- Range

So, if we wanted to plot the complete path of belonging to the *Range* object, we could write it in the following way:

Range→Worksheet→Worksheet→Application (Excel)

Of course, this is only a small sample. Excel has a large number of objects that we will discover little by little as we move forward.

5.3 Collections

Another key concept in VBA are collections. A collection is a group of objects of the same type and can also be treated as an object. Examples of collections:

- Workbooks
- Worksheets
- Charts

Notice how all the names of the collections are in plural.

5.4 Objects and how to refer to them

When I started programming, I was so eager to learn that I never learned how everything was called in the programming language. I learned as I was writing code and seeing how it worked and what each instruction did. I do not know how practical this method is for you, but I think it's worth taking the risk. So let's try to learn by doing.

To refer to an object, we must use its full and exact name.

For example in figure 5.2 we see a newly created Excel file. The Excel object will be called according to the name we choose for it. For example, we save the file with the name "Test.xlsm" (with the extension .xlsm we tell Excel that it is a file that contains macros and that you can execute them).

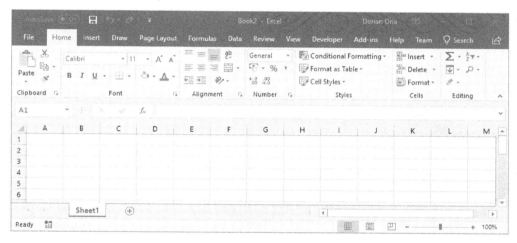

Figure 5.2. Application (Excel) showing a spreadsheet.

After changing the name, the Excel file will look as shown in figure 5.3.

So, to refer to our newly created Excel file, the following expression is used:

Application.Workbooks ("Test.xlsm")

As can be seen in figure 5.3, our Excel file has a spreadsheet called "Sheet1". This name can be preserved or changed, but regardless of that, Excel has already assigned the number 1 to that spreadsheet internally. If we add another sheet, Excel will automatically add the name "Sheet2" and if we change the name, Excel can also refer to it as number 2.

If we wish to refer to spreadsheet number 1, we can do it in one of the following ways: (based on the file shown in figure 5.4)

Application.Workbooks("Test.xlsm").Worksheets("Main") or

Application.Workbooks("Test.xlsm").Worksheets(1)

Now, if we wanted to refer to cell "A1", we could write:

Application.Workbooks("Test.xlsm").Worksheets("Main").Range("A1") or

Application.Workbooks("Test.xlsm").Worksheets(1).Range("A1")

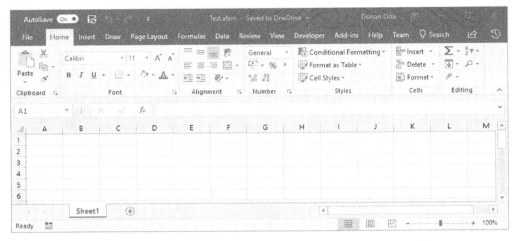

Figure 5.3. Application with updated name for the Excel file (book).

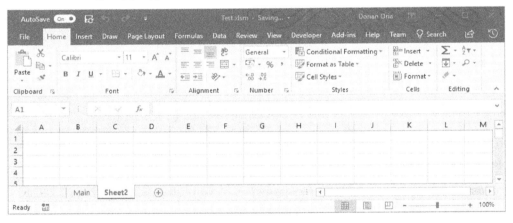

Figure 5.4. Excel file (Workbook object) showing two spreadsheets (which are objects of the Worksheets collection).

Imagine for a moment that you want to assign the value 100 to cell A1. For this, we use the following instruction:

Application.Workbooks("Test.xlsm").Worksheets(1).Range("A1") = 100.

If you want to be more specific, you can write:

Application.Workbooks("Test.xlsm").Worksheets(1).Range("A1").Value = 100.

You do not always have to write so much code to refer to an object. When VBA code is executed and no detail of the location of an object is specified, VBA assumes that all code must be executed taking into account the worksheets that are active. For example, let's see the following code.

Subroutine 5.1.

```
1   Sub firstSteps()
2   Range("A1") = 300
3   End Sub
```

If the active sheet is "Main" (in the example shown in figure 5.4), then the number 300 will be written in cell A1 of that sheet. Now, if the active sheet was Sheet2, then the number 300 was written in cell A1 of this sheet.

t is clear that this is a very simple example. However, there may be a time in the complexity of a program that a very simple way to refer a cell can complicate the handling of the application, because you should be aware of the active spreadsheet on which you want to work and, in many cases, a program works with several spreadsheets at a time. So, in this case, it is advisable that, whenever you are working with a single Excel file, you to add to the address of a cell, the worksheet on which you want to work

Thus, by rewriting the code shown above for the sheet "Main", the code would remain that way:

Subroutine 5.2.

```
1   Sub firstSteps2()
2   Worksheets("Main").Range("A1") = 300
3   End Sub
```

With this way of referring to cell A1, it is not necessary to be aware of the spreadsheet that is active.

All objects can be customized in their corresponding hierarchy.

5.5 Properties of objects

Each object in Excel has properties. Properties describe characteristics of an object: color, font, size, etc. Through VBA it is possible to:

- Check the current property of an object.
- Set or change the property of that object.

For example, a simple cell in a spreadsheet has a property called *Value* (which is a default property of the cells, meaning it was not necessary to indicate it explicitly to assign the value to the cell). This property stores the value contained in the cell. Then, you can write code to assign a value to a cell, (as shown in the previous code) or you can write code to retrieve the value in a cell. We are going to modify the previous code to illustrate it.

Subroutine 5.3.

```
1   Sub firstSteps3()
2   Worksheets("Main").Range("A1") = 300
3   MsgBox Worksheets("Main").Range("A1").Value
4   End Sub
```

Note in the code as I purposely obviated the *Value* property in the instruction in line 2 and how I added it in line 3. In both cases the instruction refers to the same property.

When executing this code, the window shown in figure 5.5 appears.

Figure 5.5. Result of the execution of the subroutine 5.3.

Each object has a set of properties, but they are not exclusive to them. There are many properties that are common to other objects. The collections also have properties. For example, the code in the 5.4 subroutine lets you know how many Excel files are open in a session.

Subroutine 5.4.

```
1   Sub firstSteps4()
2   MsgBox "There are " & Workbooks.Count & " Excel files open"
3   End Sub
```

In my session I have two opened books. Figure 5.6 shows the result of the execution of the 5.4 subroutine.

Figure 5.6. Result of the execution of the 5.4 sub-routine.

5.6 Object methods

In addition to properties, objects have methods. A method is an action that is executed with an object. A method can change the properties of an object or cause the object to do something.

For example, the following code when executed, adds a new Excel book.

Subroutine 5.5.

```
1   Sub firstSteps5()
2   Workbooks.Add
3   End Sub
```

VBA Excel has a way to help us know what the properties and methods of an object are and helps us differentiate them from each other.

If you wrote the previous code in the VBA editor, once you finished writing a point after the word *Workbooks* a submenu will come up, as shown in figure 5.7. As you can see, some words appear with a green icon on the left side and others with an icon that has a hand. The words with the green icon correspond to the methods and the others correspond to the properties.

Some methods can take one or more parameters, that is, a value that can give more detail to the action to be executed. The parameter is added to a method after it, separated by a comma. VBA comes back to our aid in this case. When placing the space after the instruction of line 2, VBA tells us that it expects that what is entered as an argument is a *template* (figure 5.8). If we do not put the argument, VBA assumes that we want to add a standard template. The 5.6 subroutine shows what the code looks like when we ask you to specifically add a *template*.

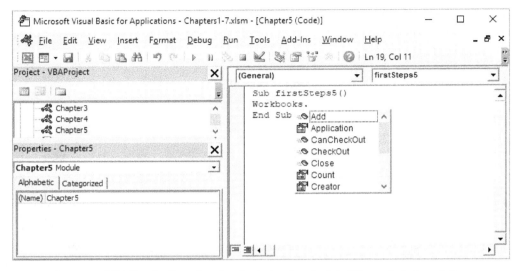

Figure 5.7. VBA-Excel editor showing the help given by *IntelliSense Code Completion*.

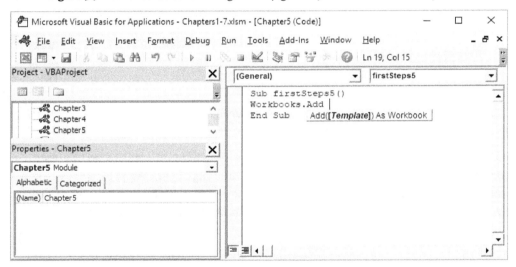

Figure 5.8. More detail on the operation of *IntelliSense Code Completion*.

Subroutine 5.6.

1	Sub firstSteps6()
2	Workbooks.Add template:= _
3	"C:\Users\dorian\AppData\Roaming\Microsoft\Templates\Welcome to Excel.xltx"
4	End Sub

5.7 Events in VBA - Excel

An event is an action that the user generates when, for example, he presses a key or clicks with the mouse or selects an object (such as a spreadsheet, an excel book or a cell). An Event Procedure is a subroutine written by the user that VBA Excel automatically calls when the event is presented. Let's see the following code.

Subroutine 5.7.

1	Private Sub worksheet_change(ByVal target As Range)
2	MsgBox ("You have changed something in this sheet")
3	End Sub

The code of the subroutine 5.7 was written in the code window of the object Sheet1. To add this subroutine, it is necessary to do the following steps:

1. Double-click on the object Sheet1 (listed in the Project window of the VBA programming environment). This causes the code window for that object to open.

2. Select the Worksheet object, as shown in figure 5.9. This is necessary so that the events associated with this object are listed in the *combo-box* next to it.

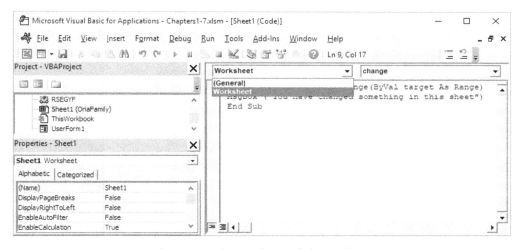

Figure 5.9. Selecting the Worksheet object.

3. Select, as shown in figure 5.10, the event that you wish to program. In our exercise, we want to program a subroutine that will be executed when the user makes a change in the object Sheet1 (Change).

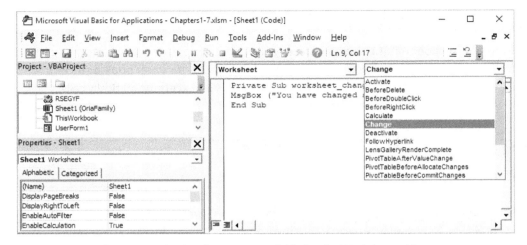

Figure 5.10. Viewing the events available for the Worksheet object.

4. Once the previous step is completed, VBA-Excel automatically adds a subroutine where the instructions will be and that will be executed when the Change event occurs in the worksheet Sheet1.

For example, writing something in any cell of the worksheet "Sheet1" will cause the message shown in figure 5.11 to appear (according to the instruction in line 2 of the 5.7 subroutine).

Figure 5.11. Response to events that generate changes in the object "Sheet1".

It is important to note that the subroutines of the events are declared **Private**. This is because events are always related to an object. You can not program a subroutine for an event in a code window other than the one that belongs to the object.

5.8 Additional help

VBA Excel is a mature programming language. If you need additional help on properties and methods of each object in Excel, you can turn to the Object Browser (figure 5.12). It can be accessed by pressing the F2 key, from the Menu Bar (View menu) or from the Standard toolbar using the button highlighted in figure 5.13.

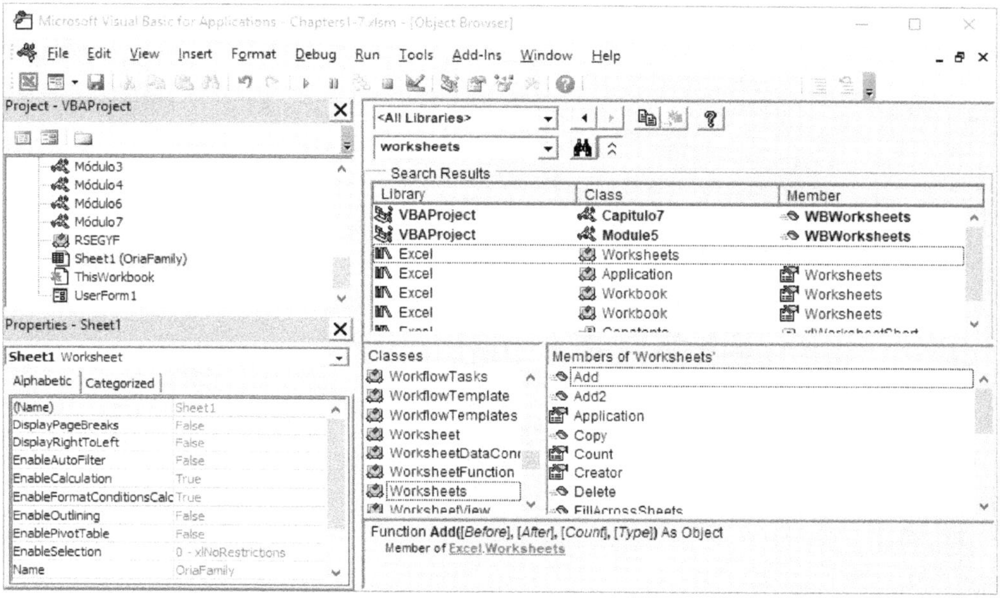

Figure 5.12. Object Browser.

Suppose you want to get information about the properties and methods of the Worksheets collection (figure 5.12). Write in the textbox, next to the binoculars, the name of the collection and in the *Search* results select the topic that fits what you are looking for. Figure 5.12 shows the properties and methods of the Worksheets collection within the "Members of the 'Worksheets' window. If one of the members is selected, the arguments taken by that member (if applicable) can be seen in the lower part of the window.

Figure 5.13. Button to display the Object Browser.

Chapter 6. Application Object

6.1 Introduction

As already mentioned in the previous chapter, the Application object represents the Excel application completely. It is possible, with the properties and methods of this object, to make your application look and behave in a very professional way, different from a conventional Excel file or book.

6.2 Properties of the Application object

Next, we will describe the properties that I consider most important for this object. However, if you want to know more about the properties of this object, you can consult the information available in the following link: https://msdn.microsoft.com/en-us/vba/excel-vba/articles/application-object-excel

6.2.1 Caption property

Returns or sets a text string that represents the name that appears in the title bar of the main Excel window.

Subroutine 6.1.

```
1  Sub AppCaption()
2  Application.Caption = "My own application"
3  End Sub
```

Figure 6.1 shows the result of the execution of the previous subroutine. The text string that has been added from line 2 of the code is displayed inside the rectangle.

6.2.2 DisplayAlerts property

This property, if it takes the value *True*, shows certain alerts and messages while a subroutine is running. For example, when a change is made to an Excel file and an attempt is made to close it without first saving the changes, the application displays a message similar to the one shown in figure 6.2.

On the other hand, if we make *DisplayAlerts* take the False value, with the subroutine that follows we can close the file without the alert being displayed. If changes were made and not saved before executing the subroutine, they will be lost.

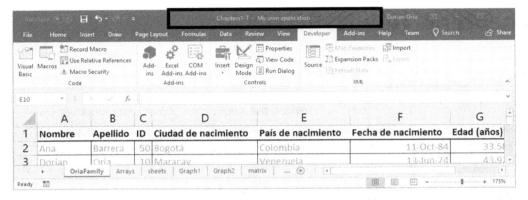

Figure 6.1. Result of the execution of the subroutine 6.1.

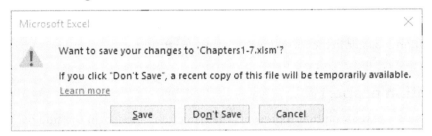

Figure 6.2. Excel alert about changes without saving in a book that is going to be closed.

Subroutine 6.2.

1	Sub DispAlert()
2	Application.DisplayAlerts = False
3	Workbooks("Test.xlsm").Close
4	End Sub

6.2.3 DisplayFormulaBar property

Shows or hides the Excel formula bar.

Subroutine 6.3.

1	Sub ShowFormulaBar()
2	Application.DisplayFormulaBar = False
3	End Sub

Figure 6.3 shows how Excel looks with the toolbar not visible, after having executed the subroutine 6.3.

6.2.4 DisplayFullScreen property

If the property is set to True, it makes Excel enter full-screen mode. This means that only spreadsheets and their cells will be seen. Excel will occupy the entire screen and none of the bars will be visible: toolbars, menus, formulas or status bar (figure 6.4).

Subroutine 6.4.

```
1   Sub DispFullScreen()
2   Application.DisplayFullScreen = True
3   End Sub
```

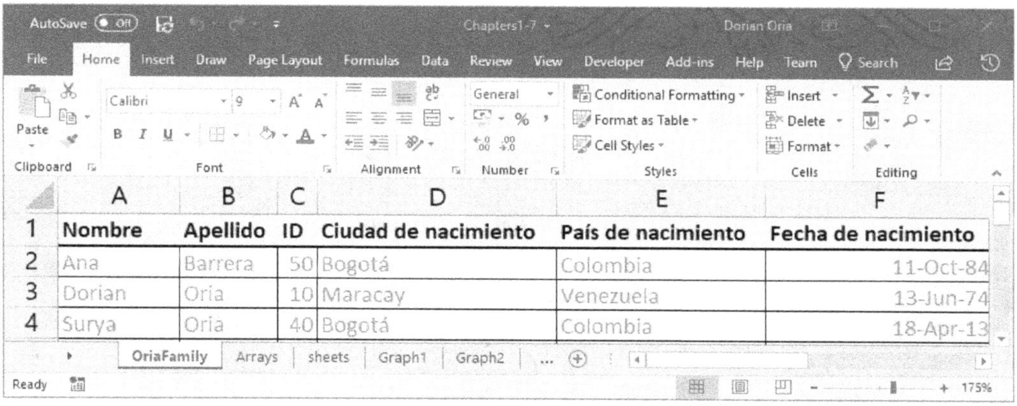

Figure 6.3. Excel with the formula bar hidden.

6.2.5 ScrollBars property

Scrollbars are a couple of bars that are usually located at the bottom and at the right side of the application. They allow you to scroll down and to the right of the spreadsheets. The following subroutine causes the scrollbars not to be visible.

Subroutine 6.5.

```
1   Sub DispScrollBars()
2   Application.DisplayScrollBars = False
3   End Sub
```

Figure 6.5 shows the result of the execution of the subroutine 6.5.

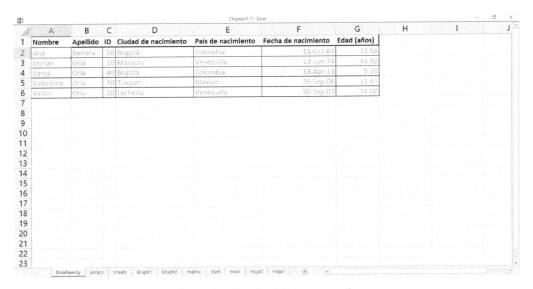

Figure 6.4. Excel in full-screen mode.

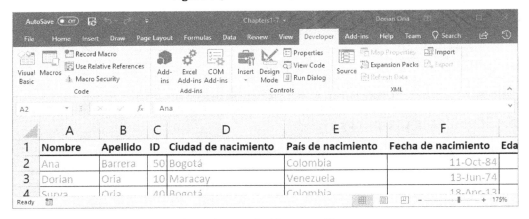

Figure 6.5. Excel without scrollbars.

6.2.6 DisplayStatusBar property

In Excel, the status bar is located at the bottom of the application (below inclusive of scroll bars) and displays information such as *zoom* within a spreadsheet. If there is selected data in a spreadsheet, as shown in figure 6.6 (inside the rectangle), the status bar shows the sum of those values, the average and the amount of data selected. You can choose the information that it shows by clicking with the right mouse button on top of it.

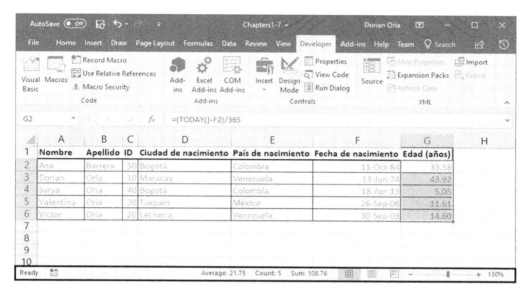

Figure 6.6. Excel showing status bar.

The following subroutine hides the status bar.

Subroutine 6.6.

1	Sub DispStatusBar()
2	Application.DisplayStatusBar = False
3	End Sub

Figure 6.7 shows the application without the status bar after executing the subroutine 6.6.

6.2.7 FileDialog property

Returns a *FileDialog* object that represents an instance of dialog boxes. These dialog boxes allow you to choose files to open them, save them or simply choose a file or choose a folder.

The following subroutine shows the *FileDialog* option to open a file of any extension that can be recognized by Excel (*msoFileDialogOpen*).

Subroutine 6.7.

1	Sub EjFileDialog1()
2	With Application.FileDialog(msoFileDialogOpen)
3	.Title = "My own window to open Excel files"
4	.AllowMultiSelect = False
5	.Filters.Add "Excel files", "*.xls;*.xlsx;*.xlsm", 1
6	.Show
7	.Execute

8	End With
9	End Sub

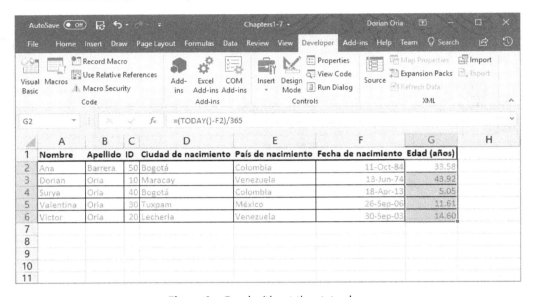

Figure 6.7. Excel without the status bar.

In line 3, the title of the dialog window has been customized.

By default, Windows allows to select several files at the same time in the windows used to open or select them. To avoid this, the *AllowMultiSelect* property was made to take the *False* value (line 4). This variable by default is *True*.

Line 5 has added filters that are the extensions of the files that the dialog window will show first when it is displayed as shown in figure 6.8.

In line 6 the instruction to show the window is given and in line 7 the order is given so that the selected file is opened.

If the command to open the file is not given (Execute on line 7), then the window works as if the *msoFileDialogFilePicker* option had been used in line 2 (instead of *msoFileDialogOpen*).

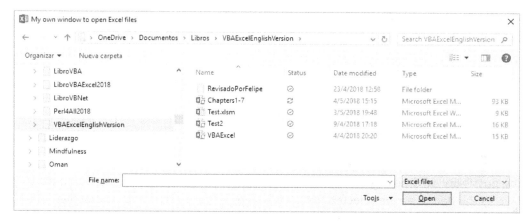

Figure 6.8. Dialog window to open files recognized by Excel.

The following subroutine allows you to choose a file regardless of the extension (*msoFileDialogFilePicker*).

Subroutine 6.8.

1	Sub EjFileDialog2()
2	Dim file As String
3	With Application.FileDialog(msoFileDialogFilePicker)
4	.AllowMultiSelect = False
5	.Show
6	If .SelectedItems.Count > 0 Then
7	file = .SelectedItems(1)
8	MsgBox "You have selected the file" & _
9	vbNewLine & file
10	Else
11	MsgBox "You have not selected any file"
12	End If
13	End With
14	End Sub

In line 6, an **If** condition was added to prevent an error in case the user does not choose any file (choose to press the "Cancel" button in the dialog window). If the user does not choose any file, then the number of items in the collection *.SelectedItems* is zero.

If *.SelectedItems* is greater than zero, then the subroutine shows the selected file, as shown in figure 6.9.

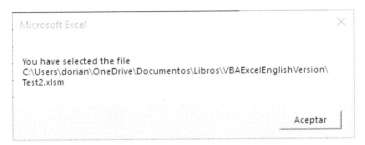

Figure 6.9. Result of the execution of subroutine 6.8, in case of having selected a file.

If the possibility of choosing several files had been allowed, the subroutine would have shown us the first of all the selected files. It is suggested to try selecting several files, but first change the index of the *SelectedItems* property.

Let's see below what the code would look like to show several selected files.

Subroutine 6.9.

1	Sub EjFileDialog3()
2	Dim file As Variant
3	Dim message As String
4	With Application.FileDialog(msoFileDialogFilePicker)
5	.AllowMultiSelect = True
6	.Show
7	For Each file In .SelectedItems
8	message = message & file & vbNewLine
9	Next file
10	End With
11	MsgBox "You have selected the files" & _
12	vbNewLine & message
13	End Sub

Between lines 7 and 9, through the use of a **For-Each** structure, each of the elements of the *SelectedItems* collection was accessed and a text string was created that will contain each of the names of the selected files (and its full route). Remember that the variable to be used in this structure must have been declared Variant (line 2).

The following subroutine shows the option of *FileDialog (msoFileDialogSaveAs)* to save information from an open file that Excel recognizes. It works as the "Save as" option.

Figure 6.10 shows the result of the execution of the subroutine 6.9.

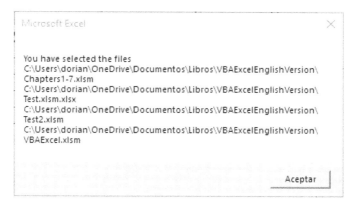

Figure 6.10. Result of the execution of the subroutine 6.9.

Subroutine 6.10.

1	Sub EjFileDialog4()
2	With Application.FileDialog(msoFileDialogSaveAs)
3	.Title = "My own window to save as"
4	.Show
5	.Execute
6	End With
7	End Sub

Figure 6.11 shows the "Save as" window as it was configured in the subroutine 6.10.

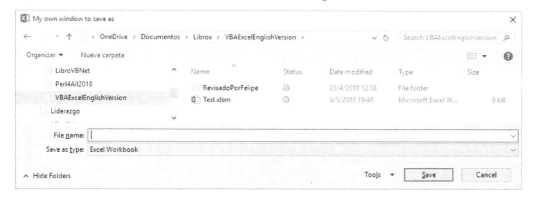

Figure 6.11. "Save as" window, result of the execution of the subroutine 6.10.

The following subroutine shows the *FileDialog* option that allows you to choose a folder (*msoFileDialogFolderPicker*).

Subroutine 6.11.

1	Sub EjFileDialog5()

2	Dim folder As String
3	With Application.FileDialog(msoFileDialogFolderPicker)
4	.AllowMultiSelect = False
5	.Title = "Select a folder"
6	.Show
7	If .SelectedItems.Count > 0 Then
8	folder = .SelectedItems(1)
9	MsgBox "You have selected a folder" & _
10	vbNewLine & folder
11	Else
12	MsgBox "You have not selected a folder"
13	End If
14	End With
15	End Sub

Figure 6.12 shows the selected folder after having executed the subroutine 6.11.

Figure 6.12. Folder selected after having executed the subroutine 6.11.

6.2.8 StatusBar property

Returns or sets the text that will be displayed in the status bar.

Subroutine 6.12.

1	Sub EjStatusBar()
2	Application.DisplayStatusBar = True
3	Application.StatusBar = "Working..."
4	End Sub

6.3 Events of the Application object

In this case we are going to explain some interesting events of the *Application* object before knowing about the methods since there are some that work more conveniently with the events.

In order to program any event for the *Application* object, it is necessary beforehand to declare a variable whose type is *Application*. Through it will be available events that can be programmed.

The steps to follow are the following:

In the code window of the ThisWorkbook object insert the following line:

Public WithEvents App As Application

With this instruction we are saying that an object variable (*App*) is created which will be of the *Application* type. The *App* variable is created with the keyword *WithEvents* in order to allow the object to receive events from *Application*.

Once this is done, the code window will look as shown in figure 6.13.

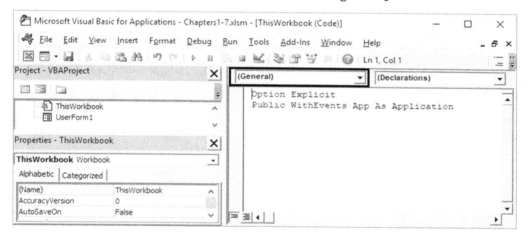

Figure 6.13. Declaration of the *App* variable in the code window of the *ThisWorkbook* object.

We are going to continue with the introduction of the *WorkbookOpen* event of the *Workbook* object, which occurs when an Excel workbook is opened.

Events must be inserted from those available in the *ThisWorkBook* object and must be done from the VBA editor. To do this, click inside the *combobox* that is enclosed in a rectangle in figure 6.13. By doing so, the *combobox* will look like the combo box in figure 6.14.

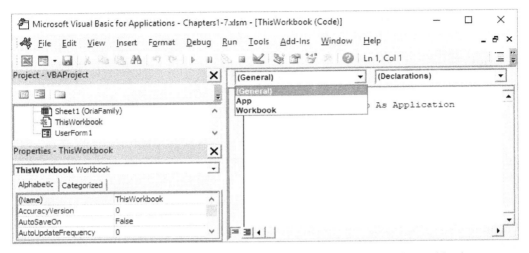

Figure 6.14. Displaying *combobox* to show the available objects in *ThisWorkbook*.

In that combobox we select *Workbook*. When doing so, by default the VBA-Excel editor adds the *Workbook_Open* event. The code window will look as shown in figure 6.15.

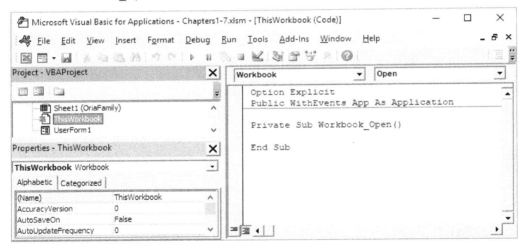

Figure 6.15. Code window of the *ThisWorkbook* object after selecting the *Workbook* object.

Within that event we will write the following line of code:

Set App = Application

With this instruction, the *Application* object is assigned to the App variable.

After this, the code will look as shown in figure 6.16.

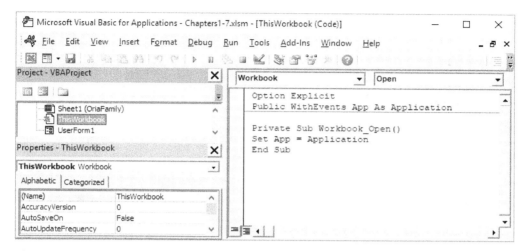

Figure 6.16. Code window of the *ThisWorkbook* object after setting the *App* variable as *Application*.

This step is necessary since these events are activated when the application is first opened. So, for these events to take effect, it is necessary to close the Excel book where the code is and reopen it. While the file is open, Excel loads in memory all the code (events) that is defined in the *ThisWorkbook* object and leaves them available for the case in which they are invoked.

6.3.1 NewWorkbook event

Occurs when a new Excel Workbook is created.

In the combo box that is enclosed in the rectangle of figure 6.13 we select **App**. By doing so, the VBA-Excel editor will add the *NewWorkbook* event (figure 6.17) by default.

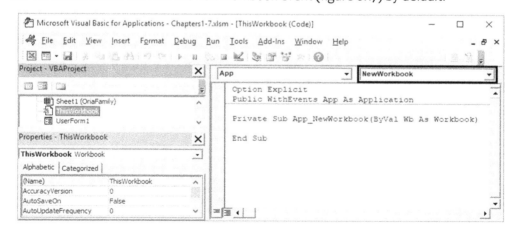

Figure 6.17. Code window of the *ThisWorkbook* object after selecting the **App** object.

In the combo box that is shown enclosed in the rectangle of figure 6.17 are all the events associated with the *Application* object declared with the **App** variable.

Subroutine 6.13.

1	Private Sub App_NewWorkbook(ByVal wb As Workbook)
2	wb.Worksheets.Add
3	wb.Worksheets(1).Name = "Main"
4	MsgBox "New Workbook: " & wb.Name
5	End Sub

It is interesting in this example that the event allows to recover the object that is being added (wb as Workbook object, line 1) and makes it available for the rest of the content that we want to add inside the subroutine of the event.

In this case the example is very simple: add a new spreadsheet (line 2), then assign a name to the spreadsheet number 1 (line 3) and finally show the name of the new book that is being added (line 4).

6.3.2 WorkbookOpen event

This event is similar to the *Workbook_Open* event of the *Workbook* object described in the introduction to this numeral (figures 6.15 and 6.16). The fundamental difference is that in the *WorkbookOpen* event of the **App** object the *Application* object cannot be assigned to the **App** variable. Otherwise, you can place any other instruction that you want to run when the application or a book is open. Events or instructions in the *Workbook_Open* event of the Workbook object occur first than those declared in the *WorkbookOpen* event of the **App** object.

Let's see the following example (figure 6.18). The subroutines enclosed in the rectangles show instructions to be executed when the book is opened: one associated with the application and the other associated with the *Workbook* object. When the file is opened, you will see that the first message that is displayed is the one that comes from the *Workbook_Open* event and then the event that comes from the *App_WorkbookOpen* event will be displayed.

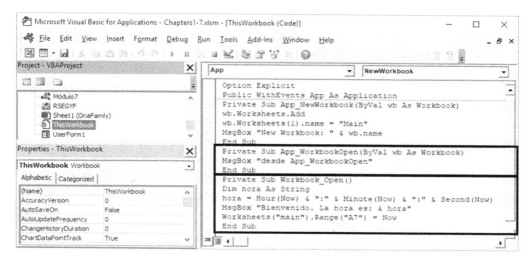

Figure 6.18. Subroutines of the *Workbook_Open* and *App_WorkbookOpen* events.

6.4 Methods of the Application object

6.4.1 FindFile method

This method displays the standard window for opening Excel files (***Open*** dialog box) or their compatible ones. It cannot be customized and it requires not as much programming compared to the *FileDialog* property.

Subroutine 6.14.

1	Sub EjFindFile()
2	Application.FindFile
3	End Sub

6.4.2 GetOpenFilename method

This method displays the standard window in order to open Excel files (or compatible) and to get a file name without actually opening it. In a way, it looks like the *FileDialog* property when it takes the *msoFileDialogFilePicker* value.

Subroutine 6.15.

1	Sub EjGetOpenFilename()
2	Dim file As String
3	Dim filters As String
4	filters = "Excel Files (*.xls;*.xlsx;*.xlsm),*.xls;*.xlsx;*.xlsm," & _
5	"Text Files (*.txt;*.prn;*.csv),*.txt;*.prn;*.csv"
6	file = Application.GetOpenFilename(filters, 2, "My customized window to open files", False)

```
7   MsgBox "The selected file is: " & vbNewLine & _
8       file
9   End Sub
```

In the previous subroutine a novelty has been introduced: the possibility of making the filter as a text string. The variable containing the filters was defined in line 4. Another interesting aspect of this subroutine is that the number 2 that appears as a parameter for the *GetOpenFilename* method indicates which filter will appear by default when the window is displayed, regardless of the order in which it has been defined in the text string that defines them. The word *False* at the end of the parameters indicates that the option that allows selecting more than one file at a time is disabled.

6.4.3 GetSaveAsFilename method

This method is used to display the standard "Save as" window to save Excel or compatible files, ask for a name for the file to save, without actually saving anything.

Subroutine 6.16.

```
1   Sub EjGetSaveAsFilename()
2   Dim file As String
3   Dim filters As String
4   filters = "Excel Files (*.xls;*.xlsx;*.xlsm),*.xls;*.xlsx;*.xlsm," & _
5       "Text Files (*.txt;*.prn;*.csv),*.txt;*.prn;*.csv"
6   file = Application.GetSaveAsFilename("", filters, 2, "My customized window to save files")
7   MsgBox "The file will be saved as with the name: " & vbNewLine & _
8       file
9   End Sub
```

The structure of the *GetSaveAsFilename* method is similar to that of the *GetOpenFilename* method, except that the first parameter is the tentative name that you want to give the file. In our example, an empty string has been assigned (line 6). Additionally the concept of eligibility of one or more files does not apply.

6.4.4 OnKey method

The OnKey method is used to execute a subroutine if you press a key or a combination of keys. This method is useful for assigning a shortcut to a subroutine, for cases in which the macro recorder was not used to generate it.

The table below shows the keys that can be used. Each one of them can be used without the need to be combined with others.

Table 6.1. Keys and their programming codes.

Key	Code
BACKSPACE	{BACKSPACE} o {BS}
BREAK	{BREAK}
CAPS LOCK	{CAPSLOCK}
CLEAR	{CLEAR}
DELETE or DEL	{DELETE} o {DEL}
DOWN ARROW	{DOWN}
END	{END}
ENTER (teclado numérico)	{ENTER}
ENTER	~ (tilde)
ESC	{ESCAPE} o {ESC}
HELP	{HELP}
HOME	{HOME}
INS	{INSERT}
LEFT ARROW	{LEFT}
NUM LOCK	{NUMLOCK}
PAGE DOWN	{PGDN}
PAGE UP	{PGUP}
RETURN	{RETURN}
RIGHT ARROW	{RIGHT}
SCROLL LOCK	{SCROLLLOCK}
TAB	{TAB}
UP ARROW	{UP}
F1 hasta F15	{F1} hasta {F15}

The following table shows the keys that can be combined with those in table 6.1.

Table 6.2. Secondary keys and their programming codes.

Key	Code
SHIFT	+
CTRL	^
ALT	%

Subroutine 6.17.

```
1   Sub EjOnKey()
2   Application.OnKey "^+{ENTER}", "EjGetSaveAsFilename"
3   End Sub
```

The parameters of the method must be enclosed in double quotes ("). The first parameter consists of the combination of keys that will invoke the subroutine that is after the comma.

6.4.5 Quit method

Exit Excel.

Subroutine 6.18.

1	Sub AppQUit()
2	Application.Quit
3	End Sub

Chapter 7. Workbook Object

7.1 Introduction

The Workbook object corresponds to an Excel workbook. It belongs to the Workbooks collection, which will contain all the books currently open in Excel. When working individually, the Workbook object has properties, methods and events that are different from those in the Workbooks collection. We will work first with the Workbook object and then with the collection.

7.2 Properties of the Workbook object

7.2.1 Property Charts

Returns a collection of graphics that occupy a sheet. Does not include graphics that are inside spreadsheets.

Subroutine 7.1.

```
1   Sub WBCharts()
2   Dim nwb As Integer
3   With ActiveWorkbook.Charts
4       nwb = .Count
5       MsgBox "This workbook has " & nwb & " charts and will be deleted"
6       If nwb > 0 Then
7           .Delete
8       End If
9   End With
10  End Sub
```

This subroutine deletes all the graphics that occupy a complete sheet in the active book (*ActiveWorkbook*). There must be at least one graphic to be deleted. This is verified first by counting the charts (line 4) and then in line 6 it is verified that there is at least one (condition nwb> 0). If there is at least 1, the subroutine will delete it (line 7).

7.2.2 Property FileFormat

Returns or assigns the file format or book type (Excel, text separated by tabs, commas, etc). The value is returned in numerical form. To know the name of the format, you can use the Object Browser and search the possible values of the *XlFileFormat* variable, as shown in figure 7.1.

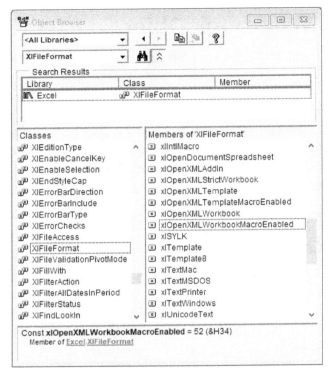

Figure 7.1. Object Browser.

The following subroutine determines the format of the active Excel workbook and displays it through an MsgBox window.

Subroutine 7.2.

1	Sub WBFileFormat()
2	Dim FF As Integer
3	With ActiveWorkbook
4	FF = .FileFormat
5	End With
6	MsgBox "The file format is " & FF
7	End Sub

7.2.3 Property FullName.

Returns the name of the Workbook object, including its full path to disk. The following subroutine shows the name and path of the Excel file that is active.

Subroutine 7.3.

1	Sub WBFullName()

2	MsgBox "The name of this file is: " & ActiveWorkbook.FullName
3	End Sub

7.2.4 Property Path

Returns the full path to disk in which the specified Excel file is located.

Subroutine 7.4.

1	Sub WBPath()
2	MsgBox "The path in which this file is located is : " & ActiveWorkbook.Path
3	End Sub

7.2.5 Property Sheets

Returns a collection of sheets that represent all spreadsheets and charts in a specified workbook.

Subroutine 7.5.

1	Sub WBSheets()
2	Dim h As Sheets
3	Dim n As Integer
4	Dim textString As String
5	textString = ""
6	Set h = ActiveWorkbook.Sheets
7	For n = 1 To h.Count
8	textString = textString & h(n).name & vbNewLine
9	Next n
10	MsgBox "The sheets in this workbook area: " & vbNewLine & textString
11	End Sub

The previous subroutine shows the names of the sheets that belong to the specified book, which in our example is the active book. In line 2 we declare the variable "h" as Sheets type. In line 6 we make the variable "h" equal to the entire collection of Sheets that are in the active book. Remember that Sheets is an object, so the variable "h" will really contain a reference to that object (remember that a collection is also an object). Then in line 7 the Count property is used to know how many sheets are in the collection and use that amount as the upper limit of the **For-Next** loop. In line 8 a text string is constructed which will contain the names of the sheets.

The subroutine 7.6 allows to determine the type of sheet present in an Excel book: spreadsheet, chart, etc. The sheet types are given by the variable *XlSheetType*, whose possible values can be found in the Object Browser, as shown in figure 7.2.

135

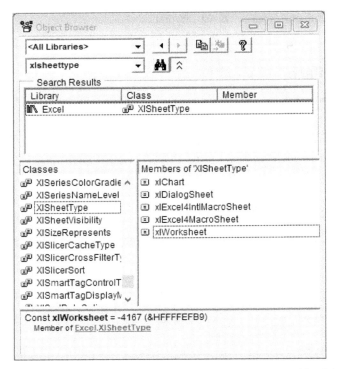

Figure 7.2. Object Browser showing the possible values of the variable *xlSheetType*.

Subroutine 7.6.

1	Sub WBTypeSheets()
2	Dim n, i, TypexlChart, TypexlDialogSheet, TypexlWorksheet, _
3	TipoxlExcel4IntlMacroSheet, TipoxlExcel4MacroSheet As Integer
4	TypexlChart = 0
5	TypexlDialogSheet = 0
6	TipoxlExcel4IntlMacroSheet = 0
7	TipoxlExcel4MacroSheet = 0
8	TypexlWorksheet = 0
9	n = Sheets.Count
10	For i = 1 To n
11	If Sheets(i).Type = -4169 Then
12	TypexlChart = TypexlChart + 1
13	End If
14	If Sheets(i).Type = -4116 Then
15	TypexlDialogSheet = TypexlDialogSheet + 1
16	End If
17	If Sheets(i).Type = 4 Then
18	TipoxlExcel4IntlMacroSheet = TipoxlExcel4IntlMacroSheet + 1

```
19   End If
20   If Sheets(i).Type = 3 Then
21      TipoxlExcel4MacroSheet = TipoxlExcel4MacroSheet + 1
22   End If
23   If Sheets(i).Type = -4167 Then
24      TypexlWorksheet = TypexlWorksheet + 1
25   End If
26   Next i
27   MsgBox "The following sheet types were found: " & vbNewLine & _
28      vbNewLine & "xlChart: " & TypexlChart & _
29      vbNewLine & "xlDialogSheet: " & TypexlDialogSheet & _
30      vbNewLine & "xlExcel4IntlMacroSheet: " & TipoxlExcel4IntlMacroSheet & _
31      vbNewLine & "xlExcel4MacroSheet: " & TipoxlExcel4MacroSheet & _
32      vbNewLine & "xlWorksheet: " & TypexlWorksheet
33   End Sub
```

Figure 7.3 shows the result of the execution of subroutine 7.6.

Figure 7.3. Result of the execution of a subroutine 7.6.

The result tells us that there are two sheets that contain graphics (*xlChart*) and eight sheets that are spreadsheets (*xlWorksheet*).

7.2.6 Property Worksheets

This property is similar to the Sheets property, with the difference that it only returns sheets that are spreadsheets (*Worksheets* collection).

The subroutine 7.7 shows the names of the spreadsheets available in the active Excel workbook.

Subroutine 7.7.

```
1  Sub WBWorksheets()
2  Dim n As Integer
3  Dim textString As String
4  textString = ""
5  For n = 1 To Worksheets.Count
6     textString = textString & Worksheets(n).name & vbNewLine
7  Next n
8  MsgBox "The sheets in this workbook are: " & vbNewLine & textString
9  End Sub
```

7.3 Workbook object methods

7.3.1 Close method

This method closes the Excel workbook. In subroutine 7.8 the active book is closed and the changes made are saved.

Subroutine 7.8.

```
1  Sub WBClose()
2  ActiveWorkbook.Close savechanges:=True
3  End Sub
```

7.3.2 Save method

Save the changes in the specified book.

Subroutine 7.9.

```
1  Sub WBSave()
2  ActiveWorkbook.Save
3  End Sub
```

Instead of using *ActiveWorkbook*, you can change line 2 to:

Workbooks("TheNameOfYourFile").Save

In case you want to exit Excel, but previously save the information of all open workbooks, use the following subroutine.

Subroutine 7.10.

```
1  Sub AllWBSave()
2  Dim wb As Workbook
3  For Each wb In Application.Workbooks
4     wb.Save
```

```
5   Next wb
6   Application.Quit
7   End Sub
```

The variable wb declared in line 2 is of the Workbook type. That means that when used in the **For-Each** loop, it represents a reference to each workbook that is open in the Excel application.

In line 4 it is requested that the information of each Excel book to be saved. Once this is finished, you exit the application with the instruction in line 6.

7.3.3 SaveAs method

Saves changes to an Excel workbook with a name specified by the user. In the following subroutine the file with the specified name Filename (line 2) is saved. Notice how the name of the file points to the path on the disk where it is to be stored. If the directory does not exist, the application will return an error. In case the full path is not specified, the file will be recorded in the route from where the subroutine is running.

Subroutine 7.11.

```
1   Sub WBSaveAs()
2   ActiveWorkbook.SaveAs Filename:="c:\dorian\dorian.xlsx", _
3       FileFormat:=51, Password:="dorian", AddToMru:=True
4   End Sub
```

The output format of the file has also been specified, which in this case corresponds to *xlOpenXMLWorkbook* (code 51). A file access key was assigned and with the AddToMru parameter it has been indicated that the file appears in the list of recent files within Excel.

7.4 Workbook object events

To access the events of the *Workbook* object, it is necessary to access the code window of the Excel *ThisWorkbook* object. This object is highlighted by a rectangle in figure 7.4. Once in the code window, you must select the *Workbook* object in the combobox that is enclosed in the segmented rectangle as shown in figure 7.4. As soon as this is done, VBA adds an empty subroutine to the Open event of the *Workbook* object. To see all the available events, you can display the combobox that is to the right of the one highlighted by the segmented rectangle. The deployed combobox will look as shown in figure 7.5. Each time an event is selected, VBA automatically adds an empty subroutine for that event.

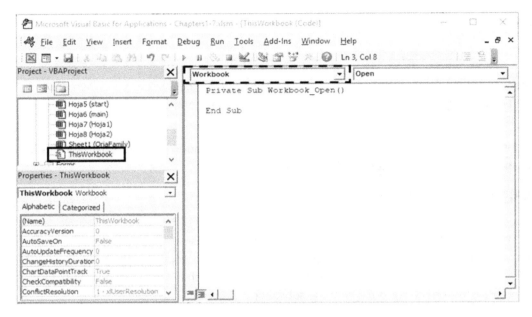

Figure 7.4. Code window of the *ThisWorkbook* object.

7.4.1 Activate event

It happens when an Excel book is activated. The following subroutine displays a message each time the Excel file containing the code is activated.

Subroutine 7.12.

1	Private Sub Workbook_Activate()
2	MsgBox "This code is running from:" _
3	& vbNewLine & ActiveWorkbook.name
4	End Sub

7.4.2 AfterSave event

It happens after the Excel book is saved. The following subroutine displays a message if the Excel file is saved successfully.

Subroutine 7.13.

1	Private Sub Workbook_AfterSave(ByVal Success As Boolean)
2	If Success = True Then
3	MsgBox "File was saved successfully"
4	End If

The variable "Success" inside the parentheses in line 1 is the one that captures the result of the process of saving the file. If successful, the "Success" variable takes the *True* value.

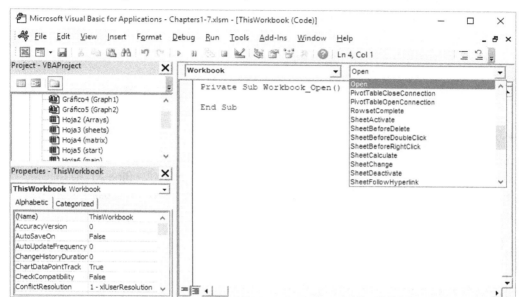

Figure 7.5. Deployment of available events for the *Workbook* object.

7.4.3 BeforeClose event

It occurs before closing the Excel file. If the book has undergone changes, this event occurs before the user is asked to save the changes. The following subroutine closes the Excel file, verifying beforehand if the file has had changes that have not been saved. If the changes have not been saved (property *Saved = False* in line 2), then they are changed before closing the file (line 3).

Subroutine 7.14.

1	Private Sub Workbook_BeforeClose(Cancel As Boolean)
2	If ActiveWorkbook.Saved = False Then
3	ActiveWorkbook.Save
4	End If
5	End Sub

7.4.4 BeforeSave event

It happens before the Excel file is saved. The following subroutine saves the file after verifying that the information has not yet been saved (*SaveAsUI = False* on line 2). Assigning *False* to the *Cancel* variable (line 3) ensures that changes to the file will be saved. Try changing the value from *Cancel* to *True* and see what happens.

Subroutine 7.15.

```
1   Private Sub Workbook_BeforeSave(ByVal SaveAsUI As Boolean, Cancel As Boolean)
2   If SaveAsUI = False Then
3       Cancel = False
4       MsgBox "When you accept it, the file will be saved"
5   End If
6   End Sub
```

7.4.5 Deactivate event

Occurs when the Excel workbook is no longer active. The following subroutine displays a message indicating the name of the Excel file that is no longer active (line 4). To do this, save the name of the active Excel file (from where the code is executed) using the Excel *ThisWorkbook* object and its *Name* property (line 3).

Subroutine 7.16.

```
1   Private Sub Workbook_Deactivate()
2   Dim book As String
3   book = ThisWorkbook.name
4   MsgBox "You have abandoned the book: " & _
5   vbNewLine & book
6   End Sub
```

7.4.6 NewChart event

It happens when a new graphic is created in the Excel file. The next subroutine displays a message saying that a new chart has been created and also indicates the name of the chart and the type. This is possible thanks to the variable "Ch" that receives input (line 1), which is the newly created graphic.

Subroutine 7.17.

```
1   Private Sub Workbook_NewChart(ByVal Ch As Chart)
2   MsgBox "The chart: " & Ch.name & ", type: " & Ch.ChartType & " has been created"
3   End Sub
```

7.4.7 NewSheet event

This event is similar to the *NewChart* event with the difference that it occurs when a new sheet is created. This sheet can be a spreadsheet or a *Chart* object. The next subroutine displays a message as soon as a sheet is created and shows the name and type of sheet.

Subroutine 7.18.

```
1  Private Sub Workbook_NewSheet(ByVal Sh As Object)
2  MsgBox "The sheet: " & Sh.name & ", type: " & Sheets(1).Type & "has been created"
3  End Sub
```

7.4.8 Open event

It happens when an Excel book is opened. In numeral 6.3 we discuss about the events of the *Application* object. The following subroutine displays a welcome message (line 4), indicating the time and also, writing the date and time in a cell of the "main" spreadsheet (line 5).

Subroutine 7.19.

```
1  Private Sub Workbook_Open()
2  Dim time As String
3  time = VBA.Hour(VBA.Now) & ":" & VBA.Minute(VBA.Now) & ":" & VBA.Second(VBA.Now)
4  MsgBox "Welcome. It's: " & time
5  Worksheets("main").Range("A7") = VBA.Now
6  End Sub
```

When the Excel file is opened, the previous subroutine is executed and the window shown in figure 7.6 is generated.

7.4.9 SheetActivate event

It happens when a sheet is activated. The following subroutine displays a message with the name of the sheet when it is activated.

Subroutine 7.20.

```
1  Private Sub Workbook_SheetActivate(ByVal Sh As Object)
2  MsgBox "The sheet: " & Sh.name & " has been activated"
3  End Sub
```

7.4.10 SheetBeforeDelete event

This event happens before deleting any sheet. The following subroutine calculates the oil production averages for the years 2013 and 2014, based on data found in a spreadsheet called "Sheet1" and writes the results in the "main" spreadsheet. All this happens before the sheet "Sheet1" is deleted.

Subroutine 7.21.

```
1  Private Sub Workbook_SheetBeforeDelete(ByVal Sh As Object)
2  Dim range2013, range2014 As Range
```

3	MsgBox "The sheet: " & Sh.name & " will be deleted" & _
4	vbNewLine & "Production averages will be written on the main sheet"
5	With Worksheets("Sheet1")
6	Set range2013 = .Range("B4:B15")
7	Set range2014 = .Range("C4:C15")
8	End With
9	With Worksheets("main")
10	.Range("A7") = "Average oil production"
11	.Range("A8") = 2013
12	.Range("B8") = 2014
13	.Range("A9") = WorksheetFunction.Average(range2013)
14	.Range("A10") = WorksheetFunction.Average(range2014)
15	End With
16	End Sub

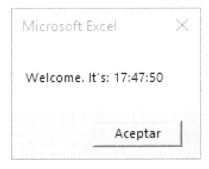

Figure 7.6. Result of the execution of the subroutine 7.19.

7.5 Methods of the Workbooks object

The *Workbooks* object is a collection of all *Workbook* objects that are currently open in an Excel session. As a collection, this object has some very important methods that we will see below.

7.5.1 Add method

Creates a new Excel book. The newly created book becomes the active book. The following subroutine creates a new Excel workbook and assigns it name and format.

Subroutine 7.22.

1	Sub EjWBAdd()
2	Workbooks.Add.SaveAs Filename:="NewFile.xlsm", _
3	FileFormat:=xlOpenXMLWorkbookMacroEnabled

4	End Sub

7.5.2 Close method

Closes the specified Excel workbook. If not specified, it closes all open Excel books. The following subroutine closes all Excel workbooks that are open.

Subroutine 7.23.

1	Sub EjWBClose()
2	workbooks.Close
3	End Sub

7.5.3 Open method

Open a book or any file that is supported by Excel. Imagine for a moment that we have a text file like the one shown in figure 7.7 in which the information is separated by tabs.

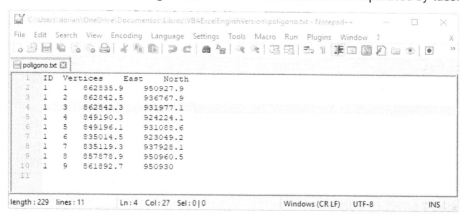

Figure 7.7. Text file.

The next subroutine opens the file in Excel.

Subroutine 7.24.

1	Sub EjWBOpen()
2	Workbooks.Open _
3	Filename:="C:\Users\doria\OneDrive\VBasic\poligono.txt", _
4	Format:=1
5	End Sub

Line 3 specifies the file name including the full path where it is located.

In line 4 the format of the text file is indicated. The format indicates the separator that is being used to sort the information within the file. According to table 7.1, the value 1 corresponds to the tabulator. Table 7.1 shows the default separators. Option 6 is used when there is another separator not included in the defaults.

Table 7.1. Possible separators to sort information within a text file.

Value	Delimiter
1	Tab
2	Comma
3	Space
4	Semicolon
5	Any
6	Specified by the user

The following subroutine shows how to open the same file shown in figure 7.7 but this time using option 6 for the file format. When this is done, it is necessary to define the character used as a separator. For that, it is necessary to use the *Delimiter* parameter (line 5) and assign the tabulator as a value. In ASCII, the tabular character is 9. In order to use it, we must use the **Chr** function, as shown in line 5 of the subroutine

Subroutine 7.25.

```
1  Sub EjWBOpen2()
2  Workbooks.Open _
3      Filename:="C:\Users\doria\OneDrive\VBasic\poligono.txt", _
4      Format:=6, _
5      Delimiter:=Chr(9)
6  End Sub
```

7.5.4 OpenText method

This method is specially designed to open text files in Excel. The following subroutine opens the text file shown in figure 7.8.

Subroutine 7.26.

```
1  Sub EjWBOpenText()
2  Workbooks.OpenText _
3      Filename:="C:\Users\doria\OneDrive\VBasic\poligono2.txt", _
4      StartRow:=4, _
5      DataType:=xlDelimited, _
6      Tab:=True, _
7      FieldInfo:=Array(Array(1, 1), Array(2, 1), Array(3, 1), Array(4, 1), Array(5, 2))
8  End Sub
```

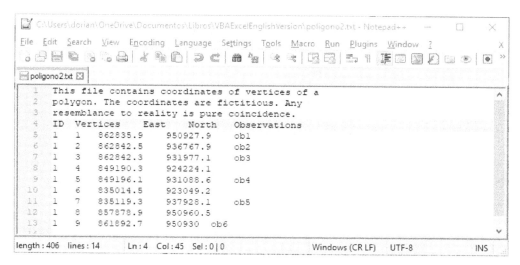

Figure 7.8. Text file with some lines with information.

The name of the file that you want to open is given in line 3, including its complete location path.

Line 4 indicates the first line containing information and where the import will begin. In our example, line 4 contains the headers of each of the data columns.

In line 5 it is indicated that the information within the file is delimited (*xlDelimited*). The other possible value for *DataType* is *xlFixedWidth*.

In line 6 it is indicated that the separator of the data is the tabulator. It is important to note that whenever the presence of a separator is indicated, the *DataType* must be equal to *xlDelimited*.

Line 7 specifies, through an array of arrays, the type of information that you want to import. Each arrangement within the main array is composed of two elements: the first one corresponds to the number of the column and the second corresponds to the type of data. For example, Array (1,1) indicates that the data type of the elements in column 1 is "General". For the case of the fifth column (Array (5,2)), the number means that the data type is "Text". More information about the supported data types can be obtained by looking for information about the variable *xlColumnDataType* in the VBA-Excel Object Browser.

Chapter 8. Worksheet Object

8.1 Introduction

The *Worksheet* object represents a spreadsheet. It belongs to the *Worksheets* collection. As we have seen previously, the *Worksheet* object also belongs to the *Sheets* collection. Remember that this collection contains all the sheets in a book, regardless of whether it is spreadsheets (*Worksheets*) or graphics occupying a sheet (*Charts*).

8.2 Properties of the Worksheet object

8.2.1 Cells property

Returns a *Range* object that represents all the cells in a spreadsheet. The following subroutine writes an Excel formula in a cell that returns the current date. It is important to be careful with these formulas since they are not portable between versions of Excel with different languages. That is, in an Excel version with a language other than English it would give an error because for Excel that function does not exist.

Cells need row and column coordinates (in that order). In our example, the row is 7 and the column is 2, which corresponds to column B, so in Excel notation, the cell in our example corresponds to cell B7.

Subroutine 8.1.

```
1   Sub EjWSCells()
2   Worksheets("main").Cells(7, 2).FormulaLocal = "=TODAY()"
3   End Sub
```

If no coordinates are specified, then the property returns all the cells in a spreadsheet. The following subroutine changes the color of all the cells in the spreadsheet "main".

Subroutine 8.2.

```
1   Sub EjWSCells2()
2   Worksheets("main").Cells.Interior.ColorIndex = 9
3   End Sub
```

8.2.2 Columns property

Returns a *Range* object that represents all the columns of a spreadsheet. The next subroutine writes the number 7 in all the rows in column 7 (which represents column G) and changes the color of the entire column.

Subroutine 8.3.

```
1  Sub EjWSColumn()
2  With Worksheets("main").Columns(7)
3     .Value = 7
4     .Interior.Color = vbRed
5  End With
6  End Sub
```

8.2.3 Name property

Returns or assigns a text string that represents the name of the object. The following subroutine shows the name of the active sheet.

Subroutine 8.4.

```
1  Sub EjWSName()
2  MsgBox "Active sheet is: " & ActiveSheet.Name
3  End Sub
```

The following subroutine changes the name of the spreadsheet "main" to "main2".

Subroutine 8.5.

```
1  Sub EjWSName2()
2  Worksheets("main").Name = "main2"
3  End Sub
```

8.2.4 Range property

Returns a Range object that represents a cell or a range of cells. The following subroutine is another way to write the subroutine 8.1.

Subroutine 8.6.

```
1  Sub EjWSRange()
2  Worksheets("main2").Range("B7").FormulaLocal = "=TODAY()"
3  End Sub
```

The *Range* object also supports a range of cells. The next subroutine works similar to the previous subroutine, but the formula writes cells B7, C7, and D7.

Subroutine 8.7.

```
1  Sub EjWSRange2()
2  Worksheets("main2").Range("B7:D7").FormulaLocal = "=TODAY()"
3  End Sub
```

Another way to write the previous code is shown in the following subroutine.

Subroutine 8.8.

```
1  Sub EjWSRange3()
2  Worksheets("main2").Range(Cells(7, 2), Cells(7, 4)).FormulaLocal = "=TODAY()"
3  End Sub
```

In the next chapter we will study the *Range* object in more detail.

8.2.5 Rows property

Returns a Range object that represents all the rows in a spreadsheet. The following subroutine writes the number 5 in all the cells in row 12 of the spreadsheet "main2".

Subroutine 8.9.

```
1  Sub EjWSRows()
2  Worksheets("main2").Rows(12) = 5
3  End Sub
```

The following code deletes the contents of all the cells written with the previous subroutine.

Subroutine 8.10.

```
1  Sub EjWSRows2()
2  Worksheets("main2").Rows(12).ClearContents
3  End Sub
```

8.2.6 Visible property

It allows the spreadsheet to be visible or not. The property can take one of the three values (*XlSheetVisibility*) that are shown in table 8.1

Table 8.1. Possible values of the Visible property (*XlSheetVisibility*) of the Worksheet object.

Name	Value	Description
xlSheetHidden	0	Hide the spreadsheet, which can be visible again via menu (Excel VIEW tab)
xlSheetVeryHidden	2	Hide the spreadsheet in such a way that the only way to make it visible again is through code.
xlSheetVisible	-1	Makes visible the spreadsheet.

The following subroutine hides the "PPColombia" spreadsheet. However, this status can be changed from Excel.

Subroutine 8.11.

```
1   Sub EjWSVisible()
2   Worksheets("PPColombia").Visible = False
3   End Sub
```

The following subroutines are equivalent ways of doing the same.

Subroutine 8.12.

```
1   Sub EjWSVisible2()
2   Worksheets("PPColombia").Visible = 0
3   End Sub
```

Subroutine 8.13.

```
1   Sub EjWSVisible2()
2   Worksheets("PPColombia").Visible = xlSheetHidden
3   End Sub
```

The way to revert the previous instruction is changing the value of the property Visible to *True, -1* or *xlSheetVisible*.

8.3 Methods of the Worksheet object

8.3.1 Activate method

Activates the indicated spreadsheet. The following subroutine makes the "PPColombia" spreadsheet active.

Subroutine 8.14.

```
1   Sub EjWSActivate()
2   Worksheets("PPColombia").Activate
3   End Sub
```

8.3.2 ChartObjects method

Returns an object that represents an embedded chart in a spreadsheet or a collection of them.

Subroutine 8.15.

```
1   Sub EjWSChartObjects()
2   With Worksheets("PPColombia").ChartObjects(1).Chart
3   .HasTitle = True
4   .ChartTitle.Text = " Oil Production Colombia 2013-2014"
5   End With
```

```
6   End Sub
```

This subroutine adds a title to a chart that is in the "PPColombia" spreadsheet. In chapter 12 we will study *ChartObjects* with more detail.

8.3.3 Copy method

Copies a sheet to another location in the Excel workbook. The next subroutine copies the "PPColombia" spreadsheet to another sheet that it creates new. The *After* parameter (optional) indicates that the new sheet will be located after the specified spreadsheet (in this case, after itself).

Subroutine 8.16.

```
1   Sub EjWSCopy()
2   Worksheets("PPColombia").Copy After:=Worksheets("PPColombia")
3   End Sub
```

The following subroutine, by not specifying *Before* or *After*, copies the spreadsheet to a new Excel workbook.

Subroutine 8.17.

```
1   Sub EjWSCopy2()
2   Worksheets("PPColombia").Copy
3   End Sub
```

8.3.4 Delete method

This method deletes the object (applies for spreadsheets and for graphics that occupy a sheet). The next subroutine deletes the spreadsheet that we created as a copy in the 8.16 subroutine.

Subroutine 8.18.

```
1   Sub EjWSDelete()
2   Worksheets("PPColombia (2)").Delete
3   End Sub
```

8.3.5 Protect method

Protects a spreadsheet in such a way that it can not be modified. The following subroutine shows the simplest way to protect a spreadsheet. In this case, no key was assigned nor was it necessary to protect the sheet. This protection prevents modifications from being made but it does not prevent the sheet from being erased.

Subroutine 8.19.

1	Sub EjWSProtect()
2	Worksheets("PPCOlombia").Protect
3	End Sub

The sheet can be unprotected from the "REVIEW" tab of Excel.

The following subroutine protects an Excel spreadsheet and assigns a password that must be entered at the time of check out.

Subroutine 8.20.

1	Sub EjWSProtect2()
2	Worksheets("PPColombia").Protect Password:="1234"
3	End Sub

The following table shows some of the parameters that can be configured in the protection as if they were exceptions (in cases of course when the parameters are assigned the value *True*).

Table 8.2. Possible parameters for spreadsheet protection.

Name	Description
DrawingObjects	*True* to protect shapes and drawings.
Contents	*True* to protect content. For a graphic the protection is complete. For a spreadsheet it only protects locked cells.
AllowFormattingCells	*True* allows the user to format any cell in a protected spreadsheet.
AllowFormattingColumns	*True* allows the user to format any column in a protected spreadsheet.
AllowFormattingRows	*True* allows the user to format any row in a protected worksheet.
AllowInsertingColumns	*True* allows the user to insert columns in a protected spreadsheet.
AllowInsertingRows	*True* allows the user to insert rows into a protected spreadsheet.
AllowDeletingColumns	*True* allows the user to delete columns in a protected spreadsheet, where each cell in the column will be deleted if it is unlocked.
AllowDeletingRows	*True* allows the user to delete rows in a protected worksheet, where each cell in the row will be deleted if it is unlocked.
AllowSorting	*True* allows the user to apply sorting processes (sort) on a protected spreadsheet.
AllowFiltering	*True* allows the user to set filters on a protected spreadsheet. Users can change the filter criteria, but they are not able to activate or deactivate a auto-filter. Users can set filter in an existing autofilter.

The following subroutine protects the spreadsheet (line 2), assigns a key (line 3) and gives permissions to modify content (line 4) and format of the cells (line 5). In line 6 it gives permission to insert columns.

Subroutine 8.21.

1	Sub EjWSProtect3()
2	Worksheets("PPColombia").Protect _
3	Password:="1234", _
4	Contents:=True, _
5	AllowFormattingCells:=True, _
6	AllowInsertingColumns:=True
7	End Sub

8.3.6 Unprotect method

Removes the protection of a sheet or Excel book. This method has no effect if the Excel sheet or book was unprotected. The following subroutine removes the protections from the "PPColombia" spreadsheet.

Subroutine 8.22.

1	Sub EjWSUnprotect()
2	Worksheets("PPColombia").Unprotect
3	End Sub

8.4 Properties of the Worksheets object

The *Worksheets* object is a collection of all worksheets (*Worksheet* objects) present in an active Excel workbook.

The *Worksheet* object is also a member of the *Sheets* collection. The *Sheets* collection in turn contain all the pages of an Excel book regardless of whether it is spreadsheets or graphics (*Charts*).

8.4.1 Count property

Returns a value that represents the number of spreadsheets present in an Excel workbook, as shown in the following subroutine.

Subroutine 8.23.

1	Sub EjWSCount()
2	MsgBox "This book has: " & Worksheets.Count & " spreadsheets"
3	End Sub

8.5 Methods of the Worksheets object

8.5.1 Add method

Creates a new spreadsheet. As soon as it is created it becomes the active spreadsheet (*ActiveSheet*). The following subroutine creates a new spreadsheet after the "PPColombia" spreadsheet (line 2) and assigns it a name (line 3).

Subroutine 8.24.

```
1  Sub EjWSAdd()
2  Worksheets.Add after:=Worksheets("PPColombia")
3  ActiveSheet.Name = " NewSheet"
4  End Sub
```

Chapter 9. Range Object

9.1 Introduction

The *Range* object becomes the lowest level within the VBA-Excel object hierarchy and is where the heavy work is actually done within a spreadsheet. It is contained within the *Worksheet* object and may consist of a single cell up to the full range of cells available in a spreadsheet (17,179,869,184 cells).

9.2 Ways to refer to a cell

There are two ways to refer to a cell or a range of them. One of those ways is using its name as you can see in the rectangle in figure 9.1.

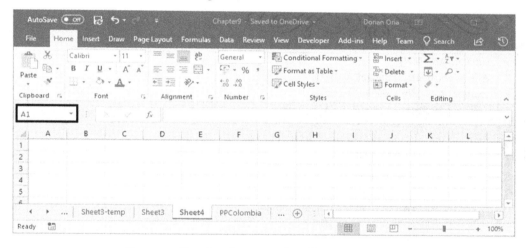

Figure 9.1. Showing the name of a cell in a spreadsheet.

In VBA-Excel code, we refer to cell A1 as Range ("A1"). If we wanted to refer to the range of cells highlighted in figure 9.2, then it would be Range ("A1: B7").

Depending on the operation that you want to do with those cells, this way of referring to the ranges of cells can be useful and easy to understand when for example, you want to format (properties) the cells: color of the sources, color of the cells, edges, alignment; or apply a method: delete information, copy, etc.

Let's see the following example. Figure 9.3 shows a range of colored cells with borders. This can be achieved with the code shown in the subroutine 9.1.

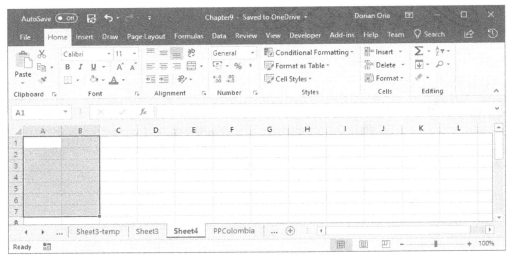

Figure 9.2. Range of cells "A1: B7" selected in a spreadsheet.

Subroutine 9.1.

1	Sub FormatCells2()
2	With Worksheets(1).Range("A1:B7")
3	.Interior.Pattern = xlSolid
4	.Interior.PatternColorIndex = xlAutomatic
5	.Interior.Color = 49407
6	.HorizontalAlignment = xlCenter
7	.VerticalAlignment = xlBottom
8	.Borders(xlEdgeLeft).LineStyle = xlContinuous
9	.Borders(xlEdgeLeft).Weight = xlMedium
10	.Borders(xlEdgeTop).LineStyle = xlContinuous
11	.Borders(xlEdgeTop).Weight = xlMedium
12	.Borders(xlEdgeBottom).LineStyle = xlContinuous
13	.Borders(xlEdgeBottom).Weight = xlMedium
14	.Borders(xlEdgeRight).LineStyle = xlContinuous
15	.Borders(xlEdgeRight).Weight = xlMedium
16	End With
17	With Worksheets(1).Range("A1:B1")
18	.Borders(xlEdgeLeft).LineStyle = xlContinuous
19	.Borders(xlEdgeLeft).Weight = xlMedium
20	.Borders(xlEdgeTop).LineStyle = xlContinuous
21	.Borders(xlEdgeTop).Weight = xlMedium
22	.Borders(xlEdgeBottom).LineStyle = xlContinuous
23	.Borders(xlEdgeBottom).Weight = xlMedium
24	.Borders(xlEdgeRight).LineStyle = xlContinuous

```
25    .Borders(xlEdgeRight).Weight = xlMedium
26  End With
27  With Worksheets(1).Range("A1:A7")
28    .Borders(xlEdgeRight).LineStyle = xlContinuous
29    .Borders(xlEdgeRight).Weight = xlMedium
30  End With
31  For i = 1 To 5
32    With Worksheets(1).Range("A" & i + 2 & ":B" & i + 2)
33      .Borders(xlEdgeTop).LineStyle = xlContinous
34      .Borders(xlEdgeTop).Weight = xlThin
35    End With
36  Next i
37  End Sub
```

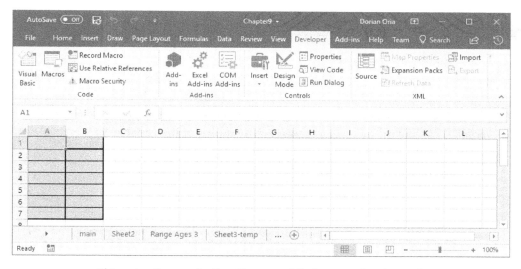

Figure 9.3. Range of cells with some of their properties changed.

If you want to work with the information contained in the cells, the notation described above may be useful if the information is organized by columns, where each of them represents different information. However, things can get complicated if the information needs more than one column. In this case, it is better to refer to the cells in their matrix form. For example, to refer to cell A1, the notation would be Cells(1,1). An example of the use of this notation can be found in the subroutine 4.11.

9.3 Offset property

This property offers another way of referring to a range of cells. It allows referring to a cell that is at a certain number of rows and columns from another cell. This offers a possibility to use the *Range* notation when working with matrix-organized information. Using the *offset* property is a way of using a cell as a pivot. Let's rewrite the code of subroutine 4.11 using this property.

Subroutine 9.2.

1	Sub transposedMatrix2()
2	Dim r, c As Integer 'r: rows, c: columns
3	With Worksheets("matrices")
4	For r = 1 To 3
5	For c = 1 To 3
6	.Range("G1").Offset(r - 1, c - 1) = .Range("B1").Offset(c - 1, r - 1)
7	Next c
8	Next r
9	End With
10	End Sub

To write the transposed matrix, we have used cell G1 as a pivot and from there we count rows and columns (it is important to note that the rows expand downwards and the columns to the right). When the variables "r" and "c" are equal to 1, then the offset is (0,0), that is, it refers to the same cell G1. From there, we move along the columns (**For-Next** loop of the variable "c") and then along the rows (**For-Next** loop of the variable "r").

This form has the advantage that Excel, by default, calls its cells with the notation of letters and numbers. As shown by the previous code, it is easy to locate within the sheet and from there move to the adjacent cells using the *offset* property. When the *Cells* notation is used, it is necessary to know the column number, which can be a bit tedious, at least for me. However, it is possible that for many of those who are involved with mathematics, the Cells notation may be more comfortable for them.

9.4 Properties of the Range object

The *Range* object has many properties. However, we will discuss some of the most common and most widely used. If you want to know what other properties this object has available, you can consult the Object Browser, as shown in figure 9.4.

9.4.1 Value property

We already discussed this property in Chapter 5. It is the default property of the *Range* object and represents the value contained in a cell. If this property is not specified, VBA-Excel will understand that the property of the *Range* object is Value. That is, the line a = Worksheets(1).Range("A1").Value

it's the same as writing:

a = Worksheets(1).Range("A1")

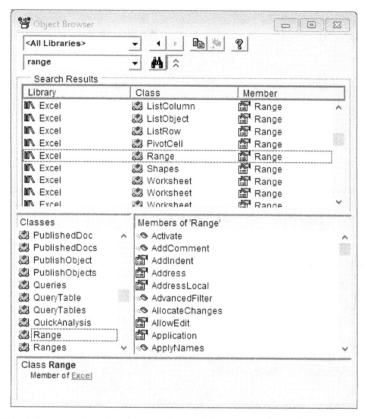

Figure 9.4. Object Browser showing the members of the Range object (methods and properties).

9.4.2 Text property

This property is read-only and returns a string that represents the text as it is displayed in a cell (including its format). For example, suppose that in cell C3 (Sheet1) the value 123.56 is written in currency format. This will look like: $123.56. Let's see how the following code shows it as text and as a value (*Text* and *Value*).

Subroutine 9.3.

1	Sub propertyTextValue()
2	MsgBox Worksheets("Hoja1").Range("C3").Text
3	MsgBox Worksheets("Hoja1").Range("C3").Value

4	End Sub

When executing this code, the following windows will appear (the one on the right side will appear after pressing Accept (Aceptar) in the window on the left).

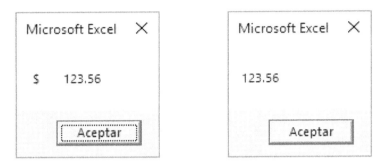

Figure 9.5. Difference between displayed information with the *Text* and *Value* property.

9.4.3 Count property

This property returns the number of cells in a range. Counts all the cells, regardless of whether they have information or not. It is read only.

Subroutine 9.4.

```
1  Sub countCells()
2  MsgBox "The cells located in the range B1: E3 are: " & Range("B1:E3").Count
3  End Sub
```

Figure 9.6 shows the result of the execution of the subroutine 9.4.

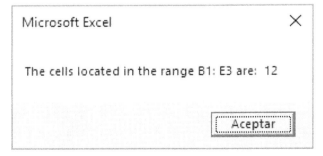

Figure 9.6. Result of the execution of the subroutine 9.4.

9.4.4 Column and Row properties

The *Column* property returns the number of the first column in the first area in the specified

162

range. The *Row* property returns the number of the first row of the first area in the specified range. Let's see the following example.

Subroutine 9.5.

```
1  Sub ColumnAndRow()
2  MsgBox "The column of F3 is: " & Range("F3").Column & vbNewLine & _
3     "The row of F3 is: " & Range("F3").Row
4  End Sub
```

When you execute this code, the window shown in figure 9.7 appears.

Figure 9.7. Result of the execution of subroutine 9.5.

9.4.5 Font property

This property returns a *Font* object that represents the font of the specified object. This object in turn has other properties. To change some aspect of the source within a range, it is necessary to first access the object and then manipulate its properties. Let's see an example. Figure 9.8 shows the names and surnames of my family members. We are going to make a subroutine that changes the names to **bold**, *italics* to the surnames and also change the colors of the letters.

Subroutine 9.6.

```
1  Sub FontProperty()
2  With Worksheets("Sheet2")
3     .Range("A1:A6").Font.Bold = True
4     .Range("A1:A6").Font.ColorIndex = 3 'change the color of the font to red
5     .Range("B1:B6").Font.Italic = True
6     .Range("B1:B6").Font.ColorIndex = 10 'change the color of the font to green
7  End With
8  End Sub
```

Figure 9.9 shows the changes made in the information of names and surnames, once the subroutine 9.6 has been executed.

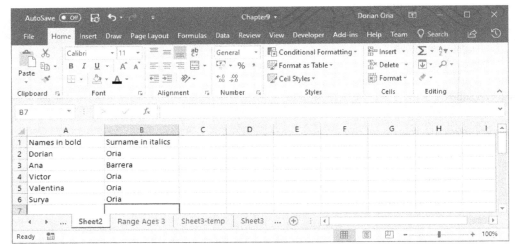

Figure 9.8. My family's first and last names.

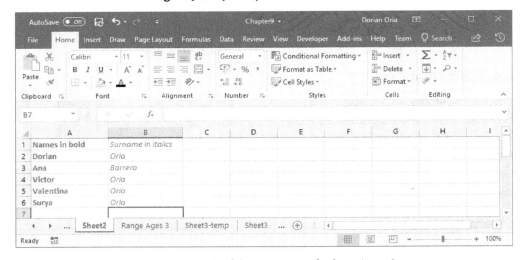

Figure 9.9. Result of the execution of subroutine 9.6.

9.4.6 Interior property

This property returns the internal qualities of an object (as if it were an object as well). For example, applied to the *Range* object, it returns the properties of its interior. Next we will take as an example the cells that have information in figure 9.9 and we are going to change the color.

Subroutine 9.7.

```
1  Sub InteriorProperty()
2  Worksheets("Sheet2").Range("A1:B1").Interior.Color = RGB(229, 229, 221)
3  Worksheets("Sheet2").Range("A2:B6").Interior.Color = RGB(247, 245, 115)
4  End Sub
```

Executing the above code causes the table of names and last names to appear as shown in figure 9.10.

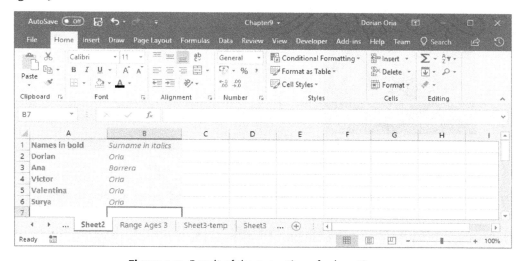

Figure 9.10. Result of the execution of subroutine 9.7.

The RGB function (lines 2 and 3) allow us to create a wide range of colors, combining the colors **R**ed, **G**reen and **B**lue. In the link https://htmlcolorcodes.com/ you can find an application (figure 9.11) in which you can select the desired color with the mouse in a color palette and you can also indicate the proportion of red, green and blue that is needed to obtain the desired color. The values of each color can range from 0 to 255.

Another way to add colors is by using the default ones for the *ColorIndex* property. There are 56 colors, which can be found at https://msdn.microsoft.com/en-us/library/cc296089%28v=office.12%29.aspx.

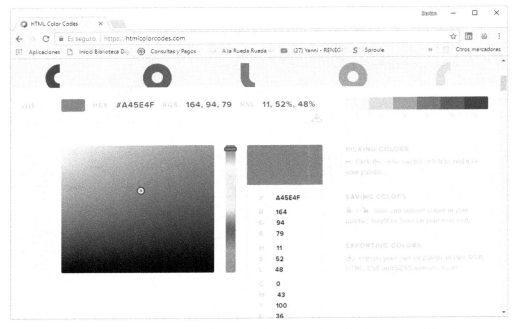

Figure 9.11. Optional Third-party app to determine the proportion of red, green and blue to generate a color with the RGB function.

The following subroutine shows an example of the use of the *ColorIndex* property.

Subroutine 9.8.

1	Sub InteriorProperty2()
2	Worksheets("Sheet2").Range("A1:B1").Interior.ColorIndex = 20
3	Worksheets("Sheet2").Range("A2:B6").Interior.ColorIndex = 6
4	End Sub

Executing this code makes the table in figure 9.10 look like in figure 9.12.

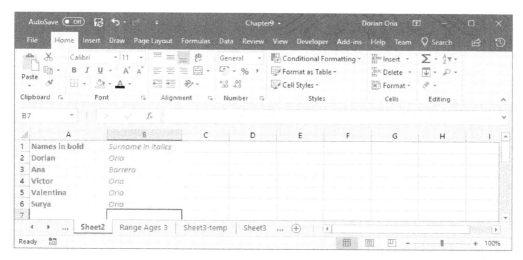

Figure 9.12. Result of the execution of the subroutine 9.8.

9.4.7 FormulaLocal property

This property represents the formula in a cell. This property is read-write, which means that it can be used to see the formula in a cell or to insert one. The following subroutine gets the average age of my family (according to the age values shown in column C, figure 9.13).

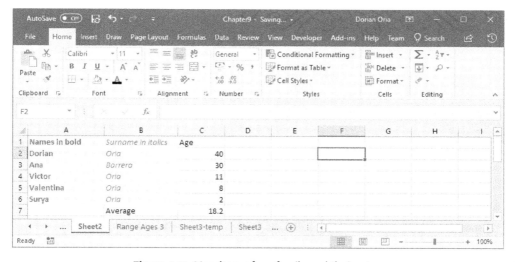

Figure 9.13. Members of my family and their ages.

Subroutine 9.9.

1	Sub propertyFormula()
2	Worksheets("Sheet2").Range("C7").FormulaLocal = "=AVERAGE(C2:C6)"
3	End Sub

The *FormulaLocal* property has a small drawback which is the language. The previous subroutine can only be executed in the English version of Excel. In Spanish, for example, the "average" function will not be recognized. Later we will see that VBA-Excel has almost all Excel functions at its disposal, but in English, which allows the code to be portable, regardless of the language of the Excel version.

9.4.8 NumberFormat property

This property returns or assigns the format to a *Range* object. The available formats can be seen in figure 9.14. To view this window from Excel, press the Ctrl + 1 keys simultaneously.

In figure 9.15 we have the list of the members of my family with additional information about height (in meters). The subroutine 9.10 will be used to format the measurements, so that each of them has two decimals.

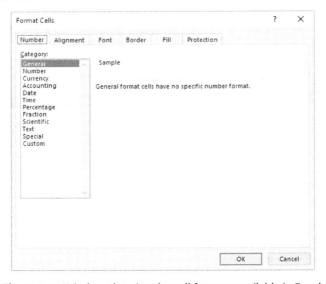

Figure 9.14. Window showing the cell formats available in Excel.

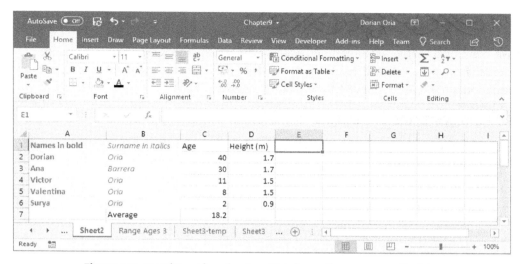

Figure 9.15. Members of my family with information on age and height.

Subroutine 9.10.

```
1   Sub numberFormat()
2   Worksheets("Sheet2").Range("D2:D6").numberFormat = "0.00"
3   End Sub
```

The height information will look like it is shown in figure 9.16 after executing the previous code.

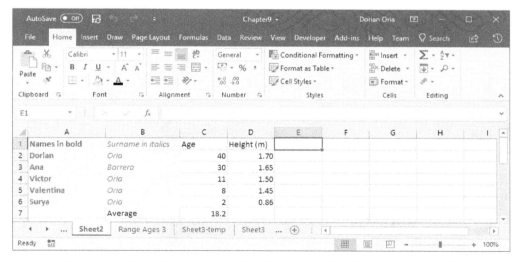

Figure 9.16. Height information with uniform format for all values (column D).

9.5 Range Object Methods

As we mentioned earlier, the methods execute an action. The *Range* object has a lot of methods. However, I will show what I consider most useful. Remember that more information is obtained in the VBA-Excel Object Browser (F2).

9.5.1 AddComment method

This method allows you to add a comment to a cell. To illustrate, let's make a small change in the subroutine code 9.9.

Subroutine 9.11.

```
1  Sub methodAddComment()
2  With Worksheets("Sheet2").Range("C7")
3     .FormulaLocal = "=AVERAGE(C2:C6)"
4     .AddComment "Average age of my family"
5  End With
6  End Sub
```

When executing this code, a comment is added to the cell where the calculation of the average age of my family is, as can be seen in figure 9.17.

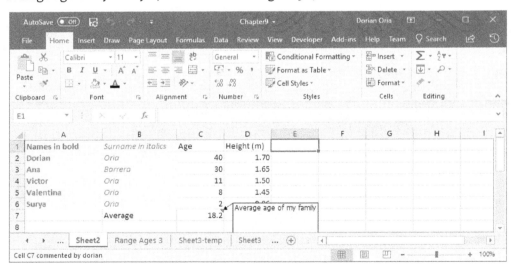

Figure 9.17. Result of the execution of the subroutine 9.11.

9.5.2 Clear method and its variants: ClearComments, ClearContents, ClearFormats

The *Clear* method cleans the *Range* object from formulas, formats, comments, basically everything. It's as if you were returning the *Range* object to its original condition.

Taking as an example what was done with the previous code, we will restore the original condition of cell C7 (which is the average of the ages and the comment). For this we use the following code.

Subroutine 9.12.

```
1  Sub methodClear()
2  Worksheets("Sheet2").Range("C7").Clear
3  End Sub
```

When executing this code you will see that in cell C7 the comment disappears.

If we wanted to delete only the comment, instead of using *Clear* we use *ClearComments*. If you want to delete only contents of the *Range* object (values or formulas), then *ClearContents* is used. If you want to delete the format of the cells, then you can use *ClearFormats* (we suggest you try this option in the range of values D2: D6).

9.5.3 ColumnDifferences method

Returns a *Range* object that contains all the cells whose contents are different from the one established in a cell located in the same column. For example, given the data shown in figure 9.18, we want to highlight in yellow all those values (ages) other than 45 (Range ("A14")). For this we are going to use the subroutine 9.13.

Subroutine 9.13.

```
1  Sub methodColumnDifferences()
2  Dim R2 As Range
3  With Worksheets("Sheet3")
4    Set R2 = .Range("A2:A16").ColumnDifferences _
5    (Comparison:=.Range("A14"))
6    R2.Interior.ColorIndex = 6
7  End With
8  End Sub
```

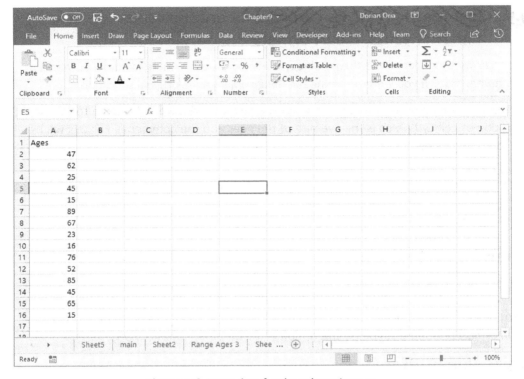

Figure 9.18. Input data for the subroutine 9.13.

When executing the previous code, the data will look as shown in figure 9.19.

9.5.4 AdvancedFilter method

This method is very powerful, since it allows to work with advanced filters using VBA code. Although this option is available in Excel through the window shown in figure 9.20 (in the "DATA" tab), it is also very useful to do so using code, as it gives more freedom to make customizations.

With the advanced filter shown in figure 9.20, the results shown in figure 9.21 were obtained.

Note that when designing advanced filters, it is very important that the variable that you want to use as a filter has the same name as the one you have in the source of the data (in our case Age). In our example, we want to extract from the data located in columns A and B, those whose Age is between 20 and 60 years old.

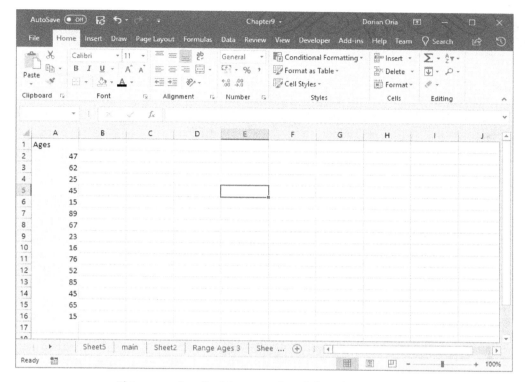

Figure 9.19. Result of the execution of the subroutine 9.13.

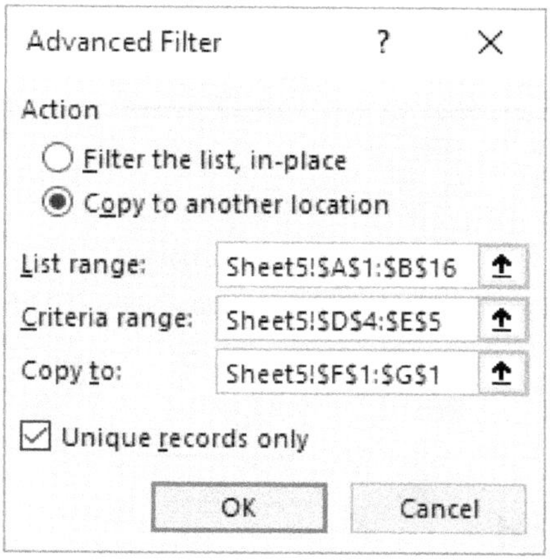

Figure 9.20. Advanced filter window available in Excel.

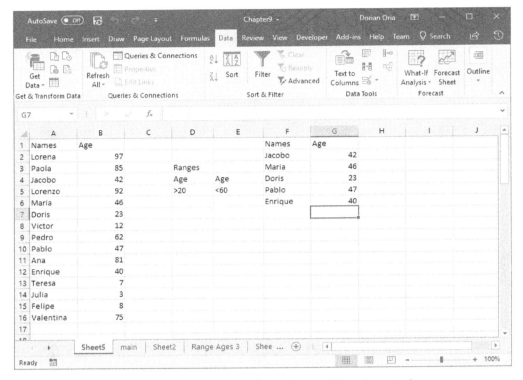

Figure 9.21. Result of the application of the advanced filter shown in figure 9.20.

The code to do this is shown below.

Subroutine 9.14.

```
1   Sub methodAdvancedFilter()
2   Dim R2 As Range
3   With Worksheets("Sheet5")
4       Set R2 = .Range("A1:B16")
5       R2.AdvancedFilter Action:=xlFilterCopy, CriteriaRange:=.Range("D4:E5"), _
6       copytorange:=.Range("F1"), Unique:=True
7   End With
8   End Sub
```

9.5.5 Autofilter method

This method allows filtering information without needing to extract it or copy it in another range of cells. Fundamentally it is only for visualization.

Suppose we want to do the same as in the previous example: we want to visualize those names whose ages are between 20 and 60 years old. For this we will use the following code.

Subroutine 9.15.

1	Sub methodAutofilter()
2	Dim R As Range
3	Set R = Worksheets("Sheet5").Range("A1")
4	R.AutoFilter field:=2, Criteria1:=">20", _
5	Criteria2:="<60", visibledropdown:=True
6	End Sub

When executing the previous subroutine we will see the names whose ages meet the condition mentioned above. Figure 9.22 shows how the results look.

9.5.6 Sort method

This method allows you to sort a range of values. Take for example the Name and Age values shown in figure 9.21. Now let's say we want to sort the information first by age and then by name. The code to do this is shown in subroutine 9.16.

Subroutine 9.16.

1	Sub methodSort()
2	Columns("A:B").Sort key1:="Age", order1:=xlAscending, _
3	key2:="Names", order2:=xlAscending, Header:=xlYes
4	End Sub

When executing the previous subroutine, the data is sorted as shown in figure 9.23.

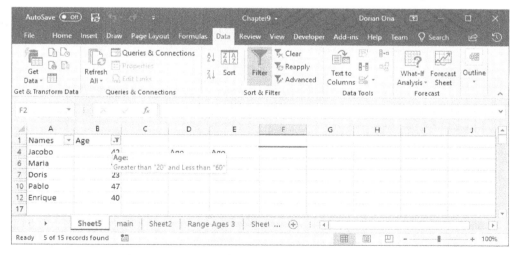

Figure 9.22. Result of the execution of subroutine 9.15.

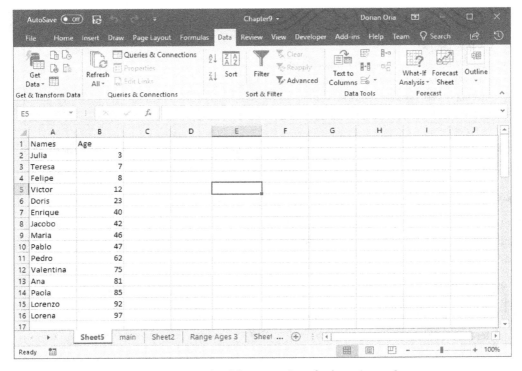

Figure 9.23. Result of the execution of subroutine 9.16.

Chapter 10. Functions of the VBA and Excel library

10.1 Introduction

In the previous chapter we saw how we can write Excel functions in a cell (item 9.4.7). Those functions can also be used within the VBA code and additionally the VBA language comes with its own built-in functions. This saves a lot of work, by not having to write lines of code that perform all those functions. All the functions available in a spreadsheet can be used in VBA-Excel. In this chapter we will see examples on how to take advantage of all this power.

10.2 Excel functions

Almost all the functions that can be used in a cell within a spreadsheet are available for use in the VBA code. The only thing that must be taken into account is that the functions in VBA are in English, which could be uncomfortable (and may confuse a bit too) if you have an Excel version in a different language (Spanish, for example). As mentioned in previous chapters, the fact that they are in English guarantees their portability to other versions of Excel that have a different language.

Let's start with the examples. Let us take the data shown in figure 9.23 and calculate the age average, standard deviation and also, let us determine which is the biggest and the smallest age. For all this we will use the functions of VBA-Excel. The following subroutine does this and shows the results on the same Sheet3 where the input data is.

Subroutine 10.1

1	Sub worksheetFunc()
2	Dim R As Range
3	Dim average, standardDev, min, max As Variant
4	Set R = Worksheets("Sheet3").Range("B2:B" & Worksheets("Sheet3").Range("C2") + 1)
5	average = WorksheetFunction.average(R)
6	standardDev = WorksheetFunction.StDev(R)
7	min = WorksheetFunction.min(R)
8	max = WorksheetFunction.max(R)
9	With Worksheets("Sheet3")
10	.Range("E1:E4").ClearFormats
11	.Range("D1") = "The average age is:"
12	.Range("E1") = VBA.Format(promedio, "0.00")

13	.Range("D2") = "The minimum age is:"
14	.Range("E2") = min
15	.Range("D3") = "The maximum age is:"
16	.Range("E3") = max
17	.Range("D4") = "The standard deviation is:"
18	.Range("E4").numberFormat = "0.00"
19	.Range("E4") = desvEstandar
20	End With
21	End Sub

To make the calculations, we use the property of the **Application** object (that is, Excel) called *WorksheetFunction*, which returns the object of the same name. All Excel functions are available within this object, which in the VBA model would be the equivalent of the methods. All the functions (or methods) available for this object can be consulted in the VBA Object Browser, as shown in figure 10.1.

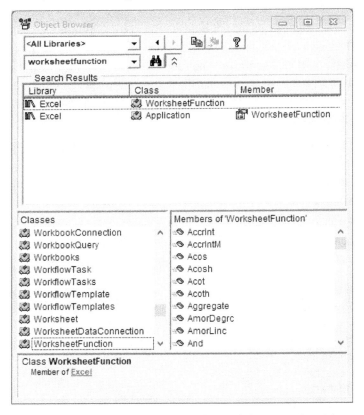

Figure 10.1. Object Browser showing the *WorksheetFunction* object.

The results of the execution of subroutine 10.1 are shown in figure 10.2.

10.3 Functions of the VBA library

These are functions of the VBA language (*bulit-in functions*). Each function is associated with a library. To know what libraries are available and their functions, you can consult to the Object Browser. There, we will select VBA in the *combobox* where the categories of objects are, as shown in figure 10.3. Classes are highlighted within the black rectangle.

Function libraries are those that have the following icon on the left side . Either way, to make things easier, we will mention the libraries of available functions: *Conversion, DateTime, FileSystem, Financial, Information, Interaction, Math* and *Strings*.

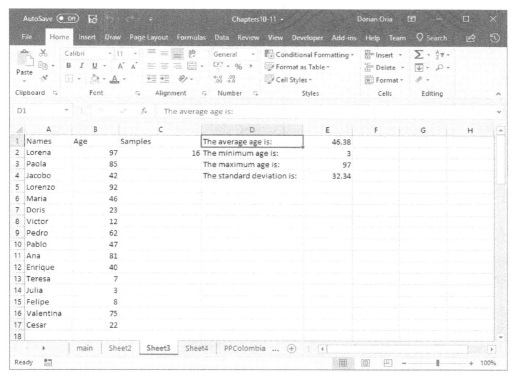

Figure 10.2. Result of the execution of subroutine 10.1.

To show how the VBA functions work, let's repeat the previous exercise with a few small variations: we will change the way we present the information and how. Instead of writing them in the spreadsheet, we will show them using an **MsgBox** window. The subroutine to do this is the following.

Figura 10.3. Functions of the VBA library.

Subroutine 10.2

1	Sub vbaFunc()
2	Dim R As Range
3	Dim average, standardDev, min, max As Variant
4	Set R = Application.InputBox(prompt:="Enter the age range without the header", _
5	Title:="My calculator", Type:=8)
6	average = WorksheetFunction.average(R)
7	standardDev = WorksheetFunction.StDev(R)
8	min = WorksheetFunction.min(R)
9	max = WorksheetFunction.max(R)
10	MsgBox "The average age is: " & VBA.Format(average, "0.00") & _
11	vbNewLine & "The minimum age is: " & min & vbNewLine & _
12	"The maximum age is: " & max & vbNewLine & _
13	"The standard deviation is: " & VBA.Format(standardDev, "0.00"), _

| 14 | vbOKOnly + vbInformation, "Results" |
| 15 | End Sub |

When executing the subroutine, a window will appear asking you to enter the age range. With the mouse, you will select the range of data (from the same page of the previous exercise) as shown in figure 10.4.

The window shown in the figure 10.4 is generated from the **InputBox** method of the *Application* object. In line 2 of subroutine 10.2 the option Type:=8 allows to use data range as input. For more information on how to configure **InputBox** and the types of input that can be configured, you can follow the following link:

https://msdn.microsoft.com/en-us/vba/excel-vba/articles/application-inputbox-method-excel

InputBox is also a function of the **Interaction** library. Remember that more information can also be obtained in the Object Browser.

The result of the execution of subroutine 10.2 is shown in figure 10.5.

Figure 10.4. VBA window to request information from the user.

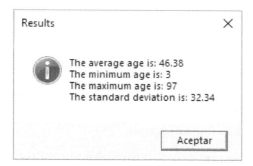

Figure 10.5. Result of the execution of subroutine 10.2.

To achieve that the average and standard deviation values showed only two decimals, the **Format** function was used. The **Format** function is part of the *Strings* library.

To present the information we used the **MsgBox** function, from the **Interaction** library. We have already introduced this function in other chapters, but here we do it formally. In previous chapters we have used it in its simplest version. However, it is possible to personalize it. For example, our window (figure 10.5) shows an information image (*vbInformation*) and also has a custom title.

For more information on how to configure MsgBox, you can visit the following link:

https://msdn.microsoft.com/en-us/vba/language-reference-vba/articles/msgbox-function

10.4 Functions designed by the user

In chapter 2 (item 2.3.2) we talk about functions and we said that, unlike a subroutine, a function executes a task and may or may not return a value or a reference. We also said that functions start with the keyword **Function**. In that context, we invoke functions from a subroutine to execute a calculation. However, that same function can also be invoked from a cell in a spreadsheet. To illustrate this, we will make our own average calculation function and use it with the same data from the previous numeral.

Subroutine 10.3.

```
1    Function myOwnAverageFunc(R As Range) As Double
2    Dim sum As Double
3    Dim i, j, rows, columna As Integer
4    rows = R.rows.Count
5    columna = R.Columns.Count
6    sum = 0
7    For i = 1 To rows
8       For j = 1 To columna
9          sum = sum + R.Cells(i, j)
10      Next j
11   Next i
12   myOwnAverageFunc = sum / (rows * columna)
13   End Function
```

Figure 10.6 shows the name of the function created in the previous subroutine and the range of the cells that will be taken into account for the execution of the calculation. Once you press the "Enter" key you will see the result.

An interesting thing in this function is the fact to receive a range as input and the use of the *Rows.Count* and *Columns.Count* properties to determine the number of rows and columns respectively that make up the selected range (lines 4 and 5). To refer to each of the cells that make up the range, the *Cells* property was used (line 9).

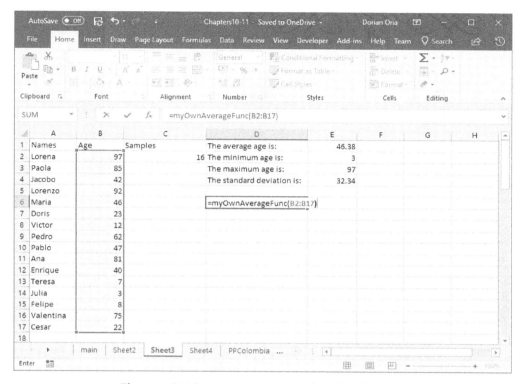

Figure 10.6. Using our own average calculation function.

Be careful not to use names for those functions that are already reserved for Excel functions. Remember that functions must be written in module code windows.

Chapter 11. Interacting with the user

11.1 Introduction

With VBA you can also make applications that look professional. So far we have worked with the fundamentals that will allow us to handle many of the strengths that make Excel and its programming language a very powerful tool for the development of applications. Now we will see how we can interact with the user of our applications, through forms (*Userforms*) that are no more than the windows in which requests for information are made or results are presented. The above can be done using either numbers, texts, images and / or graphics. VBA offers a wide variety of controls to display information to the user and to request it called *widgets*. Through these controls you can display information, show options for the user to choose, buttons that perform tasks, etc.

11.2 Userforms

Userforms are the main container which contains a graphical application. Within a form there will be labels, buttons, lists of options, text controls, etc. It is the interface with which the user interacts. Figure 11.1 shows how an empty form looks. It is composed of a main area where we will add our controls (enclosed in a rectangle). It has an "x" in the upper right corner, which allows closing the window (forever), which in turn terminates the execution of the program. This option is a "violent" way to exit the execution, since it is also a way to abort the execution of the program (or that portion of the program). In the upper left corner of the form there is a text that is often used to show the name of the application, but in general it can be customized with any message (in our figure it is where *UserForm1* says).

Figure 11.2 shows a window with all the controls that can be added to a form to customize it. We will give a brief explanation of each of them, by building an application.

The application that we are going to develop is based on the subroutine 10.2 with the difference that now we will ask the user to enter the range of data that is taken into account for the calculations. The user can choose the calculation that he wants and the result will be shown in the form, instead of using the **MsgBox** function. Additionally, the program will count the number of samples in a range of ages.

In numeral 2.5 (chapter 2) we showed how to add a form. To add a control, we select it from the Toolbox (figure 11.2) and drag it into the form. There we can move it to the position that we like and we can even change its size. Another way of adding a control is by clicking on it and moving the mouse to the form and clicking on it.

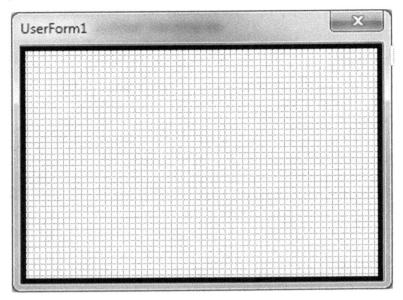

Figure 11.1. Userform.

Let's start by customizing our form. In figure 11.3 we can see it in the design phase. In case we want to modify the size we can do it by dragging one of the white squares that surround the form. It can also be done manually, modifying its *Height* and *Width* properties in the properties window (window located in the bottom left of figure 11.3).

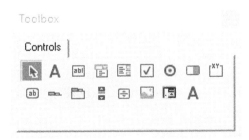

Figure 11.2. Userform Toolbox (*widgets*).

The first thing we are going to do is change the name that the form will have. To do this, we change the *Name* property.. As can be seen in figure 11.3, the name (*Name* in the properties window) and the title (*Caption*) are the same. Changing the name does not change the title. The difference between both is that the name (*Name*) will be used to refer to the form in the code. The title can be a word or sentence that we want to show.

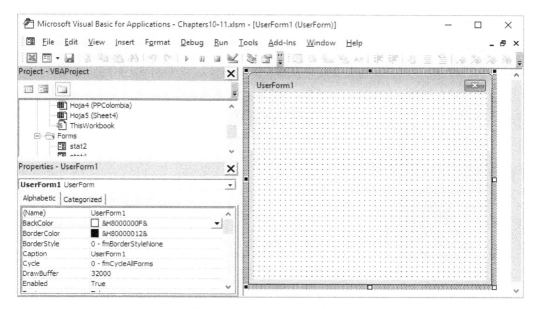

Figure 11.3. Form design phase.

The properties that we are going to change in the properties window are:

Property	Value
Name	Stat
Caption	Statistical software

We modify the size using the mouse.

11.3 Label

This control allows you to add a label with text that usually is not long. It is mostly used to give some information about another control or to show information to the user (which may vary as the application is running), such as a path to a file. The content of information in this control can not be modified directly by the user at runtime, unless the modification is made from code.

For now we are going to add a label with information about the program. In figure 11.4 you can see what the message looks like and the properties that have been modified so far (enclosed in rectangles).

As we go adding other controls we will be adding more labels.

11.4   Frame

A frame allows us to group controls within it. It helps to improve the appearance of the interface and is also very useful during the design, since just by moving the frame within the form, all the controls that are inside of it are moved at the same time.

In our example, we are going to add a frame that will later contain text boxes.

Figure 11.5 shows how the application looks with the added frame.

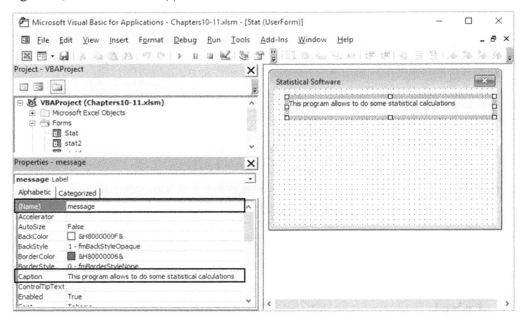

Figure 11.4. Label properties edition.

11.5   Textbox

This control allows the user to enter information into the program. This information can be a text string or a number. In our case, we are going to use this control to introduce age limits.

As can be seen in figure 11.6, we have added two text boxes, one for entering the lower age limit and one for the upper limit. One feature of our application is that it counts the number of people within those age limits.

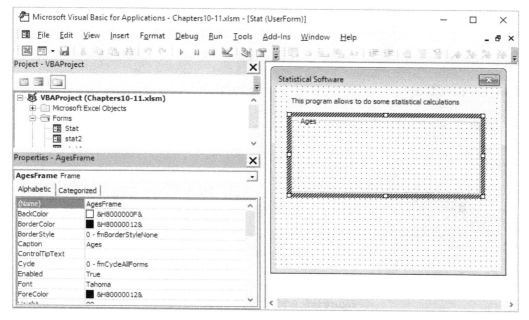

Figure 11.5. Frame properties edition.

11.6 Checkbox

This control allows us to offer the user several options to take into account in the execution of a program. It is especially useful when the options are not many. It is a question of space available to offer the options and maybe also of aesthetics. If there are many options, you can use the list box which we will see later.

For purposes of our example, we will use checkboxes to offer the user the calculation options of our program, as shown in figure 11.7.

As you can see, we have grouped the checkboxes within a frame. Sometimes it can happen that we add some controls and then we realized that we wanted to group them in a frame. No problem. You can create the frame afterwards and drag the controls inside it.

11.7 RefEdit

This control is exclusive of VBA-Excel. Through it, the range of cells of an Excel spreadsheet that contains the input data for our application is chosen.

Figure 11.8 shows how the application looks with this control that has been added. As you may have noticed, we have expanded the height of the form. The new control was called DataRange.

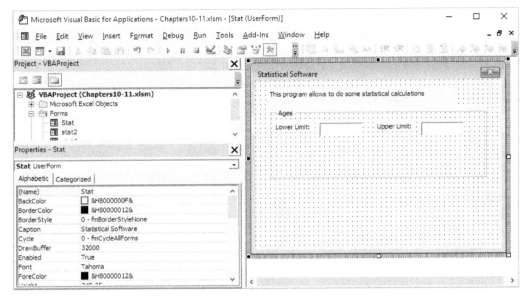

Figure 11.6. Adding textboxes.

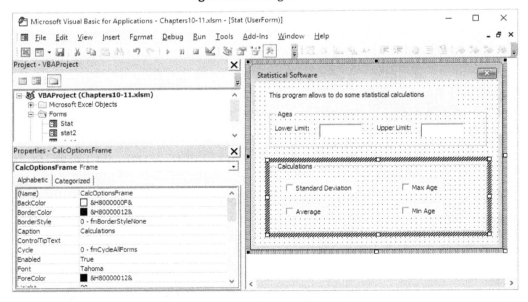

Figure 11.7. Adding checkboxes.

11.8   CommandButton

This button allows you to start the execution of a program. In its programming we have all the necessary code to make the calculations of our application. Although the execution of tasks is not exclusive of this control, it is what is most commonly practiced. You can also write code for events associated with other controls.

Figure 11.9 shows how our finally designed application looks now. It can also be noticed that we have added more labels, which are the ones that will show the results. These labels do not show text at the beginning of the execution. As the information they display may be of different sizes, you must change the **AutoSize** property of each label to *True* (as shown in figure 11.9) and the **WordWrap** property to *False*. Additionally we have added a button to close the application (Exit). We will program this button using the *Click* event.

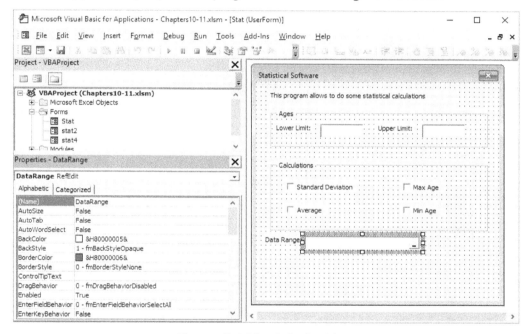

Figure 11.8. Adding Ref Edit widget.

To add the code that will be executed when you press the "Run" button, double-click on the button. This will automatically create the subroutine where the code will be contained (figure 11.10). By default, the subroutine that is created will be associated with the "Click" event. This means that the subroutine will be executed when the user makes a single click on the button. However, it is possible to associate another event.

In figure 11.10, inside the rectangle, two combo boxes can be observed. The one on the left contains all the controls that make up the application (figure 11.11). The one on the right contains all the events that can be programmed for the control selected in the combo box on the left.

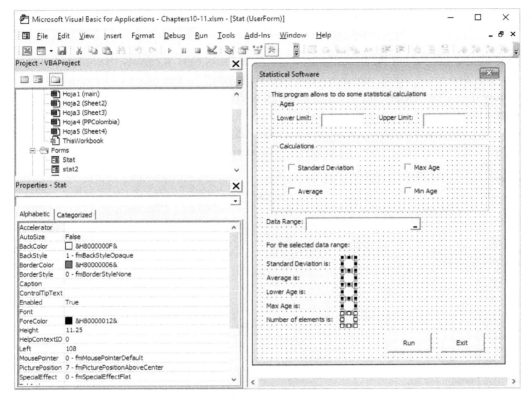

Figure 11.9. Adding command button and other labels.

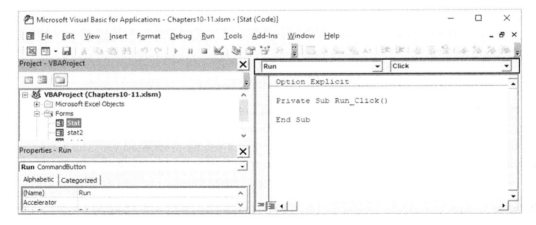

Figure 11.10. Window where the code of the "Run" button will be written.

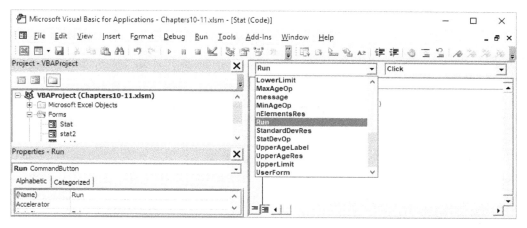

Figure 11.11. Controls that make up our application.

For example, in the case of the "Run" button, the possible events to program are those shown in figure 11.12.

Just to illustrate how events work, we will program our "Run" button to respond to the double-click of the mouse.

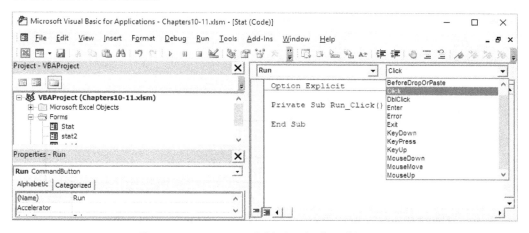

Figure 11.12. Events available for the "Run" button.

To add a subroutine associated with another event, select the event from the combo box on the right. Selecting the double-click event (*DblClick*) generates the space that will contain the subroutine, as shown in figure 11.13 (enclosed in the rectangle)

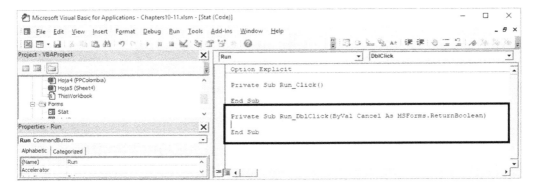

Figure 11.13. Space for the subroutine of the "Run" button associated with the *Dblclick* event.

We are also going to program the *KeyPress* event, which will be activated when the user, after clicking the "Run" button, now press any key. The program will show a message that this option is not valid to run the application. Figure 11.14 shows the body of the subroutine, associated with the *KeyPress* event (rectangle).

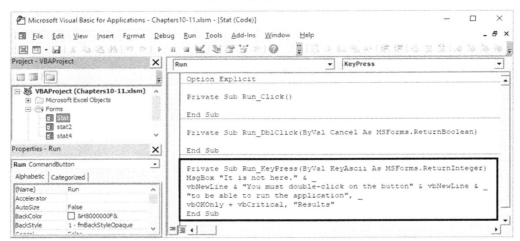

Figure 11.14. Subroutine for the *KeyPress* event of the "Run" button.

Subroutine 11.1 shows the code for the *KeyPress* event.

Subroutine 11.1.

1	Private Sub Run_KeyPress(ByVal KeyAscii As MSForms.ReturnInteger)
2	MsgBox "It is not here." & _
3	vbNewLine & "You must double-click on the button" & vbNewLine & _
4	"to be able to run the application", _
5	vbOKOnly + vbCritical, "Results"
6	End Sub

The subroutine 11.2 shows the code associated with the DblClick event of the "Run" button. This code is the one that will execute the calculations of the application.

Subroutine 11.2.

```
1   Private Sub Run_DblClick(ByVal Cancel As MSForms.ReturnBoolean)
2   Dim R As Range
3   Dim i, rows, n, lla, ula As Integer
4
5   Set R = Range(DataRange.Value)
6   rows = R.rows.Count
7   n = 0
8   lla = CInt(LowerLimit.Value)    'Min Age
9   ula = CInt(UpperLimit.Value)   'Max Age
10
11  If lla >= WorksheetFunction.min(R) _
12  And ula <= WorksheetFunction.max(R) Then
13      For i = 1 To rows + 1
14          If R.Cells(i, 1).Value >= lla And _
15              R.Cells(i, 1).Value <= ula Then
16              n = n + 1
17          End If
18      Next i
19  End If
20
21  If StatDevOp.Value = True Then
22      StandardDevRes = VBA.Format(WorksheetFunction.StDev(R), "0.00")
23  End If
24  If AverageOp.Value = True Then
25      AverageRes = VBA.Format(WorksheetFunction.average(R), "0.00")
26  End If
27  If MinAgeOp.Value = True Then
28      LowerAgeRes = WorksheetFunction.min(R)
29  End If
30  If MaxAgeOp.Value = True Then
31      UpperAgeRes = WorksheetFunction.max(R)
32  End If
33  nElementsRes = n    'elements in the age range
34  End Sub
```

Some interesting comments about this code:

- To select the range of cells, we place the mouse inside the DataRange control. Once there, we go to the spreadsheet and select the range of cells with the information we want to use as input.

- That range of cells is read as a text string. In order to be used as a Range object, it is necessary to use the Range instruction (line 5). This range is assigned to the variable "R". Remember that in this case, the use of the reserved word Set is similar to use a nickname to make it easier and more practical to refer to the Range object.

- In lines 8 and 9, we used the **CInt** instruction so that text strings read from text boxes are converted to numbers.

- The checkboxes can only have two values: *True* or *False* (selected or not). This is what is evaluated in lines 21, 24, 27 and 30, for each of the four checkboxes used in the program.

To execute this program, you can press **F5** or the button Execute macro (it is easy to recognize this button in the standard toolbar: it is a green triangle pointing to the right). This should be done in this way, since a form is not in itself a complete program, but part of a larger one. In order for an application with windows (forms) to be launched without having to be in the programming environment, its invocation must be done from (or be part of) a subroutine.

In figure 11.15 you can see a stage during the execution of the program, in which the selection of the range of cells to be used in the calculations is shown. Figure 11.16 shows the window with the results.

To exit the application, the "Exit" button was programmed. The code that is executed when pressing it is the one that is shown in subroutine 11.3.

Subroutine 11.3.

```
1   Private Sub ExitStat_Click()
2   Unload Me
3   End Sub
```

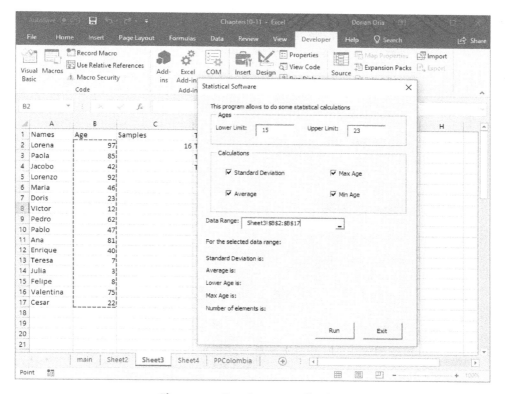

Figure 11.15. Running our application.

Interesting in this code is that the instruction to end the application refers to the object itself (**Me**). However, it can be changed by the name of the form: Stat. This means that the **Unload** statement can close any other form. Simply change the word Me for the name of the Userform (try changing **Me** by *Stat* on line 2).

11.9 Running a form application

Running an application from the programming environment may not be very elegant or practical. Not to mention the fact that probably this application will be executed by people with little or no knowledge of programming (which in fact they do not have to have it considering that they are end users). Even, you may want nobody to have access to the code.

Regardless of how you want to give access to the application, you need to create a subroutine that launches the program, like the one shown below.

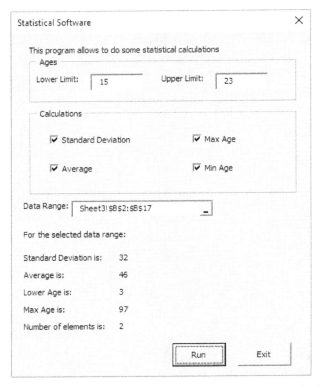

Figure 11.16. Result of the execution of the subroutine 11.2 (after pressing the "Run" button).

Subroutine 11.4.

1	Sub RunStat()
2	Stat.Show
3	End Sub

This subroutine was written in a module. In a strict sense, you can write in any code window of any object (except in the code window of the form). If for some reason you want to write the subroutine in a code window different from the modules, add the word **Public** before the word **Sub**.

We will present four ways to access the application from Excel. The first one is using the Macros button that is in the "Developer" tab (figure 11.17), which launches the window shown in figure 11.18. The Macro window can also be launched using the **Alt + F8** keys as a shortcut. To execute the application, press the "Run" button once the application (RunStat) has been selected.

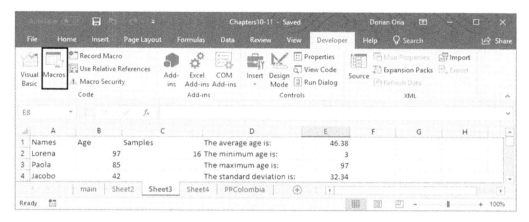

Figure 11.17. Button that activates the Macro window.

The second way to launch the application is using a shortcut through the combination of keys. To do this, in the window shown in figure 11.18 press the "Options" button (having previously selected the subroutine to which you want to add the shortcut). When you do this, the window shown in figure 11.19 appears.

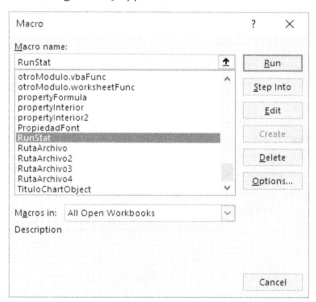

Figure 11.18. Macro window, showing the subroutine highlighted to launch our application.

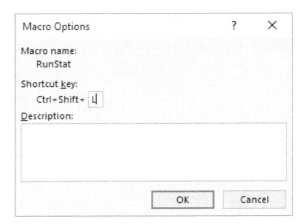

Figure 11.19. Adding a shortcut to the subroutine that launches the Stat application.

In the upper part of the window you can see the name of the subroutine to which we are going to add the key combination for its invocation. Pressing that set of keys will execute the subroutine that the application launches.

The third option is to do it using a button in the Excel toolbar. You can create the button in any of the available tabs or you can create a new, customized one. To do this we follow the path File -> Options -> Customize Ribbon. By doing this, the window that appeared will look like it is shown in figure 11.20.

Once in this window, we select Macros in the "Choose commands from:" combo box (enclosed in the rectangle in figure 11.20). Once this is done, the window will look as shown in figure 11.21. On the right side of the window, click on the "New tab" button (enclosed in the rectangle). A new tab is automatically added, as can be seen in figure 11.22 (enclosed in the rectangle). To change the name of this tab, click on the button that says "Rename". This will bring up the window shown in figure 11.23. Change the name to "Own Apps" as shown in the same figure. Right below we will see that there is a new group. Change the name to Chapter 11. This time, the Window to rename will be seen as shown in figure 11.24. In addition to changing the name, you can choose an icon for the group. Once these steps are completed, the window will look as shown in figure 11.25.

Figure 11.20. Window to customize ribbon (toolbar).

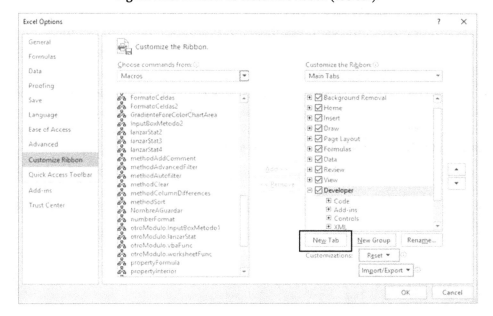

Figure 11.21. Customization window showing the macros (subroutines) available in the Excel workbook.

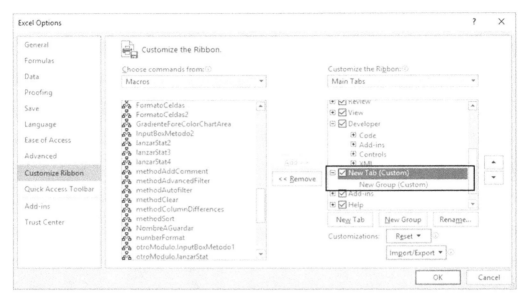

Figure 11.22. Excel options window, showing the added tab.

Figure 11.23. Window to change the name of the tab.

Having selected the new group, we go to the left side of the window where the available macros (subroutines) are displayed and we select the one that interests us (in our case, RunStat). We press the "Add >>" button and now the window will look as shown in figure 11.26. Once this is finished, the Excel toolbar will look like the one shown in figure 11.27.

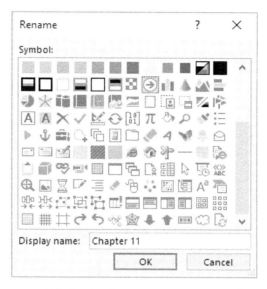

Figure 11.24. Window to change name and icon to the group.

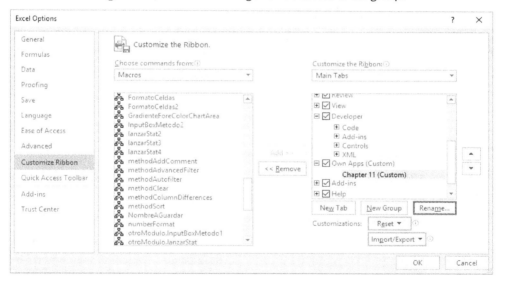

Figure 11.25. Window showing the new tab and the new group added, with the final names.

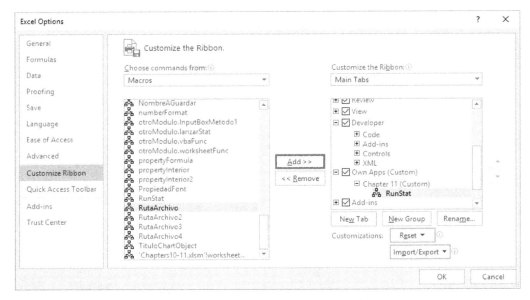

Figure 11.26. Button for RunStat added.

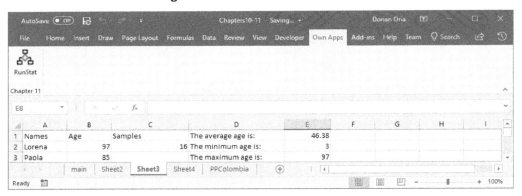

Figure 11.27. Own apps tab added with the button to launch our application.

The fourth option is to add a command button in a spreadsheet. To access the controls in this area, we go to the "Developer" tab and there we press the "Insert" button. When you do this, the window shown in figure 11.28 appears. I suggest to do this in the spreadsheet named "main".

Figure 11.28. Activex controls available for spreadsheet.

The command button is selected (enclosed in the rectangle in figure 11.28) and the mouse takes the form of a small cross. Excel is waiting for you to click with the mouse at the point where you want to add the button. Either way, the button can then be configured, including the change of position. Once the button has been added, it looks as shown in figure 11.29.

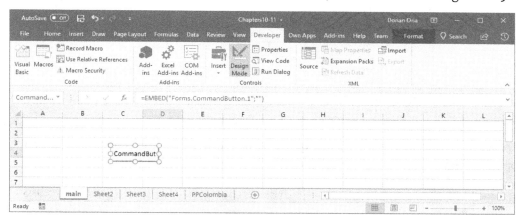

Figura 11.29. Adding a command button in a spreadsheet.

Notice that the button next to the "Insert" button (Design Mode) is now activated. This means that while in that mode the instructions of any control that is inside the spreadsheet will not be executed.

To modify the properties of the newly added button, press the button that says "Properties" that is next to the "Design Mode" button. When doing so, the window shown in figure 11.30 appears.

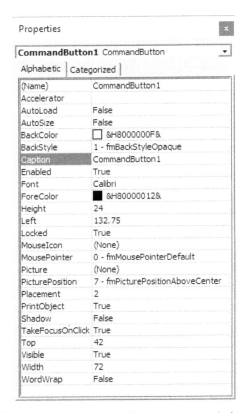

Figure 11.30. Command button properties window.

In this case, we can ignore the change of the *Name* property. We can change the *Caption* property to **Stat**. By doing so, our button will look as shown in figure 11.31.

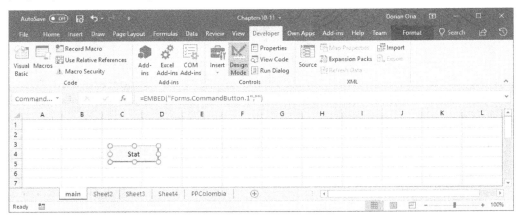

Figure 11.31. Appearance of the command button with the custom *Caption* property.

Finally, we double-click on our button and a code window will appear. Within the subroutine that was automatically created, we write the name of the subroutine that we want to invoke. The code window will look like the figure 11.32.

Figure 11.32. Programming the command button.

It is interesting to note that, because since the button is contained within the "main" worksheet, the code of this button will be in the code window of this spreadsheet.

To be able to execute the instructions of the newly added button, we must deactivate the Design Mode. Once this is done, by clicking on the button, the RunStat instruction will be executed, which in turn will execute the subroutine 11.4. If you wish, try changing the line 2 in the subroutine shown in figure 11.32 by *Stat.Show* and see what happens.

11.10 Protection of an application code

It is my duty to show you that Excel has a way to protect the code, so that it is not visible. However, it is also my duty to tell you that Microsoft has not yet improved the way to do this and there is already a lot of code out there that allows you to unlock a protected macro. If you want to know how to do it, subscribe to my web page: http://infiniterand.com/es/

To protect the code, so that it is not visible, we will do the following:

-   From the programming environment, we go to Tools -> VBAProject Properties. When you do this, the window shown in figure 11.33 appears.

-   In the window of the previous figure we select the tab that says "Protection". The window will now look as shown in figure 11.34.

-   Select "Lock project for viewing" and assign a password.

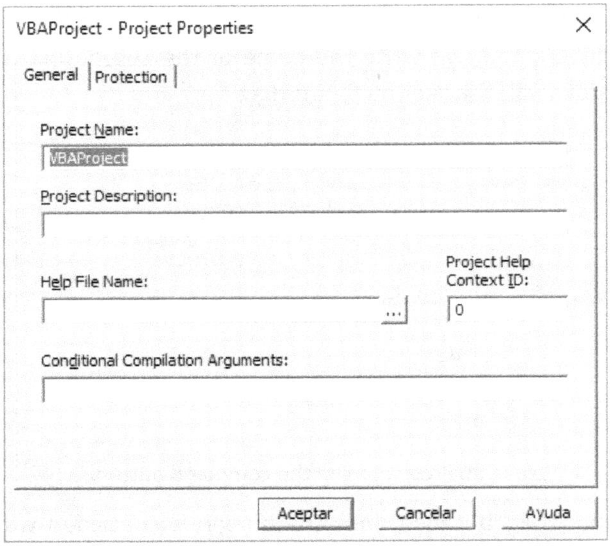

Figure 11.33. VBA project properties window.

Figure 11.34. VBA project properties window, showing the option to protect code.

11.11 ListBox

We are going to make a small variation in our application. We are going to change the checkboxes for a list box. This control offers all the calculation options. Figure 11.35 shows how the empty control looks.

Statistical Software   ×

This program allows to do some statistical calculations
┌─ Ages ──┐
│ Lower Limit: [│   ]   Upper Limit: [   ] │
└───┘

┌─ Calculations ──────────────────────────────────────┐
│ ┌───┐ │
│ │   │ │
│ │   │ │
│ │   │ │
│ └───┘ │
└───┘

Data Range: [▾]

For the selected data range:

Standard Deviation is:

Average is:

Lower Age is:

Max Age is:

Number of elements is:

                        [Run]   [Exit]

Figure 11.35. Version of the Stat application, now with a list box.

To make this version of the form, I exported *Stat* and then changed the name of the user form to *Stat2*. To export a form, click with the left button on top of the form and select "Export File". The user form will be saved with extension **.frm**.

As can be seen in figure 11.35, the list box offers no options. This occurs because this control requires the information to be entered into it before the user form that contains it is displayed.

For this, we have made a modification in the subroutine 11.4 (RunStat). The new routine can be seen below.

Subroutine 11.5.

1	Sub RunStat2()
2	With Stat2
3	With .CalcList
4	.AddItem "Standard Deviation"
5	.AddItem "Average"
6	.AddItem "Max Age"

7	.AddItem "Min Age"
8	End With
9	.Show
10	End With
11	End Sub

We have called our list box "CalcList". Remember that a control is an object, so to refer to the objects that compose it, its properties or methods we use a point after the object. In our case, since the application is being launched from a subroutine that is in a module, it is necessary to invoke the complete path to each object. Our user form has been called "Stat2". Then, with structures **With - End With** nested we have made reference to the object "CalcList" and we have populated it with the method *AddItem*. Internally, the list box assigns an index (in runtime) to each of the elements that comprise it, starting from 0. Just to serve as a reminder, the subroutine 11.6 shows how the code would look without using the structures **With - End With** nested.

Subroutine 11.6.

1	Sub RunStat3()
2	Stat2.CalcList.AddItem "Standard Deviation"
3	Stat2.CalcList.AddItem "Average"
4	Stat2.CalcList.AddItem "Max Age"
5	Stat2.CalcList.AddItem "Min Age"
6	Stat2.Show
7	End Sub

To execute the program with these changes in the form, change the code shown in figure 11.32 by the following instruction:

Call Chapter11.RunStat2

Now when we launch our application from any of these subroutines (11.5 or 11.6), it looks as shown in figure 11.36.

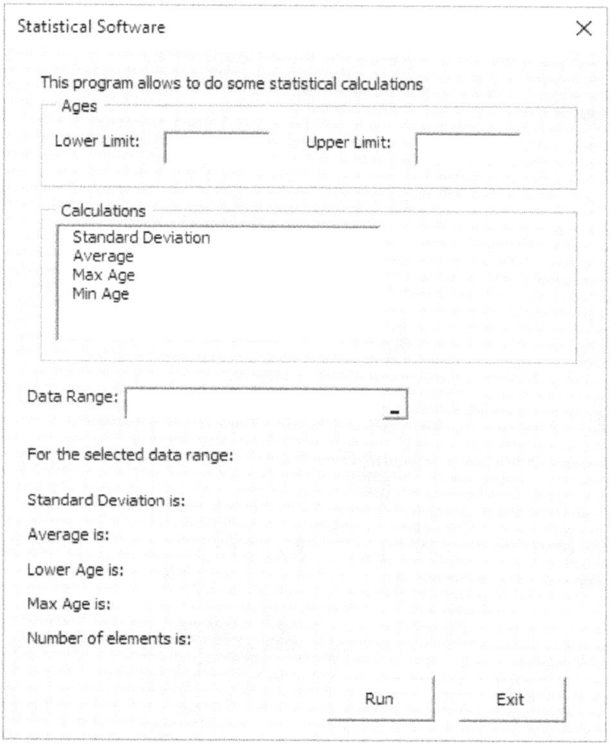

Figure 11.36. Stat2 application using list box to show options.

The way in which the list box was configured is an extended version that allows you to choose one option at a time, or all of them (leaving the mouse pressed or using the **Shift +** **click** combination of the left mouse button), or to choose several options but not consecutive (using the **Ctrl + click** combination with the left mouse button). For this, the *MultiSelect* property of the list box "CalcList" was changed to *fmMultiSelectExtended*. Another way of doing this is during the execution of the subroutine RunStat (11.5). To do this, add the following instruction below line 7:

```
    . MultiSelect= fmMultiSelectExtended
```

When you are writing this instruction, at some point your code window will look as shown in figure 11.37.

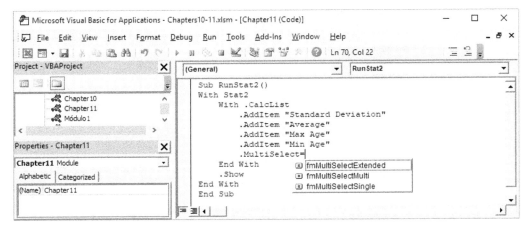

Figure 11.37. Code window showing the operation of *IntelliSense* technology.

The subroutine that follows is the code that will be executed when clicking on the "Calculate" button of our new user form (Stat2). In this case, as it is the same button, we are going to program the Click event only.

Subroutine 11.7.

```vba
1   Private Sub Run_Click()
2   Dim R As Range
3   Dim i, rows, n, lla, ula As Integer
4
5   Set R = Range(DataRange.Value)
6   rows = R.rows.Count
7   n = 0
8   lla = CInt(LowerLimit.Value)    'Min Age
9   ula = CInt(UpperLimit.Value)   'Max Age
10
11  If lla >= WorksheetFunction.min(R) _
12  And ula <= WorksheetFunction.max(R) Then
13      For i = 1 To rows + 1
14          If R.Cells(i, 1).Value >= lla And _
15              R.Cells(i, 1).Value <= ula Then
16              n = n + 1
17          End If
18      Next i
19  End If
20
21  If CalcList.Selected(0) = True Then
22      StandardDevRes = VBA.Format(WorksheetFunction.StDev(R), "0.00")
```

```
23    End If
24    If CalcList.Selected(1) = True Then
25        AverageRes = VBA.Format(WorksheetFunction.average(R), "0.00")
26    End If
27    If CalcList.Selected(2) = True Then
28        LowerAgeRes = WorksheetFunction.min(R)
29    End If
30    If CalcList.Selected(3) = True Then
31        UpperAgeRes = WorksheetFunction.max(R)
32    End If
33    nElementsRes = n    'elements in the age range
34    End Sub
```

The difference between this subroutine and the subroutine 11.2 is between lines 21 to 32. Now, instead of validating *checkboxes*, the options shown in the list box are validated. As mentioned above, each of the elements in the list box has an index assigned at run time. Thus, the option "Standard Deviation" is option 0 and we refer to it as "CalcList.Selected (0)". Notice how it was not necessary to add the name of the object that contains it (ie the user form Stat2) because it is already inside the object and its code.

11.12   Scrollbar

This bar allows you to scroll through a control when its size is not large enough to show all its content. In this case, the scroll bar is embedded within the control.

There are other cases in which the scroll bar can be used as an individual control. For example, in cases where you want the user to choose from a range of values.

Let's see first how a scroll bar looks inside another control. For this case, we will take as an example the list box that we used in the previous subroutine. In this case, we know that we have four options available. Reduce the size of the list box (*Height*), so that only two options can be seen. Now execute the application again. After doing so, the window will look as shown in figure 11.38. As you can see, the scroll bar appears automatically.

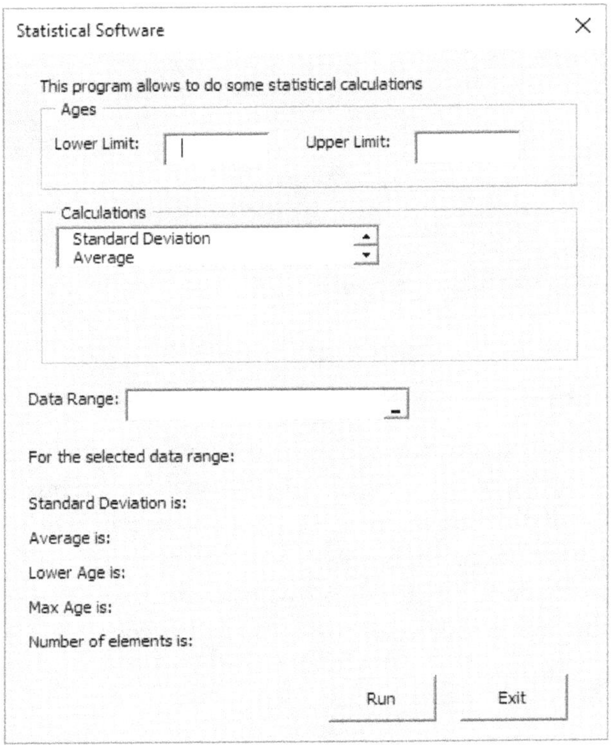

Figure 11.38. Smaller list box cannot show all the elements that contain it, we add a scroll bar to navigate in it.

Let's go with another example. Imagine that our user form was smaller. Something like the image shown in figure 11.39.

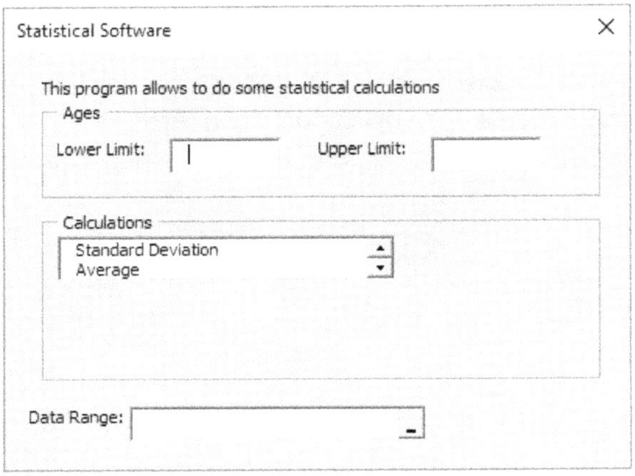

Figure 11.39. Smallest user form.

As you can see, you cannot see the labels or buttons at the bottom of the application. If you try to access that part of the application, it will not be possible.

Taking into account this window size, we are going to modify a couple of properties of the user form. The first one is the *ScrollBars* property. Remember that this is done from the Properties window, having the form selected. Let's select the *fmScrollBarsVertical* value here. Now, change the value of the *ScrollHeight* property to 366 (this value is estimated so that the scroll bar can cover the entire height of the window. I suggest you start by assigning a value of 100 and see what happens). When you run the application again, it will look as shown in figure 11.40.

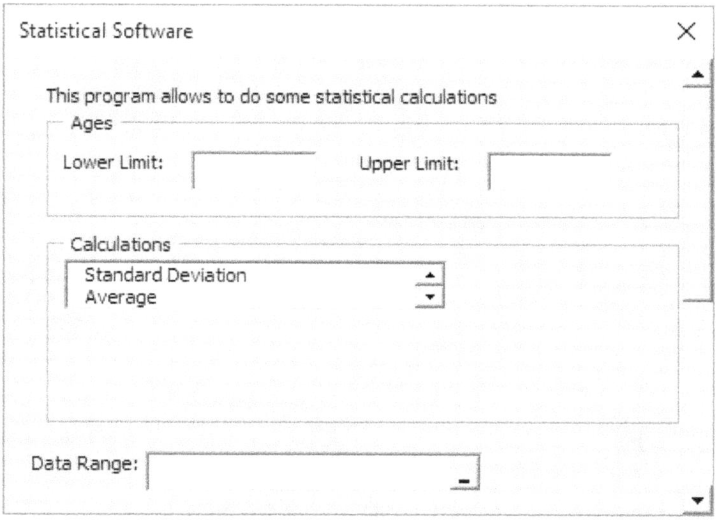

Figure 11.40. Smaller form, now with vertical scroll bar.

Now you can use the scroll bar to move to the end of the window.

This can also be done with code. Add the following lines of code to subroutine 11.5 just before line 9. It is important to do it this way. If the lines of code are added after the instruction that is in line 9 (*.Show*) it will be too late and the changes will not be taken into account.

```
.ScrollBars = fmScrollBarsVertical
.ScrollHeight = .InsideHeight * 2
```

Interesting in these lines of code is the *InsideHeight* property. It returns the current height of the window. In this case, we assume that multiplying it by two already allows us to cover the size of the window and reach the controls that are at the bottom. Test it on your own by changing the 2 for another value or by adding values to *InsideHeight* instead of multiplying.

Let's see now the option in which the scroll bar can be used as an independent control. In this case, we are going to add a scroll bar to allow us to change the size of the letters within the list box. In addition, we add a label to indicate the size of the letter we are using. This label (it is invisible) was added next to the expression "Size Char" and we called it *SizeChar*. We have given the name of *ChangeSizeChar* (*Name* property) to the scrollbar. Once this is done, the application will look as shown in figure 11.41.

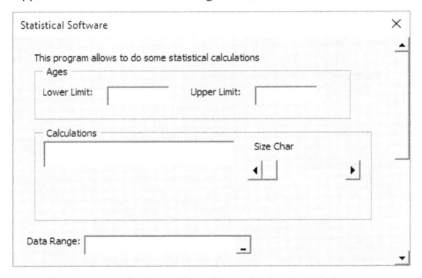

Figure 11.41. Application with scroll bar added as individual control.

Now, let's program the scroll bar. Let's start by editing a pair of properties: *Min = 8* and *Max = 14*. With this pair of values we want the smallest font to have size 8 and the largest 14. Now, let's program the bar so that before a movement in the scroll bar, a change occurs in the list box. To do this in design mode, double-click on it and automatically create the subroutine space for the code, which is shown below .

Subroutine 11.8.

1	Private Sub ChangeSizeChar_Change()
2	CalcList.Font.Size = ChangeSizeChar.Value
3	SizeChar = ChangeSizeChar.Value
4	End Sub

When executing this code and varying the values of the scrollbar, the window shown in figure 11.41 will look as shown in figure 11.42.

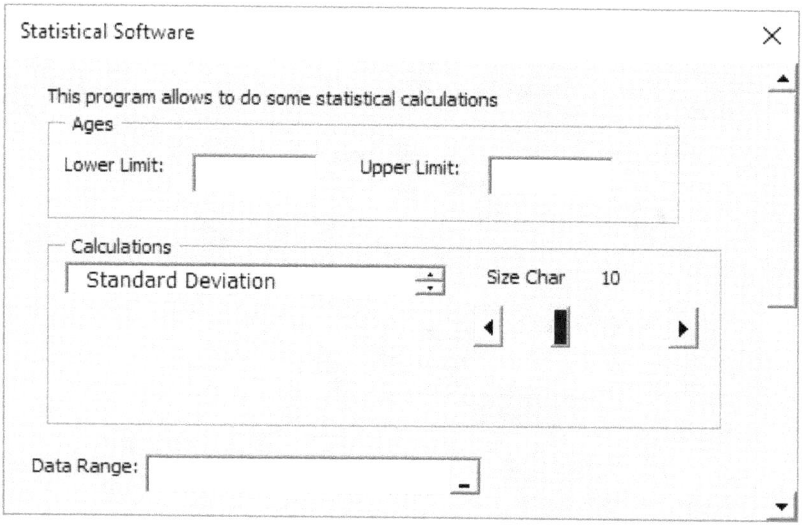

Figure 11.42. Scroll bar taking the value of 10, which is reflected in the size of the letter in the calculation list and indicated on the label that is just above it.

11.13 ComboBox

Like the list box, this control allows you to offer several options to the user, with the difference that you can only choose one. Although it may not be practical for our program, we will show it for academic purposes.

For this example, we have changed the name of the complete form to Stat3. Figure 11.43 shows what the application looks like with the added combo box. As with the list box (item 11.11), it is necessary to add the options to the combo box before displaying the application interface. To do this, we have programmed another subroutine, which we have called RunStat4. The code is shown below.

Subroutine 11.9.

```
1  Sub RunStat4()
2  Stat3.CalcCombo.AddItem "Standard Deviation"
3  Stat3.CalcCombo.AddItem "Average"
4  Stat3.CalcCombo.AddItem "Max Age"
5  Stat3.CalcCombo.AddItem "Min Age"
6  Stat3.Show
7  End Sub
```

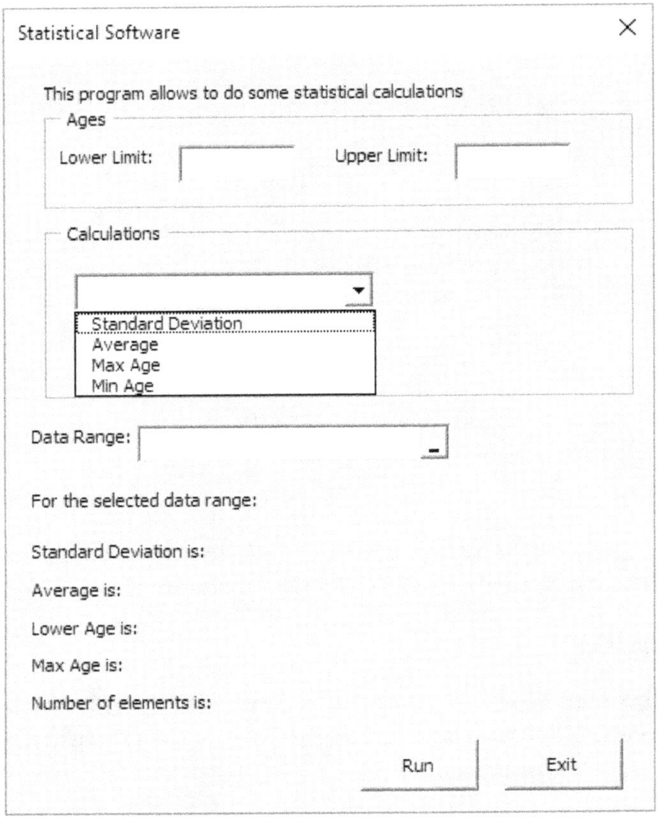

Figure 11.43. Application showing the combo box with the added options.

The code of the "Run" button is the one shown below.

Subroutine 11.10.

```
1   Private Sub Run3_Click()
2   Dim R As Range
3   Dim i, rows, n, lla, ula As Integer
4
5   Set R = Range(DataRange.Value)
6   rows = R.rows.Count
7   n = 0
8   lla = CInt(LowerLimit.Value)    'Min Age
9   ula = CInt(UpperLimit.Value)   'Max Age
10
11  If lla >= WorksheetFunction.min(R) _
12  And ula <= WorksheetFunction.max(R) Then
13     For i = 1 To rows + 1
```

```
14      If R.Cells(i, 1).Value >= lla And _
15          R.Cells(i, 1).Value <= ula Then
16         n = n + 1
17      End If
18    Next i
19  End If
20
21  If CalcCombo.ListIndex = 0 Then
22      StandardDevRes = VBA.Format(WorksheetFunction.StDev(R), "0.00")
23  End If
24  If CalcCombo.ListIndex = 1 Then
25      AverageRes = VBA.Format(WorksheetFunction.average(R), "0.00")
26  End If
27  If CalcCombo.ListIndex = 2 Then
28      UpperAgeRes = WorksheetFunction.max(R)
29  End If
30  If CalcCombo.ListIndex = 3 Then
31      LowerAgeRes = WorksheetFunction.min(R)
32  End If
33  nElementsRes = n
34
35  End Sub
```

This code is very similar to the one used for the case of the list box. In this case, the code of lines 21, 24, 27 and 30 has changed. In those lines, the object has been changed, which we call *CalcCombo*. In this control, to refer to each of the options, we use the index of each of them, as if it were an array. Thus, our first option, *Standard Deviation*, has as index the position 0, then the option *Average* has as index the position 1 and so on.

When you run the application, it will look as shown in figure 11.44.

11.14 SpinButton

This control looks like the scroll bar in terms of the ability to make a number change its value, such as the size of the letter in the example we used in numeral 11.12. However, a fundamental difference is that the scroll bar is more oriented to allow displacements in controls smaller than the contents it shows.

Let's take the same example from numeral 11.12 (subroutine 11.8) and we will replace the scroll bar that changes the size of the letter in the list box by a *SpinButton*.

Once the *SpinButton* has been added (next to the phrase "Size Char"), the window of our application will look as shown in figure 11.45.

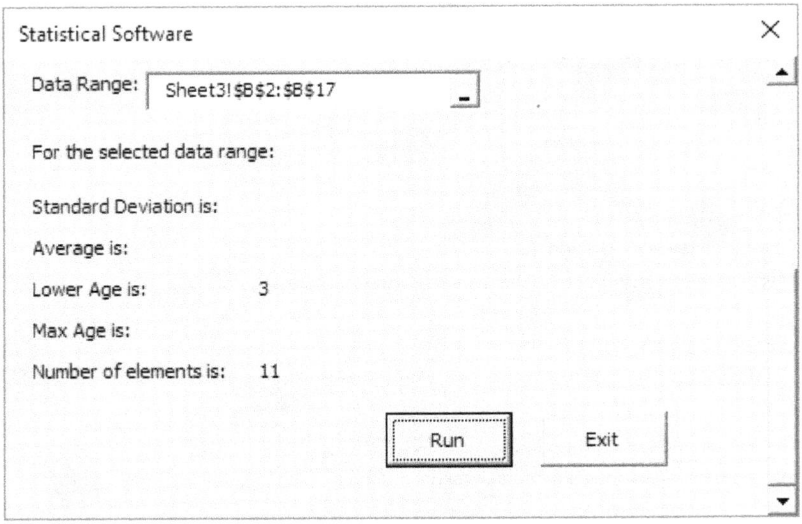

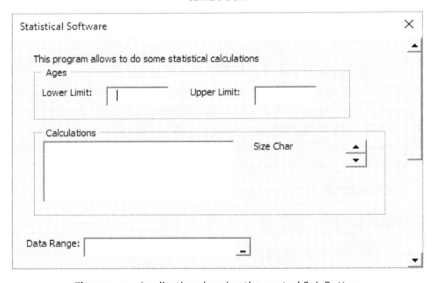

Figure 11.44. Application showing the results after having selected the *Minimum* option in the combo box.

Figure 11.45. Application showing the control *SpinButton*.

As with the scroll bar, the minimum and maximum values can be changed in the properties window of the number button. Remember that to access this window, select the control and immediately the properties of the object will be reflected in the lower left window. You can also change the orientation of the control. In our case it is oriented vertically, but it can also be placed horizontally. It is important to note that the properties of a control can be set at the design stage or at the execution time before launching the application, that is, before executing the *Show* method of the form (line 6 of subroutine 11.11, for example).

The subroutine to launch the application is shown below.

Subroutine 11.11.

```
1   Sub RunStat5()
2   Stat4.CalcList.AddItem "Standard Deviation"
3   Stat4.CalcList.AddItem "Average"
4   Stat4.CalcList.AddItem "Max Age"
5   Stat4.CalcList.AddItem "Min Age"
6   Stat4.Show
7   End Sub
```

Now, we are going to program the control in a similar way to how it was done with the scrollbar. We doubleclick on our control and the space for the code will be created automatically. In our case, we have called the CambiaTam control. The code is shown in the 11.12 subroutine.

Subroutine 11.12.

```
1   Private Sub ChangeSize_Change()
2   CalcList.Font.Size = ChangeSize.Value
3   SizeChar = ChangeSize.Value
4   End Sub
```

When you run the application, it will look as shown in figure 11.46.

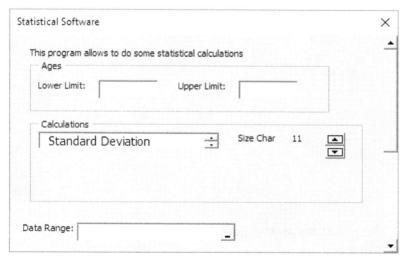

Figure 11.46. Application showing the change of the font size of the options within the list box.

11.15 Multipage

This control is quite useful when you want to organize different parts of a program, but in an elegant way, without necessarily increase the size of the form. Remember that the way to add a control is by clicking on it in the Toolbox window and then clicking on the place within the form where you want it to be. Clicking on each of the pages activates that space. Imagine for a moment that it is a collection of frames, within which you can place other controls.

Just to illustrate its operation and how to program it, we will divide the statistical calculations into two groups. Let's activate Page1. Now drag the labels corresponding to standard deviation and average to that page. Now let's do the same with the labels corresponding to the smallest and largest value, moving them to Page2. After other small adjustments that you should already be able to do on your own, the application should look as shown in figure 11.47.

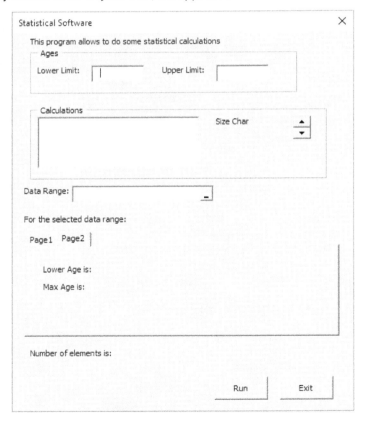

Figure 11.47. Design of the application using the *Multipage* control.

We are going to make other changes. Although this is a single control, each page will have its own attributes, as if it were an individual object tied to the main control. Thus, each page has its own attributes of name and title to be displayed (which in the properties window correspond to the *Name* and *Caption* properties). For now, we are going to change the titles of the pages (*captions*). Once this is done, the application will look as shown in figure 11.48.

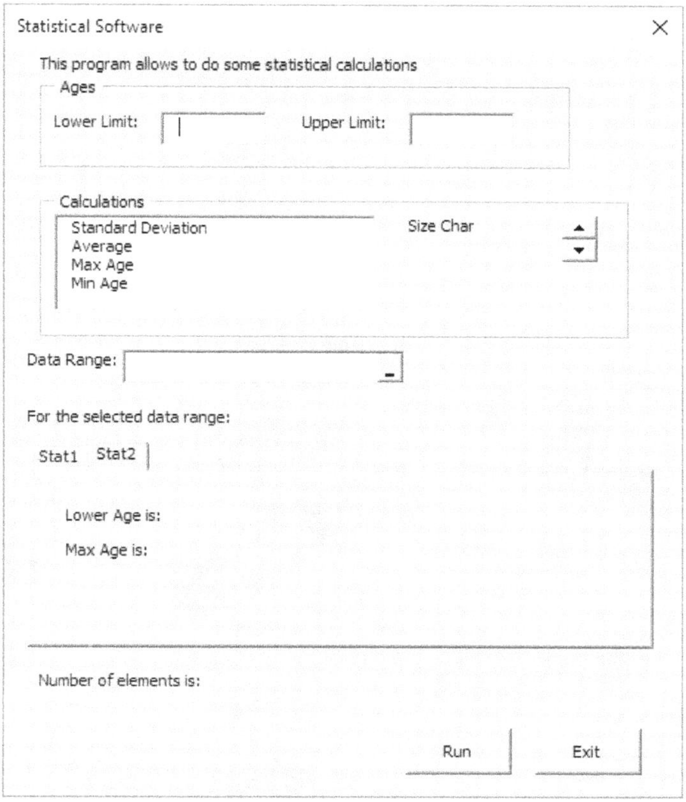

Figure 11.48. Design of the application using the *Multipage* control, with the *Caption* property modified for each page.

When you run the application, it will look as shown in figure 11.49. If we want to see the other results, we just have to select the Stat2 page. The code that will be executed with the "Run" button remained unchanged (subroutine 11.10).

If you want to add more pages to the control, right click on it. This causes a small menu to appear as shown in figure 11.50.

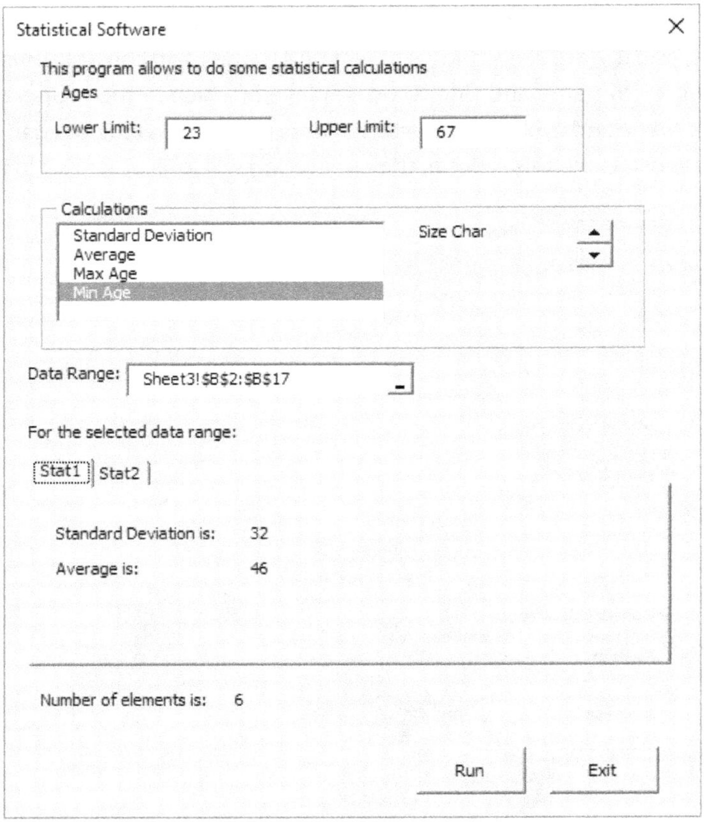

Figure 11.49. Result of the execution of the application.

11.16 Image

This control is used to insert an image within the application window. Once the control is added, it is given the path where the image that you want to show is. For this we use the *Picture* property. If the picture is larger than the container, it can be adjusted automatically by changing the values of the *PictureSizeMode* property. This property comes with three predefined values. For automatic adjustment we have selected *fmPictureSizeModeStretch*. The *PictureAligment* property was set as *fmPictureAligmentCenter* (figure 11.51).

The application will look as shown in figure 11.52.

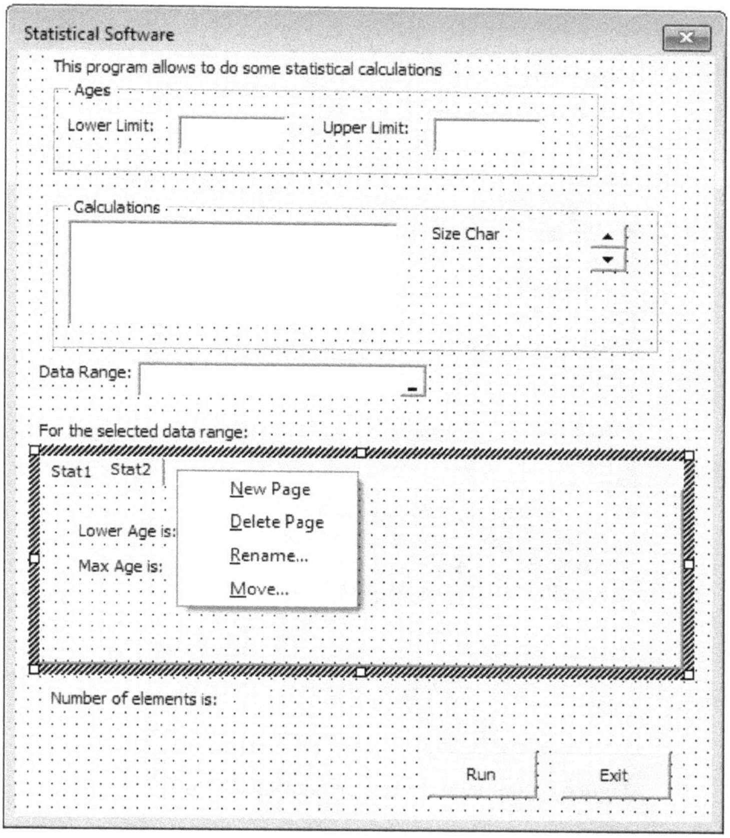

Figure 11.50. Adding more pages to the *Multipage* control.

11.17 Alternatives to user forms

VBA-Excel comes with several pre-programmed forms, some of which we have already used, such as the **InputBox** (subroutine 4.10, for example) and the **MsgBox** (subroutine 2.2). However, in this section we will see more information about these functions.

11.17.1 InputBox as function

As already mentioned, we have shown some examples of this dialog box used to capture input information by the user. When used as a function, **InputBox** can capture a number or a text string. An example of this form of use can be seen in the subroutine 4.10.

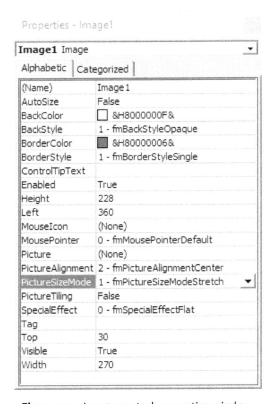

Figure 11.51. Image control properties window.

11.17.2 InputBox as method

When used as a method, *InputBox* offers many more features. It allows to capture a wider variety of data types, as shown in Table 11.1. In this table you can see the data type and the value that is used when writing as code.

Table 11.1. List of values that can be captured.

Datatype	Value
Formula	0
Number	1
Text String	2
Logical value (True or False)	4
Reference to a cell (as **Range** object)	8
Error handling value (as #N/A)	16
Array of values	64

When used as a method, it is necessary to refer to the object to which it belongs, which in this case is *Application*. The next subroutine calculates the sum and average of values that are in a range of cells in a spreadsheet. Through the *InputBox* method the user will be asked to enter the range of cells.

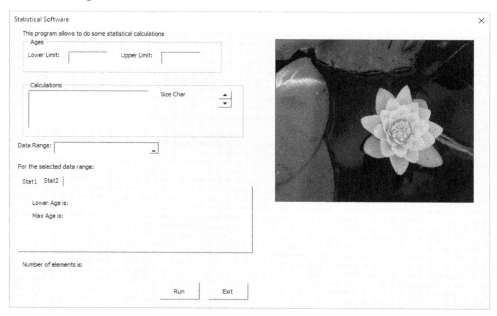

Figure 11.52. Appearance of the application with an added image.

Subroutine 11.13.

1	Sub InputBoxMethod1()
2	Dim R As Range
3	Dim sum As Integer
4	Dim Average As Single
5	Set R = Application.InputBox(_
6	prompt:="Calculate sum and average (Select data range)", _
7	Title:="Sum and average", _
8	Left:=50, Top:=50, _
9	Type:=8)
10	sum = WorksheetFunction.sum(R)
11	Average = WorksheetFunction.Average(R)
12	MsgBox "The sum is " & sum & vbNewLine & _
13	"The average is " & Average
14	End Sub

When executing the code, the program launches the window shown in figure 11.53. The figure was captured after having selected the range of cells containing the numbers to be taken into account for the calculations. It is striking that this window looks different to the **InputBox** when used as a function.

Figure 11.53. InputBox used as the method of the *Application* object.

Once the data is entered, the end of the execution shows the results in the window shown in figure 11.54.

Figure 11.54. Result of the execution of subroutine 11.13.

If in the window of figure 11.53 you decide to press the "Cancel" button, an error like the one shown in figure 11.55 will occur.

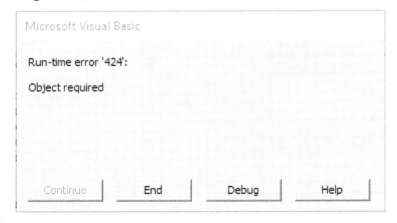

Figure 11.55. Error in the execution of subroutine 11.13 when trying to cancel its execution.

To avoid that during the cancellation of the execution this error occurs, it is necessary to add a couple of lines of code to be able to give this type of errors proper handling. Subroutine 11.14 shows the code with the added lines of code (lines 5 and 11). Line 5 captures the error just when it occurs and after it is captured, it goes to line 11 and does something with that error, which in our case is to finish the execution of the program. However, we could have placed an instruction to run something different (replacing **Exit Sub** with a **GoTo** for example).

Subroutine 11.14.

```
1   Sub InputBoxMethod2()
2   Dim R As Range
3   Dim sum As Integer
4   Dim Average As Single
5   On Error Resume Next
6   Set R = Application.InputBox( _
7       prompt:="Calculate sum and average (Select data range)", _
8       Title:="Sum and average", _
9       Left:=50, Top:=50, _
10      Type:=8)
11  If R Is Nothing Then Exit Sub
12  sum = WorksheetFunction.sum(R)
13  Average = WorksheetFunction.Average(R)
14  MsgBox "The sum is " & sum & vbNewLine & _
15          "The average is " & Average
16  End Sub
```

11.17.3 MsgBox as function

This function was discussed a little more in chapter 10. At this point we will only give an additional example of its configuration. The following subroutine shows several possible configurations of the **MsgBox** window and the form of the answers offered.

Subroutine 11.15.

```
1   Sub ExMsgBox()
2   Dim optionAnswer
3   optionAnswer = MsgBox("Are you sure of what you want to do?", vbYesNoCancel, _
4       "Security Question")
5   If optionAnswer = vbYes Then
6       MsgBox "Good Luck...", vbExclamation
7   End If
8   If optionAnswer = vbNo Then
9       MsgBox "Maybe it's the most convenient", vbInformation
```

10	End If
11	If optionAnswer = vbCancel Then
12	MsgBox "At some point you will have to make a decision", vbCritical
13	End If
14	End Sub

Chapter 12. Charts

12.1   Introduction

Graphs (*charts*) are one of the most powerful objects that Excel has. For purposes of what will be explained later, it is assumed that you are familiar with them. What will be discussed in this chapter is how to automate its creation every time you want to analyze information and want to present the information that supports it in graphical form. Excel has a wide variety of charts. We will see how to work with those that I consider the most relevant and leave the door open for you to try others. In any case, once you become familiar with the ones that will be exhibited here, surely working with others will not be so complicated.

12.2   Chart object

This object represents a graphic within a book (*Workbook*). The chart can be embedded within a spreadsheet (included in a container or *ChartObject* object) or it can be a separate chart sheet within a *Sheets* object.

12.2.1 ChartObject

This object represents a chart within a spreadsheet. The *ChartObject* object acts as a container for a *Chart* object. Additionally, this object is a member of the *ChartObjects* collection, which contains all the graphics within a spreadsheet.

Each chart that is added within a spreadsheet has an assigned index (which is actually assigned to the *ChartObject* container), so that one or more charts belong to a larger collection called *ChartObjects*. To refer to a chart within a spreadsheet, you need to know its index. I think this can be a mess when there is more than one graph inside a spreadsheet or inside a book, so I prefer to put names to each graph. However, for academic purposes, we will see the two ways of referring to a graph: with indexes and with names.

Next, we will work with the data shown in columns A and B of the spreadsheet shown in figure 12.1. Imagine for a moment that we want to analyze the age ranges of that sample. Age ranges of interest will be written in the highlighted cells. Additionally, we want to show the results in a graph. The code is shown below.

Subroutine 12.1.

```
1   Sub ChartExample1()
2   Dim R1, R2 As Range
3   With Worksheets("Sheet3")
```

4	Set R1 = .Range("B2:B16")
5	.Range("E7").Value = WorksheetFunction.CountIf(R1, "<20")
6	.Range("E8").Value = WorksheetFunction.CountIfs(R1, ">=20", R1, "<35")
7	.Range("E9").Value = WorksheetFunction.CountIfs(R1, ">=35", R1, "<50")
8	.Range("E10").Value = WorksheetFunction.CountIf(R1, ">=50")
9	Set R2 = .Range("D7:E10")
10	End With
11	With Worksheets("Sheet3").ChartObjects.Add _
12	(Left:=450, Width:=375, Top:=45, Height:=225)
13	.Chart.SetSourceData Source:=R2
14	.Chart.ChartType = xlColumnClustered
15	End With
16	End Sub

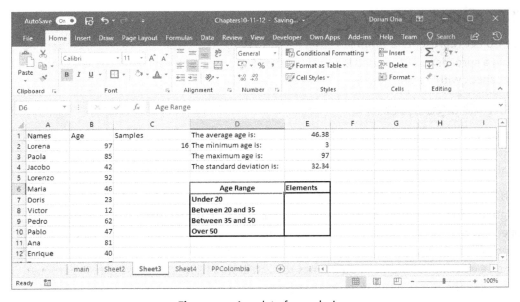

Figure 12.1. Age data for analysis.

Let's analyze the subroutine. In line 2 we have declared two variables of type range. Later we will see what each of them will contain. Between lines 3 and 10 we have the instructions that will allow us to count the elements according to the criteria specified in the ranges of column D. In line 4, we assign the range of values that we want to analyze to the variable "R1". In line 5 we use the *CountIf* spreadsheet function (the same function used in a worksheet) that will allow us to count, in this case, the ages under 20 that are within range.

Since the second top-down criterion requires two conditions (between 20 and 35), we have used the *CountIfs* function (it allows the use of two conditions). In this case, it will count the ages between greater than or equal to 20 and less than 35.

The explanation of line 7 is similar to that of the previous line and that of line 8 is similar to the explanation of line 5.

In line 9 the results are assigned to the variable "R2". Note that in addition to the data, the data headers were also added. This is necessary since this range will be used to build the graph.

Between lines 11 and 15 the graph is built.

In line 11, a **With** block is started, which will have the common instructions for the *Add* method of the *ChartObjects* collection. Line 12 establishes some parameters of the graph such as its location (upper right corner given by the *Left* and *Top* coordinates) and its dimensions (given by *Width* and *Height*).

Line 13 establishes what will be the range of data to build the graph. In line 14 the graph (Chart) is finally built, which in our case is a column chart (*xlColumnClustered*). To know what the code is for each of the types of graphics that Excel offers, remember that you can consult the VBA-Excel Object Browser. Figure 12.2 shows some of the types of graphs, which really correspond to the values that the *ChartType* property of the *Chart* object can take (class *XlChartType*).

When executing this code, a graphic will be generated within the spreadsheet, as shown in figure 12.3.

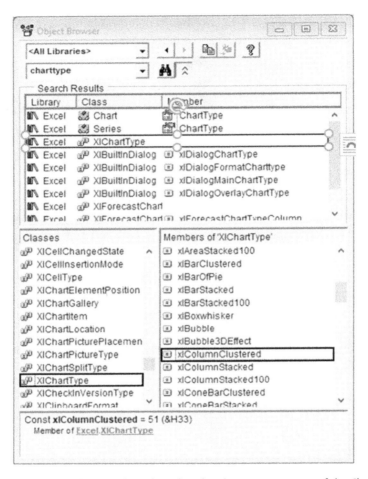

Figure 12.2. Object Browser showing the values that the *ChartType* property of the *Chart* object can take.

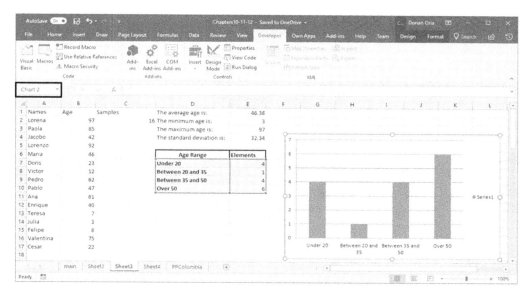

Figure 12.3. Result of the execution of the subroutine 12.1.

Note that Excel automatically assigns a name to the chart, which in this case is "Chart 2," as can be seen inside the rectangle in figure 12.3. However, the number 2 is not its identification number. As for now there is only one graphic, its identification number will be 1. This means that if, for example, you want to make the graphic active to do other operations on it, we could refer to it with any of the following instructions:

Worksheets("Sheet3").ChartObjects("Chart 2").Activate   or

Worksheets("Sheet3").ChartObjects(1).Activate

Excel never repeats the names of the graphics, but in case another was added, this new one would have the identification number 2. This can get complicated later, since it is difficult to remember the indexes. For example, assuming that we have two graphs and the one that was added first is deleted (that is, the one that has identification number or index 1), then the graph that previously had index 2 will now have index 1. With the use of the names there is no problem to refer to the graphics because it will always be unique.

"Chart 2" may not tell us much about what that graph represents. It is possible that the graph can be assigned a different name while it is being created or can be changed later.

For example, add the following statement after line 14 in subroutine 12.1 and run it again.

.Chart.Parent.Name = "Age Range"

When selecting the graph you will see that now its name changed, according to the instruction shown above.

Suppose now that the input data (ie, those in columns A and B) changed and you want to repeat the analysis. If we do not want to have two graphs, we can manually delete the existing one and execute the 12.1 subroutine again. Another alternative is to check if there are existing graphics and if they exist, delete them with code. For now, let's go with an example of this case. Imagine for a moment that you have two graphs as shown in figure 12.4.

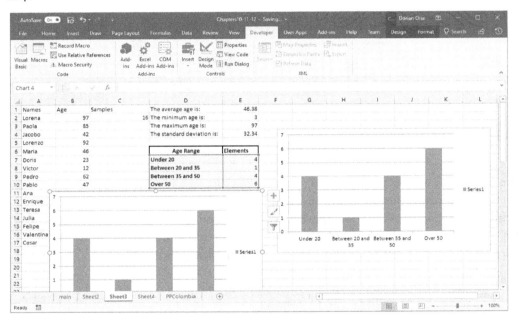

Figure 12.4. Example of input with two graphs before executing subroutine 12.2.

What we want to do is not add more graphics, but to always have one. Therefore, we are going to eliminate the existing ones and then build a new one.

Subroutine 12.2.

1	Sub ChartExample2()
2	Dim R1, R2 As Range
3	Dim n As Integer
4	n = Worksheets("Sheet3").ChartObjects.Count
5	If n <> 0 Then
6	Worksheets("Sheet3").ChartObjects.Delete
7	End If
8	With Worksheets("Sheet3")
9	Set R1 = .Range("B2:B16")

```
10    .Range("E7").Value = WorksheetFunction.CountIf(R1, "<20")
11    .Range("E8").Value = WorksheetFunction.CountIfs(R1, ">=20", R1, "<35")
12    .Range("E9").Value = WorksheetFunction.CountIfs(R1, ">=35", R1, "<50")
13    .Range("E10").Value = WorksheetFunction.CountIf(R1, ">=50")
14    Set R2 = .Range("D7:E10")
15  End With
16  With Worksheets("Sheet3").ChartObjects.Add _
17    (Left:=400, Width:=375, Top:=45, Height:=225)
18    .Chart.SetSourceData Source:=R2
19    .Chart.ChartType = xlColumnClustered
20    .Chart.Parent.Name = "Age Range"
21  End With
22  End Sub
```

When executing this subroutine, the pre-existing graphics will be deleted and a new one will be created. The spreadsheet will look the same as shown in figure 12.3.

Let's now explain how we did it. The subroutine 12.2 was based on subroutine 12.1. In fact it has the same instructions that were used to create the graphic. The only difference is the instructions that were added to evaluate the existence of other graphics within the spreadsheet and then delete them if they existed.

To check if there were other graphics we use the *Count* property of the *ChartObjects* object. If the resulting value is zero, then the instruction in line 6 will not be executed. Otherwise, the instruction in line 6 will erase all the existing graphics within the spreadsheet.

Everything that comes after is the same as what was explained for subroutine 12.1.

Another way to avoid creating a new chart every time is simply by updating the chart information. As you know, if the values that are in the E7: E10 range change, the graph will automatically update. Taking advantage of this functionality of Excel, we can check the existence of the graph and if so, do not create it again, but only do the calculations.

Let's see how the subroutine would look.

Subroutine 12.3.

```
1  Sub ChartExample3()
2  Dim R1, R2 As Range
3  Dim n As Integer
4  n = Worksheets("Sheet3").ChartObjects.Count
5  With Worksheets("Sheet3")
6    Set R1 = .Range("B2:B12")
7    .Range("E7").Value = WorksheetFunction.CountIf(R1, "<20")
```

8	.Range("E8").Value = WorksheetFunction.CountIfs(R1, ">=20", R1, "<35")
9	.Range("E9").Value = WorksheetFunction.CountIfs(R1, ">=35", R1, "<50")
10	.Range("E10").Value = WorksheetFunction.CountIf(R1, ">=50")
11	Set R2 = .Range("D7:E10")
12	End With
13	If n = 0 Then
14	With Worksheets("Sheet3").ChartObjects.Add _
15	(Left:=400, Width:=375, Top:=45, Height:=225)
16	.Chart.SetSourceData Source:=R2
17	.Chart.ChartType = xlColumnClustered
18	.Chart.Parent.Name = "Age Range"
19	End With
20	End If
21	End Sub

To show how the exercise worked, we changed the input data. After executing subroutine 12.3, the spreadsheet looks as shown in figure 12.5.

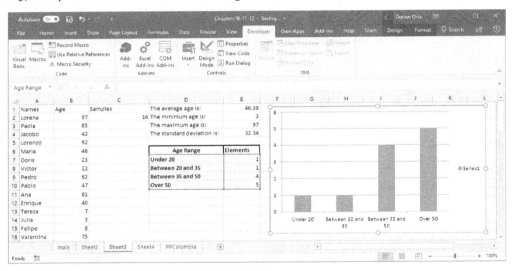

Figure 12.5. Spreadsheet after having executed subroutine 12.3.

To prove that the subroutine is really doing what you want, I suggest you delete the chart from the spreadsheet and rerun the subroutine.

12.2.2 Properties of the *ChartObject* object

Let's see the most important properties of this object. If you want to know more, please check the web pages that Microsoft has prepared for this information.

12.2.2.1 Count property

Counts the number of objects in the *ChartObjects* collection. We have an example of this property in subroutines 12.2 and 12.3.

12.2.2.2 Height property

Represents the height, in points, of the *CharObject* object.

12.2.2.3 Width property

Represents the width, in points, of the *CharObject* object.

12.2.2.4 Left property

It is the distance, in points, counted from the left edge of the *CharObject* object to the left edge of the A column (in a spreadsheet).

12.2.2.5 Top property

It is the distance, in points, counted from the top of the *CharObject* object to the top of row 1 (in a spreadsheet).

12.2.2.6 Placement property

This property represents the way in which the *CharObject* object is fixed to the spreadsheet. It can take three values:

Table 12.1. Possible values for the *Placement* property.

Name	Value	Description
xlFreeFloating	3	The graph can float freely in the spreadsheet. This means that if, for example, you change the size of any row or column, the size of the graph does not change.
xlMove	2	The graph moves along with the cells. For example, if rows or columns are inserted, the graph will move proportionally to the displacement that is caused.
xlMoveAndSize	1	The graphic moves together with the cells, for example, in the case of the insertion of rows or columns and also changes its size if the size of the rows or columns that are below it is changed. If the Placement property is not specified, this value is the one that is set by default.

When the *Placement* property is used, you can make it equal to the name or numerical value shown in the previous table. For example, in subroutine 12.4, you can change the number 3 (line 7) by *xlFreeFloating*.

12.2.2.7 ProtectChartObject property

If this property is set to *True*, the *CharObject* object can not be moved, deleted or resized through the user interface.

The subroutine 12.4 shows an example of the application of all these properties.

Subroutine 12.4.

```
1   Sub ChartExample4()
2   With Worksheets("Sheet3").ChartObjects("Age Range")
3       .Height = 175
4       .Width = 325
5       .Top = 25
6       .Left = 450
7       .Placement = 3
8   End With
9   End Sub
```

If you want to test the *ProtectChartObject* property, you can add the following statement after line 7:

.ProtectChartObject = True

12.2.3 Methods of the ChartObjects object

Let's see the most important methods of this object. If you want to know more, please check the web pages that Microsoft has arranged for this information.

12.2.3.1 Add method

Creates a new graphic. For example subroutines 12.1, 12.2 and 12.3. When used with the *ChartObjects* object, you need two compelling parameters: *Left* and *Width*.

Another way to write the instruction of the subroutines 12.1, 12.2 and 12.3 to add the graph is:

With Worksheets("Sheet3").ChartObjects.Add(400, 45, 375, 225)

That is, the instruction has the structure:

With Worksheets("Sheet3").ChartObjects.Add(*Left, Top, Width, Height*)

12.2.3.2 Delete method

Deletes the CharObject object. We use it in subroutine 12.2 (line 6).

12.2.4 Chart object occupying a sheet

So far we have created graphics that we place inside a spreadsheet. Now let's create graphics that occupy a sheet for themselves. Actually the process is quite similar. The difference lies in the container of the object. Let's see the next subroutine.

Subroutine 12.5.

```
1    Sub ChartExample5()
2    Dim R1, R2 As Range
3    Dim n As Integer
4    n = Charts.Count
5    MsgBox n
6    With Worksheets("Sheet3")
7        Set R1 = .Range("B2:B16")
8        .Range("E7").Value = WorksheetFunction.CountIf(R1, "<20")
9        .Range("E8").Value = WorksheetFunction.CountIfs(R1, ">=20", R1, "<35")
10       .Range("E9").Value = WorksheetFunction.CountIfs(R1, ">=35", R1, "<50")
11       .Range("E10").Value = WorksheetFunction.CountIf(R1, ">=50")
12       Set R2 = .Range("D7:E10")
13   End With
14   If n = 0 Then
15       With Charts.Add
16           .Name = "Age Range"
17           .ChartType = xlColumnClustered
18           .SetSourceData Source:=R2
19       End With
20   End If
21   End Sub
```

When executing the subroutine, our Excel book will look like it is shown in figure 12.6.

When we see the subroutine, we can notice that its functionality is practically the same. Let's see the differences. Now we are interested in counting the graphics that occupy separate sheets and not the graphics that are inside a spreadsheet as in the case of the *ChartObjects* object. These graphics are now in the scope of the *Workbook* object and are counted in a similar way to how the *Worksheets* objects are counted. In line 4 the charts that are in the scope of the active *Workbook* are counted. That is why no reference is made to the object that contains them. If you wish to be more specific, you could replace line 4 with any of the following instructions:

n = Workbooks("Chapters10-11-12.xlsm").Charts.Count   or

n = Activeworkbook.Charts.Count

The **MsgBox** function of line 5 can be ignored. I placed it there just to show the number of graphics the book has. The rest of the program practically varies only in the container, which is no longer in a spreadsheet but occupies practically a sheet at Excel level.

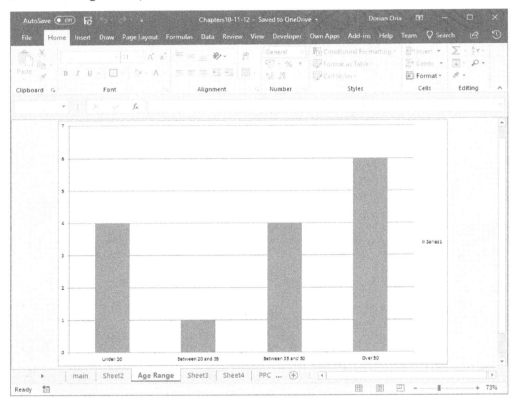

Figure 12.6. Graph created with subroutine 12.5.

12.2.5 Properties of the Charts object

Remember that when we talk about *Charts* we are referring to graphics that are not located within a spreadsheet. In my practice, I do not see a more interesting property than *Count*.

12.2.5.1 Count property

As in the case of *ChartObjects*, it also returns the number of graphics within the object or *Charts* collection. We have an example of this property in subroutine 12.5 (line 4).

12.2.6 Methods of the object Charts

As in the case of the *ChartObjects* object, the methods that I find interesting for this container are *Add* and *Delete*, which work in the same way as explained in numeral 12.2.3.1

and 12.2.3.2.

12.2.7 Properties of the Chart object

We have already seen properties and methods of the two spaces available in Excel to contain graphics. Once we have seen the two containers, we will now work specifically with the *Chart* object inside the *ChartObjects* container. Some of the *ChartObjects* properties do not apply when the *Chart* object is not inside a spreadsheet.

12.2.7.1 AutoScaling property

If the value of this property is *True*, adjust the scale of the 3D chart so that its size is close to an equivalent in 2D. For this to be possible, the value of the *RightAngleAxes* property must be *True*.

To show the operation of this property, let's change the type of graph in subroutine 12.2 (line 19) to a vertical bar graph in 3D. The line would be as shown below:

.Chart.ChartType = xl3DColumn.

Now, execute the subroutine again. The spreadsheet should look like shown in figure 12.7.

Next, let's see how the *AutoScaling* property works.

Subroutine 12.6.

```
1   Sub ChartExample6()
2   With Worksheets("Sheet3").ChartObjects("Age Range").Chart
3       .RightAngleAxes = True
4       .AutoScaling = True
5   End With
6   End Sub
```

When executing the subroutine 12.6, it makes the adjustment in the graph as shown in figure 12.8.

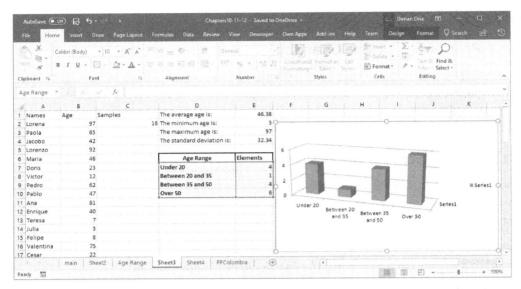

Figure 12.7. Result of the execution of the subroutine 12.2 with the change of the chart type.

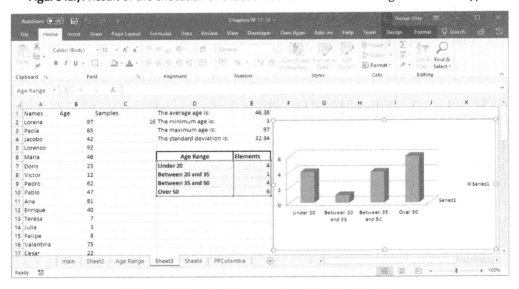

Figure 12.8. Result of the execution of subroutine 12.6.

12.2.7.2 BarShape property

Sets the shape used in the bars of the 3D graphics or in the 2D column charts.

The following table shows the possible values that you can take (*XlBarShape Enumeration*):

Table 12.2. Possible values of the *BarShape* property.

Name	Value	Description
xlBox	0	Box
xlConeToMax	5	Cone, truncated to a value
xlConeToPoint	4	Cone, coming to point at value.
xlCylinder	3	Cylinder
xlPyramidToMax	2	Pyramid, truncated to a value.
xlPyramidToPoint	1	Pyramid, coming to point at value.

When a bar graph is made, either 2D or 3D, the default shape of the bars is a box (*xlBox*).

Let's see the following example, in which a subroutine is used to change the shape of the bars shown in figure 12.8.

Subroutine 12.7.

```
1  Sub ChartExample7()
2  With Worksheets("Sheet3").ChartObjects("Age Range").Chart
3     .BarShape = xlPyramidToPoint
4  End With
5  End Sub
```

This subroutine makes the bars take the shape of a pyramid, as shown in figure 12.9.

12.2.7.3 ChartArea property

This property returns a *ChartArea* object that represents the chart area of a *Chart* object. The chart includes everything in addition to the plot area. However, the plot area (*PlotArea* object) has its own *fill*, so filling the plot area does not fill the graph area and vice versa. This seems a bit tangled. However, we are going to see examples of this.

The following subroutine changes the style of the line that borders the graphic and colors the area corresponding to the *ChartArea* object. Notice how the background of the graphic as such (*PlotArea* object) is not colored.

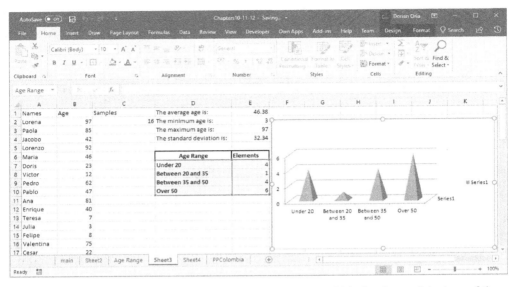

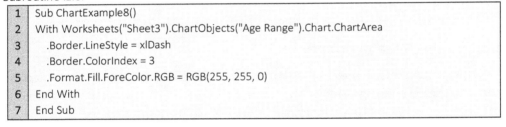

Figure 12.9. Result of the execution of the subroutine 12.7, in which the shape of the bars of the graph is changed.

Subroutine 12.8.

1	Sub ChartExample8()
2	With Worksheets("Sheet3").ChartObjects("Age Range").Chart.ChartArea
3	.Border.LineStyle = xlDash
4	.Border.ColorIndex = 3
5	.Format.Fill.ForeColor.RGB = RGB(255, 255, 0)
6	End With
7	End Sub

In line 2 we start the **With** block that will allow us to work with the *ChartArea* object of the *Chart* object inserted in the *ChartObjects* object, which is tied to the Sheet3 calculation sheet.

In line 3 we are going to modify the *LineStyle* property for the *Border* object. In this case, the line will look like segments.

In line 4 we modify the color of the *Border* object, in this case red.

In line 5 we modify the *Format* property, which actually returns the *ChartFormat* object. *Fill* is a property of the *ChartFormat* object, which in turn returns the *FillFormat* object. One of the properties of this object is *ForeColor* which in turn returns an object called *ColorFormat*. RGB is finally a property of the *ColorFormat* object.

The previous paragraph may look a bit tangled, but that's the programming language with objects. A property returns an object and this object has properties that in turn return other objects. I believe that an easy way to understand it is by making simile with the human body: a body has arms (objects). These arms have properties (length, weight, ability to hold), methods (raise or lower, bend) and at the same time have other members (objects) such as hands. Imagine the property of the arm, that ability to hold returns the hand object. And so on.

When you execute subroutine 12.8, it produces the changes in the bar graph as shown in figure 12.10.

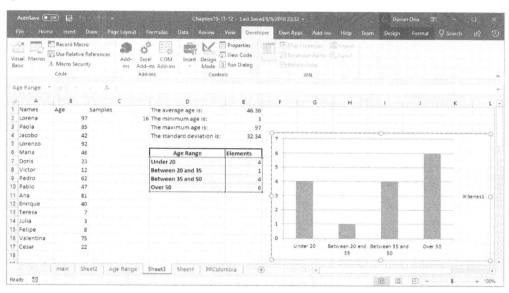

Figure 12.10. Result of the execution of a subroutine 12.8.

The next subroutine changes the color of the background using a gradient of colors.

Subroutine 12.9.

```
1   Sub ChartExample9()
2   With Worksheets("Sheet3").ChartObjects("Age Range").Chart _
3       .ChartArea.Format.Fill
4       .TwoColorGradient msoGradientVertical, 1
5       .ForeColor.RGB = RGB(255, 0, 0)
6       .BackColor.RGB = RGB(255, 255, 0)
7       .GradientStops(1).Position = 0
8       .GradientStops(2).Position = 1
9       .GradientStops.Insert RGB(255, 255, 255), 0.5
10  End With
```

11	End Sub

In line 2 begins the **With** block that we will use to work on the *Fill* property (line 3) of the *ChartFormat* object (remember that this object is returned by the *Format* property).

In line 4 we use the *TwoColorGradient* method to indicate that we want to use a gradient made up of two colors. Then comes the type of gradient that we are going to use, which in this case is vertical. The possible styles are shown in table 12.3.

Table 12.3. Possible values for gradients (*MsoGradientStyle*).

MsoGradientStyle
msoGradientDiagonalDown
msoGradientDiagonalUp
msoGradientFromCenter
msoGradientFromCorner
msoGradientFromTitle
msoGradientHorizontal
msoGradientMixed
msoGradientVertical

After the style comes a number that is called *Variant* (not to be confused with the type of variable) and it corresponds to the way in which the colors are displayed. To get an idea of its effect, change the values to 4 and see what happens. Additionally and to continue testing, comment line 9 (which we will explain) and continue testing.

In line 5 we establish the first color (which in our case is red) and in line 6 we establish the second color (which in our case is yellow).

In line 7 we establish the position where the color arrives without changing and from there the gradient begins. This value varies between 0 and 1 (you can use percentage values, for example 0.1 would be 10%, 0.5 would be 50%, etc.). In our example it starts at 0. This means that practically from there the gradient will begin and only red will be there in its purest form.

In line 8 we establish the position from where the yellow color will start. In our case it is 1, which means that only the pure yellow will be at the end. The color gradation will start at 0 and end at 1.

For example, if in line 7 we had used 0.3, we would have wanted to say that up to 30% of the length of the graph would remain red and from there begin to grade towards yellow.

In line 9 we add an intermediate color for the gradation process. In this case, the color white (**RGB (255,255,255)**). The value 0.5 corresponds to the percentage of the length of the graph where the color will be inserted, that is, in the middle. Try changing that value.

When executing subroutine 12.9, the graph changes its appearance as shown in figure 12.11.

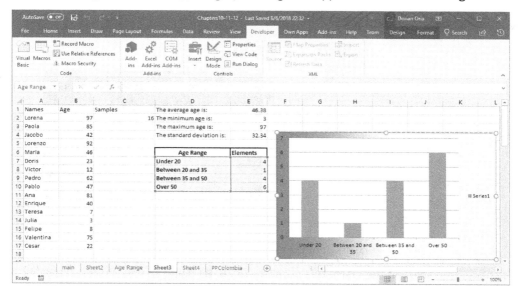

Figure 12.11. Result of the execution of the subroutine 12.9.

12.2.7.4 ChartStyle property

This property assigns a default style to the *Chart* object, including the *ChartArea* and *PlotArea* objects. There are 48 predefined styles.

We are going to see the effects that a change in this property has on the graph that was made with the subroutine 12.2.

Subroutine 12.10.

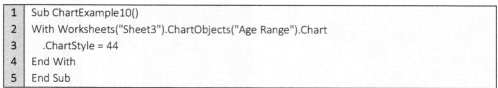

```
1   Sub ChartExample10()
2   With Worksheets("Sheet3").ChartObjects("Age Range").Chart
3       .ChartStyle = 44
4   End With
5   End Sub
```

When executing this subroutine, it will modify the style of the graph as can be seen in figure 12.12.

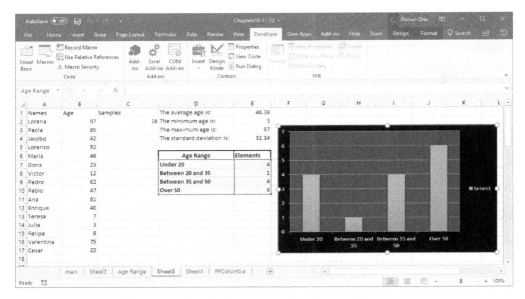

Figure 12.12. Result of the execution of subroutine 12.10.

Let's change the value of the *ChartStyle* property to 46. By doing so, the chart will look as shown in figure 12.13.

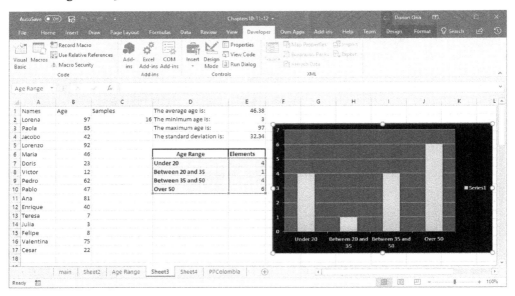

Figure 12.13. Result of the execution of subroutine 12.10, after having changed the value of the *ChartStyle* property.

12.2.7.5 ChartTitle property

This property returns the *ChartTitle* object, which represents the title of the chart. We are going to add a title to our chart and also set some properties different from those that would be established by default.

Subroutine 12.11.

```
1   Sub ChartExample11()
2   With Worksheets("Sheet3").ChartObjects("Age Range").Chart
3     .HasTitle = True
4     .ChartTitle.Text = "Study Range Ages"
5     .ChartTitle.Font.Color = vbYellow
6     .ChartTitle.Font.FontStyle = "Bold Italic"
7     .ChartTitle.Font.Size = 12
8     .ChartTitle.Font.Name = "Times New Roman"
9     .ChartTitle.Interior.ColorIndex = 3
10  End With
11  End Sub
```

The *ChartTitle* object will not exist or can not be used unless the *HasTitle* property is *True* (line 3).

In line 4 we assign the text that will contain the title of the graph.

In line 5 we assign the color to the text. In this case, we have used one of the 8 basic colors predefined in VBA-Excel, which are shown in table 12.4

Table 12.4. Basic colors and their names in VBA-Excel.

Color	Constant	Value
Black	vbBlack	&h00
Red	vbRed	&hFF
Green	vbGreen	&hFF00
Yellow	vbYellow	&hFFFF
Blue	vbBlue	&hFF0000
Magenta	vbMagenta	&hFF00FF
Cyan	vbCyan	&hFFFF00
White	vbWhite	&hFFFFFF

However, there are many more colors (in fact there are 16,581,375 possible combinations if we use the **RGB** function for color.) So, we could change line 5 to:

.ChartTitle.Font.Color = RGB(255, 255, 0)

With this instruction we will also obtain the yellow and with the **RGB** function all the possible colors. I invite you to try your own combinations.

In line 6 we make the style of the font bold and italic, using the *FontStyle* property. The possible font styles can be seen in table 12.5.

Table 12.5. Font styles.

Style	Example
Regular	Regular text
Bold	**Bold text.**
Italic	*Text in italics.*
Underline	Underlined text

In line 7 we set the size of the font with the *Size* property.

In line 8 we set the font through the *Name* property.

In line 9 we set the background color of the graphic title. Here we have used the *ColorIndex* property, which has only 56 colors available. If we want to use more colors like in the case of sources, we can change line 9 to

.ChartTitle.Interior.Color = RGB(255, 0, 0)

Notice that in order to use the **RGB** function we had to use the *Color* property and not *ColorIndex*.

12.2.7.6 ChartType property

Returns or sets the type of chart. We have already used this property in our previous subroutines. In the following link you can get all the values that this property can take, which correspond to each of the types of graph that Excel has: https://msdn.microsoft.com/EN-US/library/office/ff838409.aspx

12.2.7.7 DataTable property

This property returns a *DataTable* object that represents, in the form of a table, the data with which the chart was built.

Subroutine 12.12.

```
1   Sub ChartExample12()
2   With Worksheets("Sheet3").ChartObjects("Age Range").Chart
3       .HasDataTable = True
4       .DataTable.HasBorderOutline = True
5   End With
6   End Sub
```

In line 3 the table with the values (*DataTable* object) is added.

In line 4 we add a line as edge for each of the cells to the data table.

Figure 12.14 shows how the graph looks after the execution of subroutine 12.12.

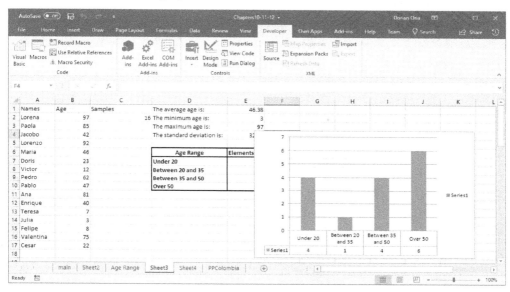

Figure 12.14. Result of the execution of subroutine 12.12.

12.2.7.8 Legend property

This property returns the *Legend* object that represents the chart legend. Excel adds it by default when the chart is created. Let's see some things that can be done with this object.

Subroutine 12.13.

```
1   Sub ChartExample13()
2   With Worksheets("Sheet3").ChartObjects("Age Range").Chart
3      .HasLegend = True
4      With .Legend
5         .Font.Color = RGB(255, 255, 0)
6         .Interior.Color = RGB(255, 0, 0)
7         .Font.Name = "Arial"
8         .Font.Size = 10
9         .Font.FontStyle = "Italic"
10        .Position = xlLegendPositionBottom
11     End With
12  End With
13  End Sub
```

In line 3 the legend becomes visible.

Line 10 establishes the position of the legend. In this case, it has been placed at the bottom of the graph, as can be seen in figure 12.15. Table 12.6 shows the possible locations that the legend can have in the graph.

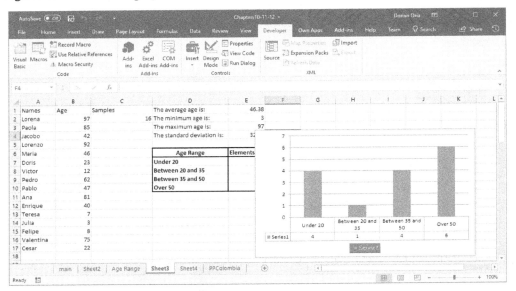

Figure 12.15. Result of the execution of subroutine 12.13.

Table 12.6. Possible locations of the legend in the chart.

Name	Description
xlLegendPositionBottom	Below the graph.
xlLegendPositionCorner	In the upper right corner of the graph.
xlLegendPositionCustom	In a position defined by the user.
xlLegendPositionLeft	To the left of the graph.
xlLegendPositionRight	To the right of the graph.
xlLegendPositionTop	On top of the graph.

The example with which we have explained this property is simple because it is only a set of data and therefore a single legend. However, it is common for a graph to represent more than one data set. Let's see an example.

The following table shows the Colombian oil production for the years 2013 and 2014. We are going to make a bar graph that shows us how the production has varied from month to month for each year.

Table 12.7. Colombian oil production in thousands of barrels.

Colombian oil production		
Month	Year	
	2013	2014
January	1015	1014
February	997	1002
March	1012	977
April	1007	938
May	1013	952
June	974	1011
July	1020	971
August	1031	1002
September	995	996
October	986	1004
November	998	1004
December	989	1009

The following subroutine generates a bar graph with this information. Additionally, you format the graphic with some of the properties that we have seen so far.

Subroutine 12.14.

```
1   Sub ChartExample14()
2   Dim R As Range
3   Dim n As Integer
4   n = Worksheets("PPColombia").ChartObjects.Count
5   If n <> 0 Then
6       Worksheets("PPColombia").ChartObjects.Delete
7   End If
8   With Worksheets("PPColombia")
9       Set R = .Range("A2:C15")
10  End With
11  With Worksheets("PPColombia").ChartObjects.Add _
12      (Left:=190, Width:=375, Top:=5, Height:=225)
13      .Chart.SetSourceData Source:=R
14      .Chart.ChartType = xlColumnClustered
15      .Chart.Parent.Name = "Petroleum Production Colombia"
16  End With
17  With Worksheets("PPColombia").ChartObjects("Petroleum Production Colombia").Chart
```

18	.HasTitle = True
19	With .ChartTitle
20	.Text = "Petroleum Production Colombia"
21	.Font.Color = RGB(255, 255, 0)
22	.Font.FontStyle = "Bold"
23	.Font.Size = 12
24	.Font.Name = "Arial Narrow"
25	.Interior.Color = RGB(0, 153, 153)
26	End With
27	.HasLegend = True
28	With .Legend
29	.LegendEntries(1).Font.Bold = True
30	.LegendEntries(1).Font.Size = 10
31	.LegendEntries(1).Font.Name = "Arial Narrow"
32	.LegendEntries(2).Font.Italic = True
33	.LegendEntries(2).Font.Size = 14
34	.LegendEntries(2).Font.Name = "Arial Narrow"
35	.Position = xlLegendPositionBottom
36	.Interior.Color = RGB(0, 200, 153)
37	End With
38	End With
39	End Sub

In this subroutine, we will comment on the lines between 29 and 34. The *Legend* object contains one or more *LegendEntry* objects. Each *LegendEntry* object contains a *LegendKey* object (we will see this later in another example). In the first graphics that we did, this object (*LegendEntry*) was also present, only in those cases, since it was a single data set, the *LegendEntry* and *Legend* objects were just one. As it was seen in the subroutine 12.13, the format that was given to the legend would have affected all the *LegendEntry* objects that had been found.

In this example I want to show how each series of data and its respective legend can be treated separately, although this can only be done practically with the sources (in this example). Between lines 29 and 31 the sources of the series 1 are formatted and between lines 32 and 34 the sources of the series 2 are formatted. The legends of each series can not be separated, so in this case the changes in the interior color (background) and its position are made at the level of the *Legend* object (lines 35 and 36).

When you execute the subroutine 12.14, you get a graph like the one shown in figure 12.16.

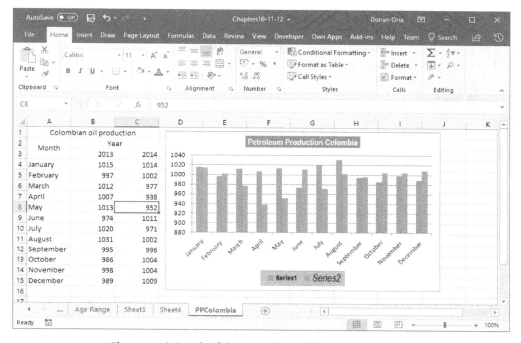

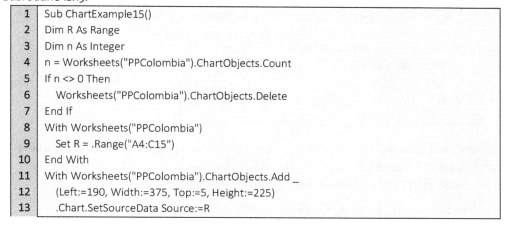

Figure 12.16. Result of the execution of the subroutine 12.14.

In the following example we will see the usefulness of the *LegendKey* object. This object visually links an entry of a legend (*LegendEntry*) with its associated data series in the chart. This means that changing the format of the entry in the legend causes a change in the format of the series represented in the graphic. In our example, we are going to graph again the data in table 12.7, but this time using a line graph.

Subroutine 12.15.

```
1   Sub ChartExample15()
2   Dim R As Range
3   Dim n As Integer
4   n = Worksheets("PPColombia").ChartObjects.Count
5   If n <> 0 Then
6       Worksheets("PPColombia").ChartObjects.Delete
7   End If
8   With Worksheets("PPColombia")
9       Set R = .Range("A4:C15")
10  End With
11  With Worksheets("PPColombia").ChartObjects.Add _
12      (Left:=190, Width:=375, Top:=5, Height:=225)
13      .Chart.SetSourceData Source:=R
```

```
14    .Chart.ChartType = xlLineMarkers
15    .Chart.Parent.Name = "Petroleum Production Colombia"
16    .Chart.FullSeriesCollection(1).Name = "=PPColombia!$B$3"
17    .Chart.FullSeriesCollection(2).Name = "=PPColombia!$C$3"
18  End With
19  With Worksheets("PPColombia").ChartObjects("Petroleum Production Colombia").Chart
20    .HasTitle = True
21    With .ChartTitle
22      .Text = "Colombian oil production"
23      .Font.Color = RGB(255, 255, 0)
24      .Font.FontStyle = "Bold"
25      .Font.Size = 12
26      .Font.Name = "Arial Narrow"
27      .Interior.Color = RGB(0, 153, 153)
28    End With
29    .HasLegend = True
30    With .Legend
31      .LegendEntries(1).Font.Bold = True
32      .LegendEntries(1).Font.Size = 10
33      .LegendEntries(1).Font.Name = "Arial Narrow"
34      .LegendEntries(1).LegendKey.MarkerStyle = xlMarkerStyleCircle
35      .LegendEntries(1).LegendKey.MarkerSize = 5
36      .LegendEntries(1).LegendKey.MarkerBackgroundColor = RGB(255, 255, 0)
37      .LegendEntries(1).LegendKey.MarkerForegroundColor = RGB(255, 0, 0)
38      .LegendEntries(2).Font.Italic = True
39      .LegendEntries(2).Font.Size = 14
40      .LegendEntries(2).Font.Name = "Arial Narrow"
41      .LegendEntries(2).LegendKey.MarkerStyle = xlMarkerStyleSquare
42      .LegendEntries(2).LegendKey.MarkerSize = 5
43      .LegendEntries(2).LegendKey.MarkerBackgroundColor = RGB(255, 0, 0)
44      .LegendEntries(2).LegendKey.MarkerForegroundColor = RGB(255, 255, 0)
45      .Position = xlLegendPositionBottom
46      .Interior.Color = RGB(0, 200, 153)
47    End With
48  End With
49  End Sub
```

Line graphs can be simply a line joining points (*xlLine* graphic type) or can include markers at each point. In our example, we are going to use a line graph with markers (*xlLineMarkers*), that is, in each value we are going to place a symbol.

In lines 16 and 17 the name is assigned to each of the series.

For the case of the legend of the series 1 in line 34, we established through the use of the *MarkerStyle* property that the points will be circles (*xlMarkerStyleCircle*). Figure 12.17 shows the Object Browser in which the available markers can be seen.

Figure 12.17. Object Browser showing the possible values of the *MarkerStyle* property.

Line 35 establishes the size of the marker.

Line 36 establishes the background color of the marker and that of the edge is established in line 37. Between lines 41 and 44, the same is done for the legend of series 2.

More properties of the *LegendKey* object can be found in the VBA-Excel Object Browser, as shown in figure 12.18.

Figure 12.19 shows the graph resulting from the execution of the subroutine 12.15.

12.2.7.9 PlotArea property

This property returns the object of the same name and represents the area within the graph where the plotted data series are (*PlotArea*). In the case of 2D graphics, *PlotArea* contains the data markers (seen in the previous point), the grid lines, data labels, data series and other optional items placed within the area of the graph. In the case of 3D graphics, *PlotArea* contains all the items mentioned above for 2D graphics plus walls, floor, axes, axis titles and *tick-marks* labels.

PlotArea is surrounded by the chart area. Unlike *PlotArea* for the case of 3D graphics, for 2D and 3D graphics, *ChartArea* contains the title of the graphic and the legend. In the case of 2D graphics, *ChartArea* contains the axes and their titles.

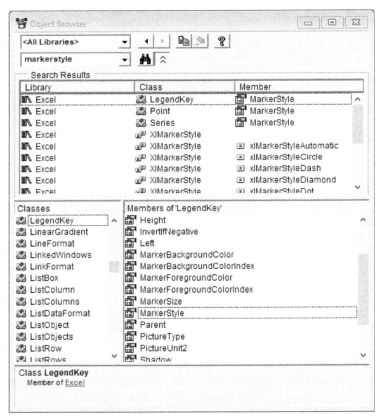

Figure 12.18. Properties of the *LegendKey* object, as seen in the VBA-Excel Object Browser.

Subroutine 12.16.

1	Sub ChartExample16()
2	With Worksheets("PPColombia").ChartObjects("Petroleum Production Colombia").Chart
3	.PlotArea.Border.LineStyle = xlDash
4	.PlotArea.Height = 150

5	.PlotArea.Width = 350
6	End With
7	End Sub

In line 3 it is established that the line of the edge of the graphic area is segmented (*xlDash*). The width and length of the area where the graph really is is established in lines 4 and 5.

When executing subroutine 12.16, the graph shown in figure 12.20 is generated.

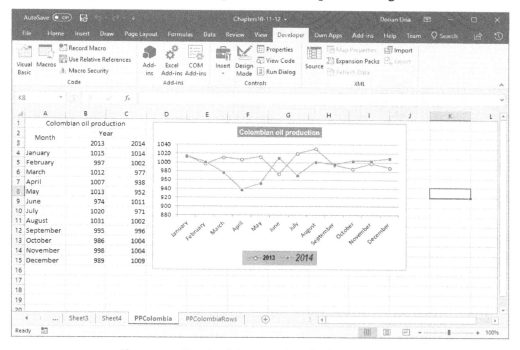

Figure 12.19. Result of the execution of subroutine 12.15.

12.2.7.10 PlotBy property

The information can be organized in columns or rows. In the previous examples, we have worked with information organized by columns. Now, Excel and VBA by default assume that the data is organized by columns. To control if we want to graph by columns or by rows, we use the *PlotBy* property. Imagine that we want to graph Colombia's oil production information, but this time it is organized by rows as can be seen in figure 12.21.

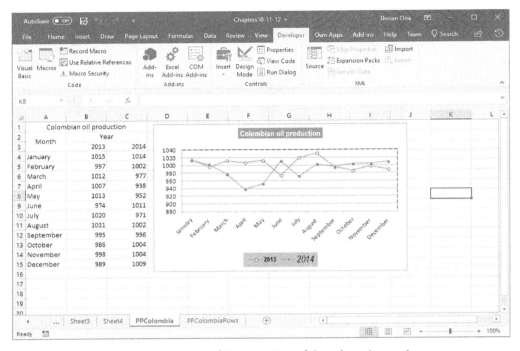

Figure 12.20. Result of the execution of the subroutine 12.16.

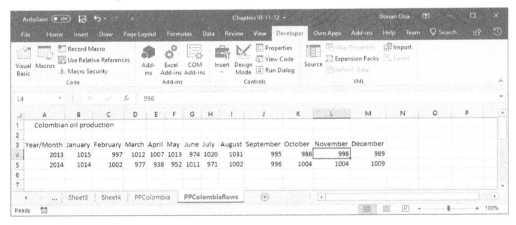

Figure 12.21. Colombian oil production organized by rows.

In case it was organized in this way and if you want to obtain a graph similar to the one in figure 12.19, it is necessary to add the instruction during the creation of the graph:

.Chart.PlotBy = xlRows

This instruction can be added after line 17 in subroutine 12.15.

Additionally, the data range must be changed. To do this, replace line 9 with

Set R = .Range("B3:M5")

And the *Left* and *Top* coordinates are changed by 10 and 90 respectively.

When executing the subroutine again, the graph will remain the same, but in a different position, as shown in figure 12.22.

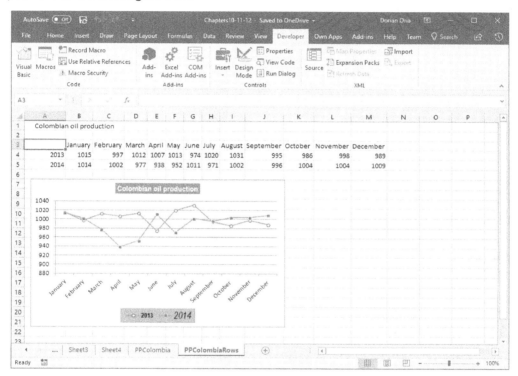

Figure 12.22. Result of the execution of subroutine 12.15 with the changes made in the data range, coordinates and form of graphing (*PlotBy*).

12.2.7.11 Rotation property

Returns or sets the rotation of a 3D chart. This rotation is really for the *PlotArea* object around the Z axis and is measured in degrees. This value can vary between 0 and 360 degrees.

To show how this property works, let's do the graph first. To do this, we are going to use subroutine 12.2 but we are going to change the type of chart to *xl3DColumn*. This is done by replacing line 19 with:

.Chart.ChartType = xl3DColumn

Let's also change the worksheet to Sheet4.

Now let's program a button to change the rotation of the graph. For this, in Sheet4, insert a *SpinButton*. This is done from the DEVELOPER tab. Press the "Insert" button and this will bring up the window shown in figure 12.23. Now the button enclosed in the square is selected.

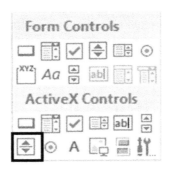

Figure 12.23. Form controls and Activex controls.

Once the control is inserted and placed in the position of interest, the orientation property of the button is modified and we make it horizontal. Then click on it with the right mouse button so that the menu shown in figure 12.24 appears.

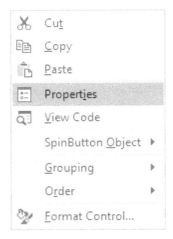

Figure 12.24. Options menu for Activex controls.

In this window we choose "Properties" and this will bring up the window shown in figure 12.25.

Now let's change some properties. Since we are working with a bar graph, we already know that the minimum value that the rotation can take is 0 and the maximum is 360. So let's edit those values in the properties window. By default, the changes in the number will be one by one. If this is to be changed, the *SmallChange* property can be edited.

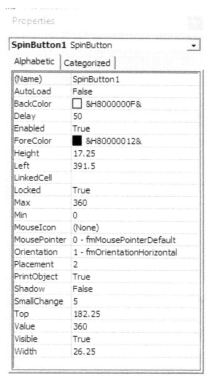

Figure 12.25. Properties window of the *SpinButton* control.

The next step is to double-click on the button and a code window will appear waiting for you to enter the instructions that you want to be executed each time there is a change in the number control. Subroutine 12.17 shows the button code.

Subroutine 12.17.

```
1  Private Sub SpinButton1_Change()
2  With Worksheets("Sheet4")
3     .ChartObjects("Age Range").Chart.Rotation = SpinButton1.Value
4     .Range("E13").Value = SpinButton1.Value
5  End With
6  End Sub
```

In line 3 we give value to the rotation.

Before executing the subroutine, you must make sure that the Design Mode button (which is next to "Insert" in the DEVELOPER tab) is deactivated. Once this is verified, you can start playing with your newly created button.

Figure 12.26 shows a moment in which the graph has been rotated 30 degrees.

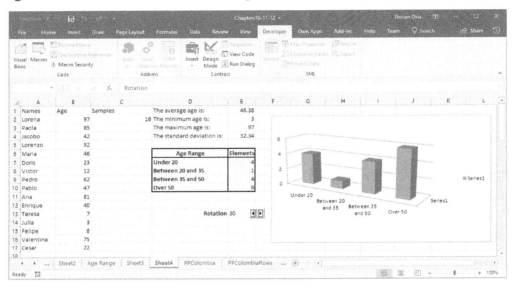

Figure 12.26. Sample of the rotation of a 3D bar graph.

12.2.8 Methods of the Chart object

We have already seen several of the most important properties that we need in order to be able to work with the *Chart* object. It is important to make clear that the properties explained above are not all. There are many more.

As with the properties, we will now see some of the most important methods that it is convenient to master to make our graphics. We will not see them all. However, I am sure that you will understand the methods that will be explained here so well, that you will then be able to extend the knowledge about them on your own. Internet is full of examples with explanations.

12.2.8.1 Axes method

Returns an object that represents, either an axis in a graph (*Axis*), or a collection of all the axes of a graph (*Axes*).

We are going to work with subroutine 12.2 to create a graph of Colombia's oil production in 3D. After modifying the subroutine, it will be as shown below:

266

Subroutine 12.18.

```
1    Sub ChartExample18()
2    Dim R1 As Range
3    Dim n As Integer
4    n = Worksheets("PPColombia").ChartObjects.Count
5    If n <> 0 Then
6       Worksheets("PPColombia").ChartObjects.Delete
7    End If
8    With Worksheets("PPColombia")
9       Set R1 = .Range("A4:C15")
10   End With
11   With Worksheets("PPColombia").ChartObjects.Add _
12      (Left:=200, Width:=375, Top:=5, Height:=225)
13      With .Chart
14         .SetSourceData Source:=R1
15         .ChartType = xl3DColumn
16         .Parent.Name = "PPColombia"
17         .Rotation = 45
18         .FullSeriesCollection(1).Name = "=PPColombia!$B$3"
19         .FullSeriesCollection(2).Name = "=PPColombia!$C$3"
20         With .Axes(xlCategory)
21            .HasTitle = True
22            .AxisTitle.Text = "Month"
23         End With
24         With .Axes(xlValue)
25            .HasTitle = True
26            .AxisTitle.Text = "Barrels x 1000"
27         End With
28         With .Axes(xlSeriesAxis)
29            .HasTitle = True
30            .AxisTitle.Text = "Years"
31         End With
32      End With
33   End With
34   End Sub
```

In this subroutine we have used several of the properties explained above. The new thing in it is the use of the *Axes* method.

Between lines 20 and 23, title is added to the X axis of the graph, which in our case corresponds to each of the months.

Between lines 24 and 27, title is added to the Z axis of the chart, which in our case corresponds to the production of oil in thousands of barrels.

Finally, between lines 28 and 31, title is added to the Y axis of the graph, showing the years that are being plotted (Series1 and Series2).

When you execute this subroutine, the chart shown in figure 12.27 is created.

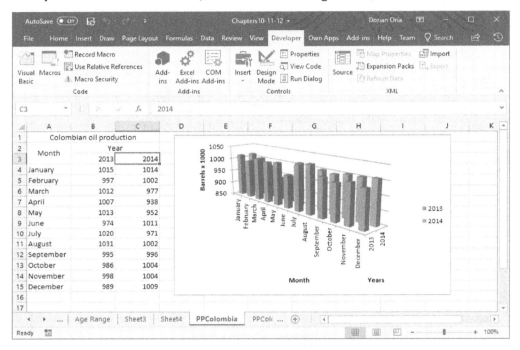

Figure 12.27. Result of the execution of subroutine 12.18.

Now, let's see another example in which we will be able to modify other attributes that depend on the collection of *Axes* objects.

Subroutine 12.19.

1	Sub ChartExample19()
2	With Worksheets("PPColombia").ChartObjects("PPColombia").Chart
3	With .Axes(xlCategory)
4	.HasMajorGridlines = True
5	.MajorGridlines.Border.Color = RGB(255, 255, 0)
6	.MajorGridlines.Border.LineStyle = xlDot
7	.HasMinorGridlines = True
8	.MinorGridlines.Border.Color = RGB(34, 100, 35)
9	With .Border
10	.LineStyle = xlDash

```
11        .Weight = xlThick
12         .Color = RGB(200, 24, 34)
13      End With
14    End With
15    With .Axes(xlValue)
16      .HasMajorGridlines = True
17      .MajorGridlines.Border.Color = RGB(255, 0, 0)
18      .MajorGridlines.Border.LineStyle = xlDot
19      .HasMinorGridlines = True
20      .MinorGridlines.Border.Color = RGB(34, 100, 35)
21      .MinimumScale = 900
22      .MaximumScale = 1050
23      With .Border
24         .LineStyle = xlDashDot
25         .Weight = xlMedium
26         .Color = RGB(150, 150, 34)
27      End With
28    End With
29  End With
30  End Sub
```

In this subroutine some of the properties of the graph shown in figure 12.27 have been changed. We only worked on the X and Z axes.

Between lines 3 and 14 the properties of the X axis were modified. With the instruction of line 4 the visualization of the main lines of the grid is allowed. In line 5 the color is changed and in line 6 the style of the line.

With the instruction in line 7, the secondary lines of the grid are visualized and in line 8 they are assigned a color.

Line 10 has changed the style of the line that defines the X axis. Line 11 has changed its thickness and line 12 has changed its color. Beyond whether this looks good or not aesthetically, the point is to show how the different properties of the *Axes* object collection work.

Between lines 15 and 28 the properties of the Z axis were modified. Here the same explanation that was given for the X axis applies with the exception of the changes that were made in the scale. The minimum and maximum values of the scale were changed in lines 21 and 22 respectively.

When executing the subroutine, the resulting graph looks like the one shown in figure 12.28 (the graph is enlarged with respect to the original to better show the changes made).

Perhaps a more practical and elegant way to establish the minimum and maximum values of the scale on the Z axis could be using the functions that allow to determine the minimum and maximum values of a range of data. So, we could change lines 21 and 22 for the following:

.MinimumScale = WorksheetFunction.Min(R)

.MaximumScale = WorksheetFunction.Max(R)

Additionally, the following lines must be added at the beginning of the subroutine:

Dim R As Range

Set R = Worksheets("PPColombia").Range("B4:C15")

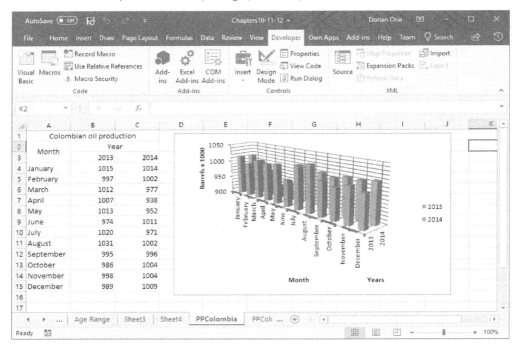

Figure 12.28. Result of the execution of subroutine 12.19.

12.2.8.2 ChartWizard method

Modify the properties of a chart. This method can be used to quickly format a graphic without the need to format each property individually.

Let's make a graph similar to the one done with subroutine 12.2, using the *ChartWizard* method.

Subroutine 12.20.

```
1    Sub ChartExample20()
2    Dim R As Range
3    Dim n As Integer
4    n = Worksheets("Sheet4").ChartObjects.Count
5    If n <> 0 Then
6       Worksheets("Sheet4").ChartObjects.Delete
7    End If
8    Set R = Worksheets("Sheet4").Range("D6:E10")
9    With Worksheets("Sheet4").ChartObjects.Add _
10      (Left:=400, Width:=375, Top:=5, Height:=225)
11      .Chart.ChartWizard _
12         Source:=R, _
13         Gallery:=xl3DColumn, _
14         Format:=1, _
15         PlotBy:=xlColumns, _
16         CategoryLabels:=1, _
17         SeriesLabels:=1, _
18         HasLegend:=True, _
19         Title:="Age Range", _
20         CategoryTitle:="Rabge", _
21         ValueTitle:="# Samples"
22      .Chart.Parent.Name = "Age Range"
23   End With
24   End Sub
```

This subroutine has code that has been explained before. We will explain what is new, which is the fact of establishing properties with the *ChartWizard* method.

Starting from line 11 and until line 21, all the properties that can be established with the *ChartWizard* method have been established except for *ExtraTitle*, which is used to add the title of the series in the case of 3D graphics or a second axis Y for the case of 2D graphics. It is the equivalent of what is set by the *.AxisTitle.Text* property of the *.Axes* object (*xlSeriesAxis*) (lines 26 and 30 of subroutine 12.18). The setting of all these parameters is optional. We could have simply used the *ChartWizard* method without parameters and VBA-Excel would have assigned default values.

A parameter that is worth commenting on is *Format* (line 14). This value can vary between 1 and 10 (depending on the type of graphic) and it is already predefined (self-formatting). Make your own experiments by changing the value of this parameter.

When executing subroutine 12.20, the graph shown in figure 12.29 is generated.

12.2.8.3 Export method

Exports the graphic in image format (GIF, JPEG, BMP).

Subroutine 12.21.

```
1   Sub ChartExample21()
2   With Worksheets("PPColombia").ChartObjects("PPColombia").Chart
3       .Export _
4       Filename:="C:\Users\dorian\OneDrive\Documentos\PPColombia.jpg", _
5       FilterName:="JPG"
6   End With
7   End Sub
```

In this way of doing the export, the *Export* method has been provided with the name and complete address where you want to locate the output file (*FileName*) and with the graphic format (*FilterName*).

Figure 12.30 shows the graphic file in *jpg* format opened with the Microsoft™ Paint program.

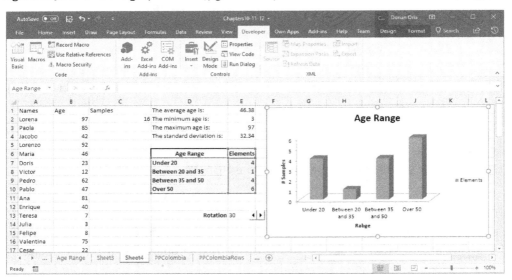

Figure 12.29. Result of the execution of subroutine 12.20.

12.2.8.4 SeriesCollection property

Returns an object that represents a simple series (*Series* object) or a collection of all series in a graphic or a group of graphics (*charts*).

Let's see some examples. We will work with the graph of the Colombian oil production information that we made with subroutine 12.18. A small change was made to the subroutine so that the graph was a little larger.

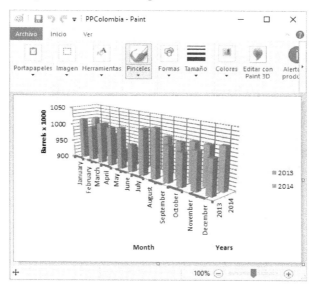

Figure 12.30. File resulting from the execution of subroutine 12.21, opened with Microsoft's Paint program.

Subroutine 12.22.

1	Sub ChartExample22()
2	Dim S As Series
3	Dim P As Points
4	Dim po As Point
5	Dim j As Integer
6	j = 0
7	With Worksheets("PPColombia").ChartObjects("PPColombia").Chart
8	With .SeriesCollection(1)
9	.BarShape = xlCylinder
10	.HasDataLabels = True
11	.ApplyDataLabels Type:=xlValue
12	.Name = Worksheets("PPColombia").Range("B3")
13	End With
14	Set S = .SeriesCollection(2)
15	Set P = S.Points
16	With S
17	.BarShape = xlBox
18	.Border.LineStyle = xlDot
19	.Border.Weight = xlThin

```
20      .Border.Color = RGB(255, 0, 0)
21      .HasDataLabels = True
22      .ApplyDataLabels Type:=xlValue
23      For Each po In P
24          j = j + 1
25          If Int(j / 2) = j / 2 Then
26              .Points(j).DataLabel.Top = xlLabelPositionBestFit
27          End If
28      Next po
29      .HasLeaderLines = True
30      .LeaderLines.Border.Color = RGB(2, 255, 89)
31      .Interior.Color = RGB(200, 230, 20)
32      .Name = Worksheets("PPColombia").Range("C3")
33    End With
34  End With
35  End Sub
```

In line 2, the variable S is declared as a variable of the *Series* type. Notice how interesting is that in addition to being an object, it also represents a type of variable. Later we will see the need to have declared this type of variable.

In line 3, the variable P is declared as a *Points* type variable. In this case, we are also declaring another variable as a type that is also an object. *Points* is a collection of *Point* objects. In line 4 a variable like this type (po) is declared.

In line 5 an integer variable was declared, which we will use later to serve as a point counter for one of the data series.

In line 6 we guarantee that before working with the data series, the value of the variable "j" always starts at zero.

From line 7 begins a **With** structure that will allow us to work with the *Chart* object of the graph.

The *Chart* object is also made up of the data series (*SeriesCollection* object), which are objects that also have properties and methods.

We can refer to the data series according to the order in which the data is entered in the graph. In our case, the first series of data which is the *SeriesCollection* (1) object, will be the one formed by the data in column "B". Between lines 8 and 13, this data series is formatted. In this case, as a 3D graph has been created, you can select the shape of the bar of that series (*BarShape*) according to the instruction of line 9. The available forms can be found in the Object Browser, as shown in figure 12.31.

In line 10 the labels of each of the samples involved in the graph are visible. These labels are the production values for each month, as established in line 11 (*xlValue*).

Figure 12.31. Object Browser showing the possible values of the *BarShape* property of the *Series* object, which belongs to the collection of *SeriesCollection* objects.

In line 14 we make the variable S to equal the *SeriesCollection(2)* object. When you use the **Set** statement, it is as if you were using a nickname so you do not have to type .*SeriesCollection(2)*. Then, in line 15, we assign to the variable P the collection of *Points* that make up the *SeriesCollection(2)* object.

Now we are going to format the second series of data (*SeriesCollection(2)*) that corresponds to the oil production of the year 2014. This will be done between lines 16 and 33.

In line 17 we assign the box shape to the bars.

From line 18 to line 20 the edges of each of the points (in this case bars) of the graph are formatted.

In lines 21 and 22 oil production values are visible for each bar of the graph (*Point*).

Between lines 23 and 28, the most optimal position is established for some of the value labels of the bars in the graph. This is achieved with the instruction in line 26 (*xlLabelPositionBestFit*).

Line 23 starts a **For** loop that allows you to move from point to point (*Point* object) in the collection of points that are in the *Points* object (which we assign to the variable po).

In line 24 we increase the value of the variable "j" by 1, each time a point in the collection is read. This was done with the idea that afterwards only the most optimal location (*xlLabelPositionBestFit*) will be applied to those tags belonging to even location points within the series. Hence the **If** condition of line 25.

Lines 29 and 30 make visible lines connecting each of the bars with their labels. As you will see later in the graph, only the lines that connect with the labels that were positioned with the condition of line 26 (*xlLabelPositionBestFit*) are seen, because they are the furthest from each of the bars. If you manually move the other bars that did not scroll, you will see that the line appears.

Table 12.8 shows other possible values for the location of the labels.

Table 12.8. Possible locations of tags (*DataLabels*).

Name	Description
xlLabelPositionCenter	Data label is centered on the data point or is inside a bar or pie chart.
xlLabelPositionAbove	Data label is positioned above the data point.
xlLabelPositionBelow	Data label is positioned below the data point.
xlLabelPositionLeft	Data label is positioned to the left of the data point.
xlLabelPositionRight	Data label is positioned to the right of the data point.
xlLabelPositionOutsideEnd	Data label is positioned outside the data point at the top edge.
xlLabelPositionInsideEnd	Data label is positioned inside the data point at the top edge.
xlLabelPositionInsideBase	Data label is positioned inside the data point at the bottom edge.
xlLabelPositionBestFit	Excel controls the position of the label.
xlLabelPositionMixed	Data labels are in multiple positions.
xlLabelPositionCustom	Data label is in a custom position.

In line 31 the bars are colored and in line 32 they are assigned a name.

When executing subroutine 12.22, the graph shown in figure 12.32 is generated.

Let's see another example based on the same oil production data, but this time plotted as 2D lines. To do this, change in subroutine 12.18, line 15, the type of graph to *xlLine* and comment (remember, with the character ') the lines from 28 to 31 (both inclusive). It is necessary to comment those lines because they only apply for 3D graphics.

Once these changes are made, executing the subroutine generates the graph shown in figure 12.33.

Now we are going to make some changes in the graph, some of them similar to those we did with the previous graphic. The novelty here is that, when dealing with line graphs, it is possible to add marks or symbols to the points.

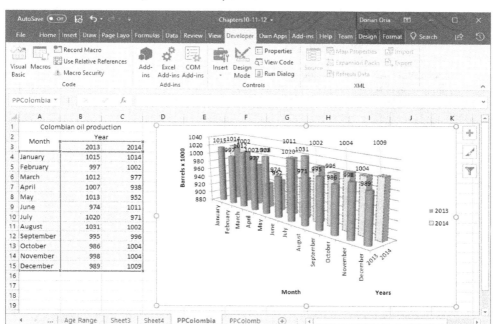

Figure 12.32. Result of the execution of subroutine 12.22.

Subroutine 12.23.

1	Sub ChartExample23()
2	Dim S As Series
3	Dim P As Points
4	Dim po As Point
5	Dim j As Integer
6	j = 0
7	With Worksheets("PPColombia").ChartObjects("PPColombia").Chart
8	With .SeriesCollection(1)
9	.HasDataLabels = True
10	.ApplyDataLabels Type:=xlValue
11	.Name = Worksheets("PPColombia").Range("B3")
12	.MarkerStyle = xlMarkerStyleStar
13	.MarkerSize = 6
14	.MarkerForegroundColor = RGB(255, 0, 255)
15	End With
16	Set S = .SeriesCollection(2)
17	Set P = S.Points

```
18    With S
19        .Border.LineStyle = xlDot
20        .Border.Weight = xlThin
21        .Border.Color = RGB(255, 0, 0)
22        .HasDataLabels = True
23        .ApplyDataLabels Type:=xlValue
24        For Each po In P
25            j = j + 1
26            .Points(j).DataLabel.Top = xlLabelPositionBestFit
27        Next po
28        .HasLeaderLines = True
29        .LeaderLines.Border.Color = RGB(2, 255, 89)
30        .Interior.Color = RGB(200, 230, 20)
31        .Name = Worksheets("PPColombia").Range("C3")
32        .MarkerStyle = xlMarkerStyleSquare
33        .MarkerSize = 6
34        .MarkerForegroundColor = RGB(255, 0, 255)
35        .MarkerBackgroundColor = RGB(255, 255, 0)
36    End With
37    With .Axes(xlValue)
38        .MinimumScale = 920
39        .MaximumScale = 1050
40    End With
41    End With
42    End Sub
```

One of the novelties in this subroutine is the fact of being able to add marks to the points that are being plotted. In the case of the oil production data for 2013 (*SeriesCollection(1)*), the marker was chosen as a star (line 12). Line 13 sets the size of the marker and line 14 establishes its color. Note that this mark does not have an interior space, so a color for the background was not established for it.

Another new feature in this subroutine is that a better location was chosen for the labels of all the points of the oil production data series for 2014 (*SeriesCollection(2)*). This can be seen in the instructions in lines 24 through 27.

Between lines 32 and 35 the marks for the second data series points are added and formatted. As the mark chosen here is a square, it was possible to assign a color to its background (*MarkerBackgroundColor*).

Figure 12.34 shows the graph that is generated when executing subroutine 12.23.

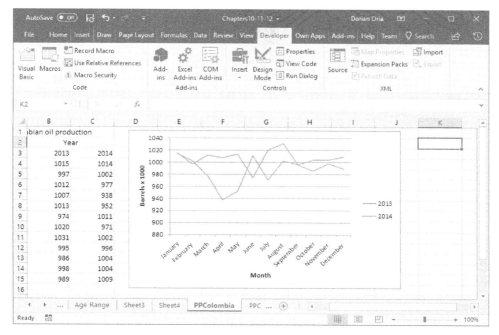

Figure 12.33. Result of the execution of subroutine 12.18 with changes made to the type of chart (2D line).

Let's now show another example when the data is plotted using 2D bars. To do this, again change the chart type in subroutine 12.18, line 15, by *xlColumnClustered*. Keep the lines commented from the 26th to the 29th.

For the next exercise, it is necessary to change the way to express input data. To do this, imagine for a moment that we want to see how much above or below was one million barrels per month. For this, we subtract a thousand from each of the values and as a result of this operation the values shown in figure 12.35 are generated. The figure also shows how the graph resulting from the execution of subroutine 12.18 is shown with the changes made.

In the example that will be shown in figure 12.35, we want to show the operation of a very interesting property of the *Series* object, called *InvertIfNegative*.

By subtracting 1000 from the production of each month, we will have negative values for the cases in which the production has been less than one million barrels.

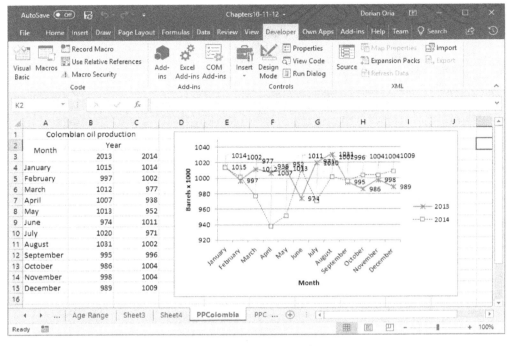

Figure 12.34. Result of the execution of subroutine 12.23.

Subroutine 12.24.

1	Sub ChartExample24()
2	Dim S As Series
3	Dim P As Points
4	Dim po As Point
5	Dim j As Integer
6	j = 0
7	With Worksheets("PPColombia").ChartObjects("PPColombia").Chart
8	With .SeriesCollection(1)
9	.HasDataLabels = True
10	.ApplyDataLabels Type:=xlValue
11	.Border.Weight = xlMedium
12	.Border.Color = RGB(0, 0, 0)
13	.Interior.Color = RGB(0, 0, 255)
14	.Name = Worksheets("PPColombia").Range("B3")
15	.InvertIfNegative = True
16	.InvertColor = RGB(255, 255, 255)
17	
18	End With
19	Set S = .SeriesCollection(2)

```
20    Set P = S.Points
21    With S
22       .Border.LineStyle = xlDot
23       .Border.Weight = xlThin
24       .Border.Color = RGB(255, 0, 0)
25       .HasDataLabels = True
26       .ApplyDataLabels Type:=xlValue
27       For Each po In P
28          j = j + 1
29          .Points(j).DataLabel.Top = xlLabelPositionOutsideEnd
30       Next po
31       .HasLeaderLines = True
32       .LeaderLines.Border.Color = RGB(2, 255, 89)
33       .Interior.Color = RGB(200, 230, 20)
34       .InvertIfNegative = True
35       .InvertColor = RGB(255, 255, 255)
36       .Name = Worksheets("PPColombia").Range("C3")
37    End With
38  End With
39  End Sub
```

Lines 15 and 16 change the properties of the bars whose values represent negative numbers in the series of production data for the year 2013. In line 15 the *InvertIfNegative* property is activated and in line 16 you have the possibility to change the color of the bars that have negative values (*InvertColor* property). In lines 34 and 35 the same is done for the bars that represent the monthly oil production of the year 2014.

When executing subroutine 12.24, the graph shown in figure 12.36 is generated.

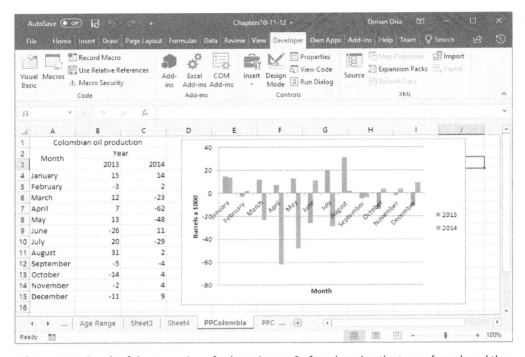

Figure 12.35. Result of the execution of subroutine 12.18 after changing the type of graph and the input data.

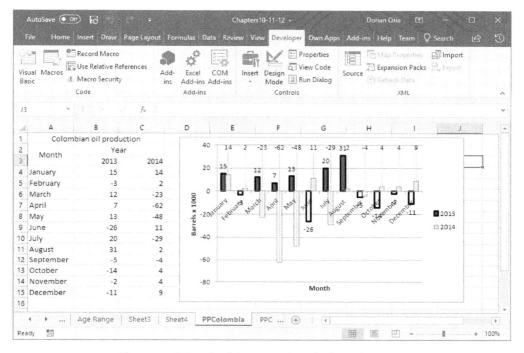

Figure 12.36. Result of the execution of subroutine 12.24.

Chapter 13. Examples of apps in VBA-Excel

13.1 Introduction

We have already gone a long way and it was time to start putting together all those pieces we have seen before. Now let's see examples with situations from various disciplines. You can not miss the examples on geophysics, which is my profession.

In the examples that we will see below, I will take the opportunity to introduce other concepts that will undoubtedly add more power to what we have seen previously.

13.2 Calculation of area under a curve

Numerical methods for integration can be used to integrate functions, whether you have your equation or a data table that describes it (Nakamura, 1998). In some cases it is even possible that the numerical solution can be faster than the analytical solution (finding the antiderivative of the function), in case you are only interested in the numeric value of the integral.

In this section, three methods for numerical integration will be described: rectangular method (or Riemann sum on the left and on the right), trapezoidal method and Simpson's rule.

The first thing to do is create a window like the one shown in figure 13.1.

This main window was given the name of Integral (remember that this is the name of the form, that is, the value of the *Name* property).

Figure 13.1 also shows the names that were given to each of the controls.

The equation text box is the one that receives the function to which the numerical integral will be calculated in the interval between *LowLim* and *UpLim*. The sample text box receives the number of divisions that will be used for the calculation.

Let's now program the *Calculate* button. To do this we double-click on the button and in the code window we will create the subroutine that will contain the code. Remember that by default, the subroutine for buttons is created with the *Click* event. That is, at run time, the subroutine will be executed by clicking on the button. Subroutine 13.1 shows the code that will be executed when you press this button. This event can be changed (respond to the *double-click* event for example).

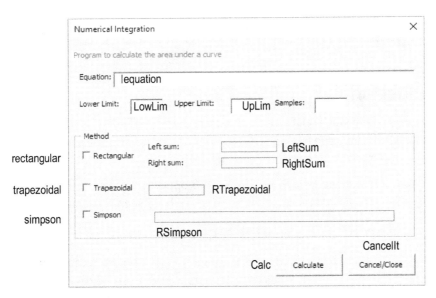

Figure 13.1. Main window of the application.

Subroutine 13.1.

1	Private Sub Calc_Click()
2	Dim i, n As Integer
3	Dim ws As Worksheet
4	Dim x, y As String
5	Dim ll, ul, sumln, deltaX As Double
6	Dim R As Range
7	n = CInt(Integral.samples)
8	ll = CDbl(Integral.LowLim.Text)
9	ul = CDbl(Integral.UpLim.Text)
10	deltaX = (ul - ll) / n
11	sumln = 0#
12	Set ws = Worksheets("function")
13	ws.Range("A:B").Clear
14	ws.Range("A1") = "x"
15	ws.Range("B1") = "f(x)"
16	For i = 0 To n
17	x = VBA.Format(ll + i * deltaX, "0.0000000")
18	ws.Range("A" & i + 2).Value = CDbl(x)
19	ws.Range("B" & i + 2).Value = VBA.Format(Application.WorksheetFunction.Substitute _
20	(Integral.equation.Text, "x", "A" & i + 2), "0.00")
21	Next i
22	If rectangular.Value = True Then

```
23    LeftSum.Caption = VBA.Format(LeftsumIn(ll, ul, n), "0.0000000")
24    RightSum.Caption = VBA.Format(RightsumIn(ll, ul, n), "0.0000000")
25  End If
26  If trapezoidal.Value = True Then
27    RTrapezoidal.Caption = VBA.Format(trapezoid(ll, ul, n), "0.0000000")
28  End If
29  If simpson.Value = True And (n / 2) = Int(n / 2) Then
30    RSimpson.Caption = VBA.Format(fsimpson(ll, ul, n), "0.0000000")
31    Else
32    RSimpson.Caption = "The number of samples must be an even number"
33  End If
34  Set R = ws.Range("A1:B" & n + 1)
35  Call ChartPaint(R, n)
36  End Sub
```

It is important to take into account that if you are going to enter a function that contains the letter x, such as EXP, it must be done using capital letters, to differentiate it from the variable "x". Additionally, the equation must begin with the "=" sign.

Now we will proceed to explain the most relevant aspects of the code.

In line 3 the variable "ws" has been declared as a *Worksheet* type. This has some advantages that I find very useful, since the Intellisense algorithm of VBA-Excel recognizes the variable as an object and it is activated when writing the name of the variable, showing its properties and methods as shown in the figure 13.2. This statement is not necessary, but it has some incredible advantages, starting with the fact that it is not necessary to write *Worksheets("function")* every time. Of course, at this point you already know that you can use a **With** block, but the Intellisense function will not be activated when using this alternative.

When textboxes are used to capture user information, it is necessary to take into account that VBA-Excel treats its contents as text strings, regardless of whether they are numbers. For this reason, in line 7, the **CInt** function was used to convert the numeric text input into an **Integer** number.

In lines 8 and 9 the **CDbl** function has been used to convert the entries of the text boxes into **Double** type variables

In line 11 we see that the variable sum is equal to 0#. This is the same as 0.0. The change is done by VBA-Excel automatically.

In line 12 we make the variable "ws" equal to the *Worksheets("function")* object. When working with objects it is necessary to use the **Set** instruction.

In line 13, we clear columns A and B so that the values of the function to be plotted can be written to them. The values of the X axis will be between *ll* and *ul* and will be spaced a distance equal to *deltaX*.

In line 19 is where the application trick is. We are used to using the letter "x" as a variable in our equations. So what the **Substitute** instruction does is to change the letter "x" that the user enters in the equation text box (figure 13.1) by A2, A3, A4 and so on ("A" & i + 2, with the variable i varying within a loop **For**) and write it in the cells of column B. These values correspond therefore to those of the function f(x).

Between lines 22 and 25 the values of the Riemann sum are calculated from the right and from the left. For each of them, a function was written. For the sum on the left, the function is shown in subroutine 13.2 and for the sum on the right, the function is shown in subroutine 13.3.

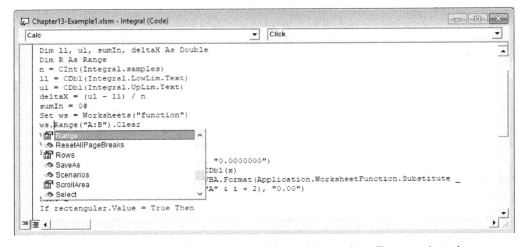

Figure 13.2. Variable declaration as *Worksheet* object and *Intellisense* activated.

Subroutine 13.2.

1	Function LeftsumIn(ByVal lowl As Double, ByVal upl As Double, ByVal s As Integer) As Double
2	Dim i As Integer
3	Dim deltaX As Double
4	LeftsumIn = 0
5	deltaX = Abs((upl - lowl) / s)
6	For i = 0 To s - 1
7	LeftsumIn = LeftsumIn + Worksheets("function").Range("B" & i + 2) * deltaX
8	Next i
9	End Function

Subroutine 13.3.

1	Function RightsumIn(ByVal lowl As Double, ByVal upl As Double, ByVal s As Integer) As Double
2	Dim i As Integer
3	Dim deltaX As Double
4	RightsumIn = 0
5	deltaX = Abs((upl - lowl) / s)
6	For i = 1 To s
7	RightsumIn = RightsumIn + Worksheets("function").Range("B" & i + 2) * deltaX
8	Next i
9	End Function

Between lines 26 and 28, the calculations are made according to the trapezoidal rule. The function that does this is shown in subroutine 13.4.

Subroutine 13.4.

1	Function trapezoid(ByVal lowl As Double, ByVal upl As Double, ByVal s As Integer) As Double
2	Dim i As Integer
3	Dim deltaX As Double
4	trapezoid = 0
5	deltaX = Abs((upl - lowl) / s)
6	For i = 0 To s
7	trapezoid = trapezoid + (Worksheets("function").Range("B" & i + 2) + _
8	Worksheets("function").Range("B" & i + 3)) * deltaX * 0.5
9	Next i
10	End Function

Between lines 29 and 33, the calculations are made using Simpson's rule. The function that does this is shown in the subroutine 13.5.

Subroutine 13.5.

1	Function fsimpson(ByVal lowl As Double, ByVal upl As Double, ByVal s As Integer) As Double
2	Dim i As Integer
3	Dim factor, f2, f4 As Double
4	fsimpson = 0
5	f2 = 0
6	f4 = 0
7	factor = Abs((upl - lowl) / (3 * s))
8	If s = 2 Then
9	fsimpson = (Worksheets("function").Range("B2") + _
10	Worksheets("function").Range("B" & s + 2)) * factor
11	End If
12	If s <> 2 Then

13	For i = 1 To s / 2
14	f4 = f4 + 4 * Worksheets("function").Range("B" & 2 * i + 1)
15	Next i
16	For j = 1 To (s / 2) - 1
17	f2 = f2 + 2 * Worksheets("function").Range("B" & 2 * j + 2)
18	Next j
19	End If
20	fsimpson = factor * (f2 + f4 + Worksheets("function").Range("B2") + _
21	Worksheets("function").Range("B" & s + 2))
22	End Function

In line 35, the subroutine which is responsible for constructing the graph of the curve and the area below it according to the specified interval is invoked. This subroutine is the one shown below.

Subroutine 13.6.

1	Sub ChartPaint(ByRef R As Range, ByVal s As Integer)
2	Dim n As Integer
3	Dim xlabels As Range
4	Set xlabels = Worksheets("function").Range("B2:B" & s + 1)
5	n = Worksheets("function").ChartObjects.Count
6	If n <> 0 Then
7	Worksheets("function").ChartObjects.Delete
8	End If
9	With Worksheets("function").ChartObjects.Add _
10	(Left:=200, Width:=375, Top:=60, Height:=225)
11	.Chart.SetSourceData Source:=R
12	.Chart.SeriesCollection(1).Delete
13	.Chart.SeriesCollection(1).XValues = xlabels
14	.Chart.ChartType = xlArea
15	.Chart.HasTitle = True
16	.Chart.ChartTitle.Text = "f(x)" & Integral.equation
17	.Chart.Parent.Name = "function"
18	End With
19	End Sub

The code for the Cancel/Close button is shown below.

Subroutine 13.7.

1	Private Sub Cancellt_Click()
2	Unload Me
3	End Sub

To show the main window of our application, we have added a command button in the spreadsheet "function", as shown in figure 13.3.

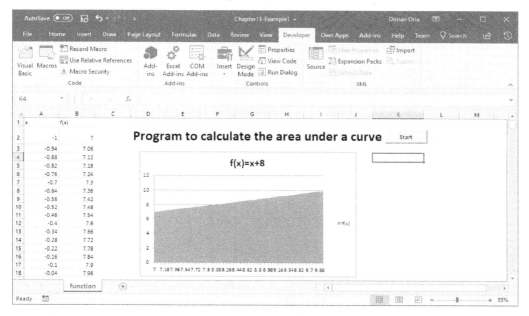

Figure 13.3. Spreadsheet that contains the application for calculating numeric integrals.

To add this button you must go to the "DEVELOPER" tab and there press the "Insert" button. When doing so, the window shown in figure 13.4 appears. The command button is inserted with the control enclosed in the black rectangle.

Figure 13.4. Form controls.

In order to edit the properties of the button, we must press the "Design Mode" button, which is next to the "Insert" button. Once this is done, click on the button with the right mouse button to see the Properties window. If you cannot do it with the right mouse button, you can also press the "Properties" button next to the "Design Mode" button. The Properties window of the button in this example is shown in figure 13.5.

Figure 13.5. Properties window of the *Start* button.

The code that will be executed when you press this button is the one shown below. To access the code window, in edit mode, double-click on it.

Subroutine 13.8.

1	Private Sub Go_Click()
2	Integral.Show
3	End Sub

Notice that "Integral" is what we have called the form shown in figure 13.1.

Remember also that since we created functions to do the calculations, these can also be used from any spreadsheet in our Excel book. Figure 13.6 shows the appearance of the spreadsheet with each of the functions used.

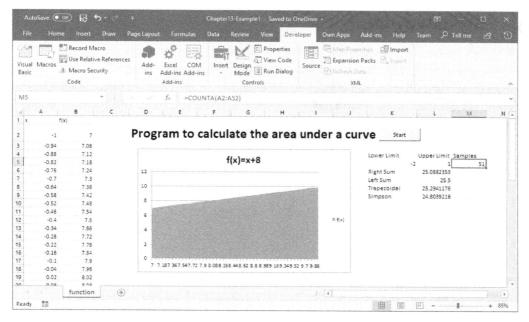

Figure 13.6. Spreadsheet showing the results of the use of each of the functions.

In cells K5 and L5 we place the extremes of the interval in which we want to calculate the integral. In cell M5, we place the following instruction:

=COUNTA(A:A)-1

This function will allow to count the quantity of values that are available for the calculation of the integral.

In cell L6 the following instruction is placed:

=RightsumIn(K5;L5;M5)

In cell L7 the following instruction is placed:

=LeftsumIn(K5;L5;M5)

In the cell L8 the following instruction is placed:

=trapezoid(K5;L5;M5)

In cell L9 the following instruction is placed:

=fsimpson(K5;L5;M5)

13.3   Brain waves

Brain waves represent the electrical activity produced by the brain. It is the repetitive or rhythmic neural activity in the central nervous system. The electrical activity of the brain changes depending on what you are doing. For example, when a person sleeps she/he has different brain waves than when she/he is awake. Broadly speaking, the types of brain waves are the following:

-   Delta (1 Hz – 3 Hz)
-   Theta (4 Hz – 7 Hz)
-   Alfa (8 Hz – 13 Hz)
-   Beta (14 Hz – 33 Hz)
-   Gamma (> 34 Hz)

The following program, graphs the different types of brain waves and changes their color depending on the frequency range. For practical purposes, we will assume the behavior of brain waves as flat waves. The main interface of the program is as shown in figure 13.7.

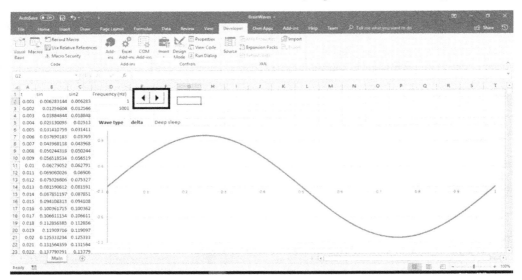

Figura 13.7. Main interface of the BrainWaves program.

In columns B and C we have added the amplitude of the wave, which is sampled every millisecond (column A). We are going to plot 1000 samples equivalent to one second of time (column B). To understand the exercise easily, we know that frequency is defined as cycles per second (Hz). Thus, if the wave has a frequency of 1 Hz, we will see only one complete cycle between 0 and 1 second as shown in figure 13.7. If the frequency is 2 Hz, then we will see two cycles in the range from 0 to 1 second as shown in figure 13.8. The dotted, gray curve plots the values in column B.

In our graph, the time is on the X axis and the amplitude is on the Y axis.

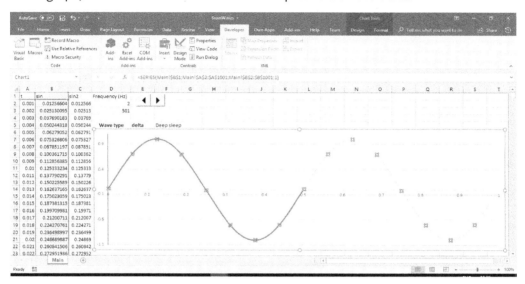

Figure 13.8. 2 Hz signal.

Equation 13.1 is the one used to calculate the amplitude.

$$A(t) = \sin(2 * \pi * \omega * t))$$

(13.1)

Where:

ω : frequency

t : time

We have added a Spin Button (black rectangle in figure 13.7) that helps us change the frequency value (Range ("D2")).

Figure 13.9 shows the properties of this button. Subroutine 13.9 shows the code that is executed each time this button is pressed.

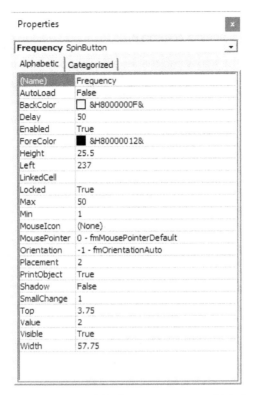

Figure 13.9. Properties of the button Frequency (Spin Button).

Subroutine 13.9.

1	Private Sub Frequency_Change()
2	Dim i As Integer
3	With Worksheets("Main")
4	.Range("D2") = Frequency.Value
5	For i = 1 To 1000
6	.Range("A" & i + 1) = i / 1000
7	.Range("B" & i + 1) = _
8	VBA.Sin(2 * WorksheetFunction.Pi * .Range("D2") * .Range("A" & i + 1))
9	.Range("C" & i + 1) = .Range("B" & i + 1)
10	Next i
11	End With
12	Macro2
13	End Sub

In line 4 we write the value that spin button has taken which for us will be each of the frequencies that we will test with the program.

Between lines 5 and 10 we have a For - Next control structure with which the values to be plotted will be generated. Line 6 generates the time values (every millisecond). In line 7 the calculations are made to generate the amplitude of the wave, according to equation 13.1.

In line 12, Macro2 (subroutine 13.10) is invoked, which aims to color a complete cycle of the wave and highlight it from the rest of the waves that are graphed up to 1 second.

Subroutine 13.10.

1	Sub Macro2()
2	Dim rango As Integer
3	Dim ws As Worksheet
4	Set ws = Worksheets("Main")
5	If ws.Range("d2") < 4 Then
6	ws.Range("e5") = "delta"
7	ws.Range("f5") = "Deep sleep"
8	ws.ChartObjects("Chart1").Chart.FullSeriesCollection(2).Format.Line.ForeColor.RGB = _
9	RGB(255, 0, 0)
10	End If
11	If ws.Range("d2") > 3 And ws.Range("d2") < 8 Then
12	ws.Range("e5") = "theta"
13	ws.Range("f5") = "First stages of sleep"
14	ws.ChartObjects("Chart1").Chart.FullSeriesCollection(2).Format.Line.ForeColor.RGB = _
15	RGB(255, 192, 0)
16	End If
17	If ws.Range("d2") > 7 And ws.Range("d2") < 14 Then
18	ws.Range("e5") = "alfa"
19	ws.Range("f5") = "Periods of relaxation, with closed eyes, but still awake"
20	ws.ChartObjects("Chart1").Chart.FullSeriesCollection(2).Format.Line.ForeColor.RGB = _
21	RGB(0, 255, 21)
22	End If
23	If ws.Range("d2") > 13 And ws.Range("d2") < 34 Then
24	ws.Range("e5") = "beta"
25	ws.Range("f5") = "Awake and aware"
26	ws.ChartObjects("Chart1").Chart.FullSeriesCollection(2).Format.Line.ForeColor.RGB = _
27	RGB(0, 26, 255)
28	End If
29	If ws.Range("d2") > 33 Then
30	ws.Range("e5") = "gamma"
31	ws.Range("f5") = "Conscious perception and expansion of attention focus"
32	ws.ChartObjects("Chart1").Chart.FullSeriesCollection(2).Format.Line.ForeColor.RGB = _
33	RGB(201, 0, 255)
34	End If
35	rango = Int(1000 / ws.Range("D2")) + 1

36	ws.Range("d3") = rango
37	ws.ChartObjects("Chart1").Chart.FullSeriesCollection(2).XValues = "=Main!$A$2:A" _
38	& rango
39	ws.ChartObjects("Chart1").Chart.FullSeriesCollection(2).Values = "=Main!$C$2:C" _
40	& rango
41	End Sub

In order to highlight how a cycle looks at different frequencies, we will paint it in different colors (lines 8, 14, 20, 26 and 32). The FullSeriesCollection named in each of those lines corresponds to a second curve that is the one painted on the chart and whose range of values we define in line 35 and assign it to the creation of curve 2 (FullSeriesCollection (2)) in lines 37 and 39.

The if - end if structures are used to know the type of brain wave according to the frequency. In cell E5 the type of brain wave will be written and in cell F5 a description of the state in which we are when that frequency is present.

If we see the data that make up the sin2 series, even though column C contains the same data as column B, to make the curve that is painted in colors we do not select all the data, but those that complete a cycle. Figure 13.10 shows what the Edit Series window looks like and the data that is used to draw it (Frequency 3 Hz).

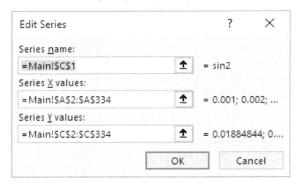

Figure 13.10. Range of data for the curve that is painted in colors (sin2, column C).

13.4 Functions designed by the user

It is possible that at some point you have found spreadsheets filled with formulas, in which a result depends on the calculations made in other cells. Many times it is difficult to understand the equations. If for some reason someone makes a mistake and modifies the equation, then the consequences can be disastrous. So, when dealing with complex formulas, I recommend to program them as functions in VBA-Excel.

In line 7 of subroutine 13.9 we generate the amplitude values for the brainwave exercise. Now let's see what the function looks like in VBA code.

Subroutine 13.11.

1	Function Amplitude(ByVal w As Single, ByVal t As Single) As Double
2	Dim pi As Single
3	pi = WorksheetFunction.pi
4	Amplitude = Math.Sin(2 * pi * w * t)
5	End Function

To invoke this function in the spreadsheet, we write in any cell:

=Amplitude($D$2;A2)

It is important to respect the order in which the arguments are placed in the function. $D$2 corresponds to the value of the frequency, which the function receives as the value w (**ByVal** w) and A2 corresponds to the value of time, which the function receives as the value t (**ByVal** t). Since the function returns a value, it is important to indicate what type of value it returns. In this case, it returns a **Double** type value, even if the values it receives are of type **Single**.

In line 2 we define the variable pi (which really is a constant) and in line 3 we assign the value returned by the Excel function PI(), which in VBA code is **WorksheetFunction.pi**. Remember that all the functions that are used in the spreadsheet have their corresponding function in the programming language. Remember also that the advantage of using the VBA-Excel functions is that they will work regardless of the Excel language. The programming language is unique.

Line 4 contains the equation that will be used to calculate the Amplitude. It is important that the variable has the same function name.

We will work with an Excel file, in which functions are programmed to calculate derivatives.

Figure 13.11 shows how the spreadsheet looks after using the Amplitude function.

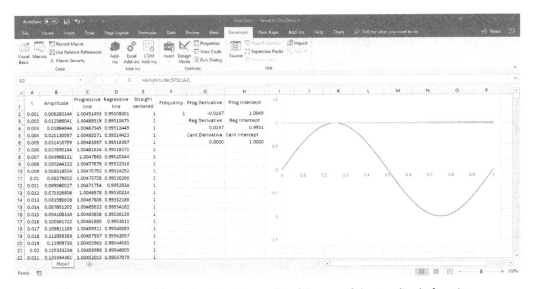

Figure 13.11. Spreadsheet showing the results of the use of the Amplitude function.

Let's see another example of a function designed by the user. We are going to create several functions that calculate the derivative of a function at a certain point. Remember that in mathematics, the derivative of a function measures the speed with which the value of that function changes, as the value of its independent variable changes (https://en.wikipedia.org/wiki/Derivative). The derivative of a function f in x_0 is defined as follows:

$$f'(x_0) = \lim_{h \to 0} \frac{f(x_0 + h) - f(x_0)}{h} \qquad 13.2$$

For small values of h, we can approximate the derivative of f in x_0 in the following way:

$$f'(x_0) \approx \frac{f(x_0 + h) - f(x_0)}{h}, h \neq 0 \qquad 13.3$$

Equation 13.3 is known as the first finite difference forward or progressive difference. You can also get the finite difference backwards or regressive difference:

$$f'(x_0) \approx \frac{f(x_0) - f(x_0 - h)}{h}, h \neq 0 \qquad 13.4$$

If we add equations 13.3 and 13.4, we will obtain the finite difference centered as follows:

$$f'(x_0) \approx \frac{f(x_0 + h) - f(x_0 - h)}{2h}, h \neq 0 \qquad 13.5$$

We will create a function for each of the ways to approximate the value of the derivative. The 13.12 subroutine shows the function to calculate the derivative according to equation 13.3.

Subroutine 13.12.

1	Function Progressive(ByRef t As Range) As Single
2	Dim ws As Worksheet
3	Dim f As Integer
4	Set ws = Worksheets(1)
5	f = t.Row
6	Progressive = (ws.Cells(f + 1, 2) - ws.Cells(f, 2)) / (ws.Cells(f + 1, 1) - ws.Cells(f, 1))
7	End Function

Subroutine 13.13 shows the function used to calculate the derivative according to equation 13.4.

Subroutine 13.13.

1	Function Regressive(ByRef t As Range) As Single
2	Dim ws As Worksheet
3	Dim f As Integer
4	Set ws = Worksheets(1)
5	f = t.Row
6	Regressive = (ws.Cells(f, 2) - ws.Cells(f - 1, 2)) / (ws.Cells(f, 1) - ws.Cells(f - 1, 1))
7	End Function

Subroutine 13.14 shows the function used to calculate the derivative according to equation 13.5.

Subroutine 13.14.

1	Function Centered(ByRef t As Range) As Single
2	Dim ws As Worksheet
3	Dim f As Integer
4	Set ws = Worksheets(1)
5	f = t.Row
6	Centered = (ws.Cells(f + 1, 2) - ws.Cells(f - 1, 2)) / (ws.Cells(f + 1, 1) - ws.Cells(f - 1, 1))
7	End Function

In addition to creating functions to calculate the derivative of the function at a certain point, we have created functions for calculating the intercepts of the tangent lines that pass through the point at which the derivative is calculated. With all this information, we can generate points from these lines using the following equation:

$$y = mx + b \qquad\qquad 13.6$$

Where m is the slope of the line (derived at the point of interest) and b is the intercept and we will calculate it using the following subroutines, depending on which derivative we use. Subroutine 13.15 shows the function to calculate the intercept of the line in case the derivative calculated by progressive difference is used.

Subroutine 13.15.

```
1   Function interProg(ByRef t As Range) As Single
2   Dim ws As Worksheet
3   Dim f As Integer
4   f = t.Row
5   Set ws = Worksheets(1)
6   interProg = ws.Cells(f, 2) - ws.Range("G2") * ws.Cells(f, 1)
7   End Function
```

Subroutine 13.16 shows the function used to calculate the intercept of the line in case the derivative calculated by the regressive difference is used.

Subroutine 13.16.

```
1   Function interReg(ByRef t As Range) As Single
2   Dim ws As Worksheet
3   Dim f As Integer
4   f = t.Row
5   Set ws = Worksheets(1)
6   interReg = ws.Cells(f, 2) - ws.Range("G4") * ws.Cells(f, 1)
7   End Function
```

Subroutine 13.17 shows the function used to calculate the intercept of the line in case the derivative calculated by finite difference centered is used.

Subroutine 13.17.

```
1   Function interCen(ByRef t As Range) As Single
2   Dim ws As Worksheet
3   Dim f As Integer
```

```
4   f = t.Row
5   Set ws = Worksheets(1)
6   interCen = ws.Cells(f, 2) - ws.Range("G6") * ws.Cells(f, 1)
7   End Function
```

Figure 13.12 shows how the spreadsheet looks after using all functions.

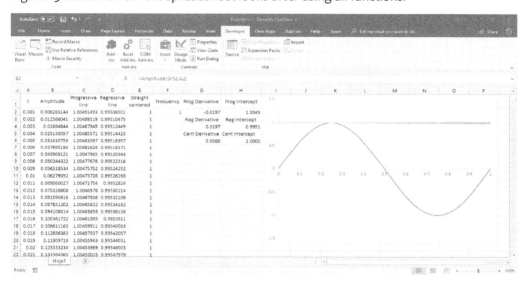

Figure 13.12. Spreadsheet showing the results of the use of functions for calculation of derivatives and intercepts of tangent lines.

As shown in figure 13.12, the calculations were made for the coordinate point $x = 0.25$, $y = 1$. The straight lines that appear above the sinusoidal curve correspond to the lines tangent to the curve at that point, generated with each one of the derivation functions. Note the simplicity of the function in the spreadsheet and that additionally that function can be used in another Excel file. The functions programmed in this way are much easier to export and reuse.

13.5   Reading text files

Microsoft Excel already comes with several utilities to import information from text files, which can have information ordered by columns and separated by commas, spaces, tabs, etc. You can record a macro while the import wizard is running and then some adjustments can be made to make a more flexible macro.

However, there is another way to access information from text files and is using VBA-Excel code. I particularly like this option, because the import process is faster. Either way, you can try it and draw your own conclusions.

Subroutine 13.18 shows an example of how to read information from a text file like the one shown in figure 13.13.

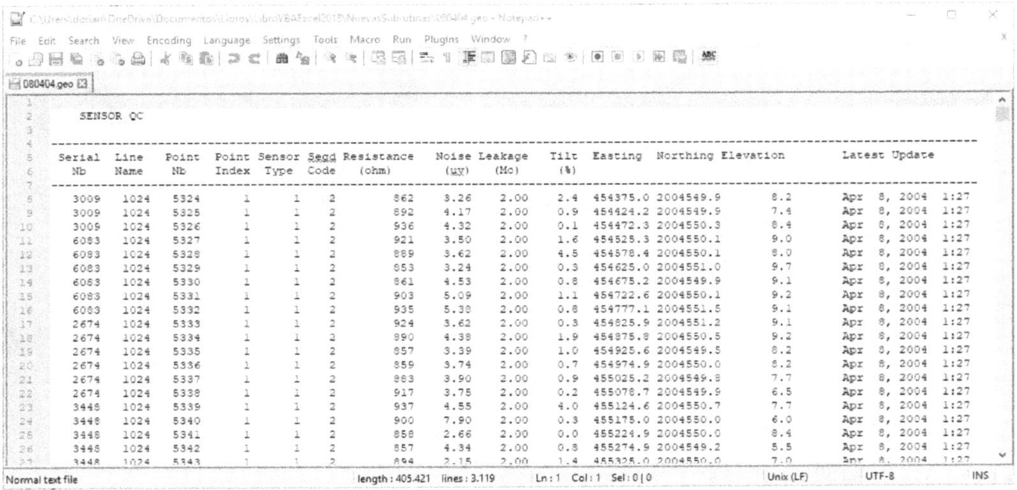

Figure 13.13. Text file that contains results of a test of instruments that are used in seismic land data acquisition.

Subroutine 13.18.

1	Sub ReadTextFile()
2	Dim file As String
3	Dim line As String
4	Dim ws As Worksheet
5	Dim i, j, n As Integer
6	Dim FileNumber As Integer
7	Set ws = Worksheets(1)
8	Dim arrayOfElements
9	Dim r As Range
10	Set r = ws.Range("A:A")
11	i = 0
12	FileNumber = FreeFile
13	file = ws.Range("B1")
14	Open file For Input As #FileNumber
15	Do While Not EOF(FileNumber)
16	i = i + 1
17	Line Input # FileNumber, line
18	line = WorksheetFunction.Trim(line)
19	arrayOfElements = Split(line, " ")

20	If i = 5 Then
21	n = UBound(arrayOfElements) - LBound(arrayOfElements) + 1
22	For j = 1 To n - 2
23	ws.Cells(2, j) = arrayOfElements(j - 1)
24	Next j
25	End If
26	If i >= 8 Then
27	n = UBound(arrayOfElements) - LBound(arrayOfElements) + 1
28	If n > 6 Then
29	For j = 0 To 12
30	ws.Cells(i - 5, j + 1) = arrayOfElements(j)
31	Next j
32	End If
33	End If
34	Loop
35	Close #FileNumber
36	ws.Range("L1") = WorksheetFunction.CountA(r) - 2
37	End Sub

In line 14 we open the text file in read-only mode and the number 1 is the way we will refer to the file in the future. As it is the first file that we are reading (and the only one, we must assign it the number 1). In case you are going to work with several files, then it is better to use the **FreeFile** function, which returns an integer with the next file number available.

With the control structure **Do While Not EOF - Loop** (line 15 to line 34), the text file is read line by line.

In line 16 we increase by 1 the value of the variable i, which will be used to keep track of the line that is being read from the text file.

In line 17 we assign to the variable *line* the entire text string that is currently being read in the current line.

In line 18 we use the **WorksheetFunction.Trim** function to eliminate all spaces that are in excess (more than 1 between text strings). Thus, no matter how many spaces there are between each element of the line, a new text string is created with a single space between each of the elements.

In line 19 we create an array that will contain (temporarily) each of the text strings without spaces that it finds, either text or numbers. The **Split** function divides the text string taking into account that each element is separated by a single space and generates an arrangement with that. That is why the instruction of the previous line is important, since the elements of the line are not separated by the same number of spaces.

In line 5 (of the text file that is being read) is where the header of each of the columns is contained. That's why we have that **If - Then** in line 20, so that it extracts the headers from the text file and writes them to the spreadsheet (line 23).

In line 21 we calculate the number of elements that the array has and assign it to the variable n.

Starting from line 8 of the text file, the values resulting from the instrument test begin. Between lines 26 and 33, each of the values that are organized by columns are read. These values are then written to the spreadsheet.

In line 35 we close the file and in line 36, using the **WorksheetFunction.CountA** function, we count the number of lines with information contained in the text file. We write this information in cell L1.

Figure 13.14 shows how the Excel file looks after reading the text file information.

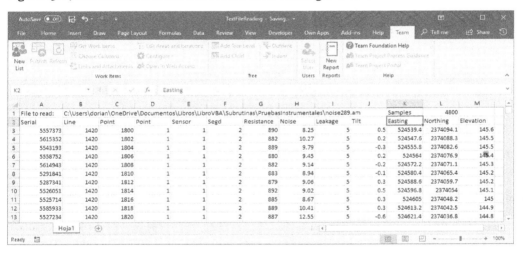

Figure 13.14. Information read from the text file.

Chapter 14. Examples of apps in Visual Basic .NET and VBA-Excel

14.1   Introduction

In the previous chapter we were able to realize the power that VBA-Excel has to make powerful applications. Now, we already know that VBA-Excel is a fairly small version of VB.Net. So, can you imagine making applications in VB.Net or C # that can be incorporated into our programs with VBA-Excel? This would cause the power of our macros to multiply by 1000! (or maybe more). This is what we are going to work on in this chapter. I will show you step by step how to make a library in VB.Net (DLL), how to make add-ons (Add-in) and how they are incorporated into our applications in VBA-Excel.

14.2   Dynamic-Link Libraries (DLL for its acronym in English)

A DLL can be defined as a module that contains functions and data that can be used by other modules. DLL's provide a way to modularize applications whose functionality can be updated and reused more easily. The DLL's also help in reducing the excessive memory drain when several applications use the same functionality at the same time, because, although each application receives its own copy of the DLL data, the applications share the code of the DLL.

In this section we will see some examples of DLL's and how they are invoked from VBA-Excel. At this point, you must have Microsorft Visual Studio installed. For all the examples that will be seen in this book, the Community 2017 version was used. When executing Visual Studio, it is necessary that you do it as Administrator, as can be seen in figure 14.1. This is necessary so that Visual Studio can write in the system registry and so that libraries can be invoked from VBA-Excel.

14.3   Add-In for Excel

An add-in is a library very similar to a dynamic library.It is especially compiled for use in Excel (**.xll**). It allows adding new functionalities to Excel. In this section we will see some examples of Add-Ins that can be used as formulas from a cell in an Excel spreadsheet.

14.4 Simple calculator

Let's start with a simple example. It is a calculator that performs four basic operations: add, subtract, multiply and divide. When running Visual Studio, the first window that appears is like the one shown in figure 14.2.

On the left side of the interface, we select *New Project*. When you do this, the window shown in figure 14.3 appears. In this window we will select the Visual Basic template (left side of the window) -> Windows Classic Desktop -> Class Library (.NET Framework), enclosed in a rectangle in figure 14.3.

Figure 14.1. Running Visual Studio as Administrator.

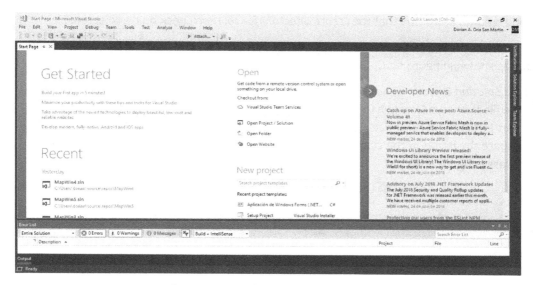

Figure 14.2. Visual Studio main interface.

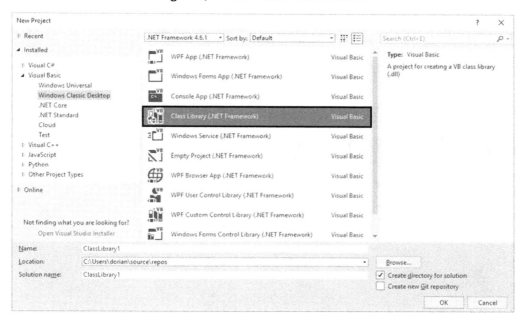

Figure 14.3. Window to select the type of project you want to create.

We are going to call the solution we are creating **CalcSimpleDLL**. This name is added in the *Name* text box. You will notice that as you type here, the contents of the *Solution name* text box are also modified. Select with the *Browse* button the location of the solution that is being created and verify that the *Create directory for solution* check box is selected.

Once this is done, start the creation of the solution. The environment of the solution will look as shown in figure 14.4.

In the *Solution Explorer* window (right side of the window in figure 14.4), change the name of the file that says **Class1.vb** to **calc.vb**. By doing so, the code window will look like the one shown in figure 14.5. Notice how the name of the class changed in the code window (compare the name of the class enclosed in the rectangle of figure 14.5 with the name of the class in figure 14.4).

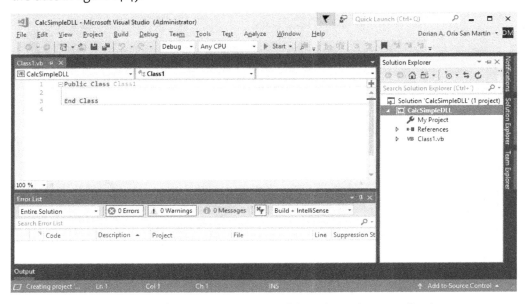

Figure 14.4. Development environment of the CalcSimpleDLL application.

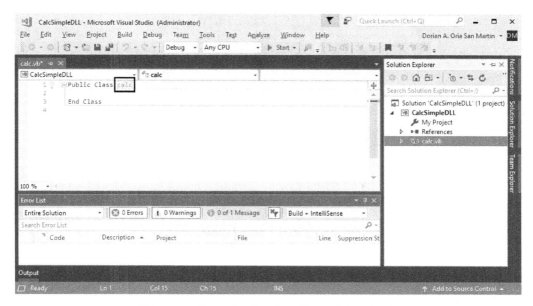

Figure 14.5. Renaming the class Class1.vb by calc.vb.

In the class code window, type the instructions that are between lines 2 and 13 of the code shown below.

Code 14.1.

1	Public Class calc
2	Public Function suma(ByVal a As Double, ByVal b As Double) As Double
3	Return a + b
4	End Function
5	Public Function resta(ByVal a As Double, ByVal b As Double) As Double
6	Return a - b
7	End Function
8	Public Function producto(ByVal a As Double, ByVal b As Double) As Double
9	Return a * b
10	End Function
11	Public Function division(ByVal a As Double, ByVal b As Double) As Double
12	Return a / b
13	End Function
14	End Class

The code window should look as shown in figure 14.6.

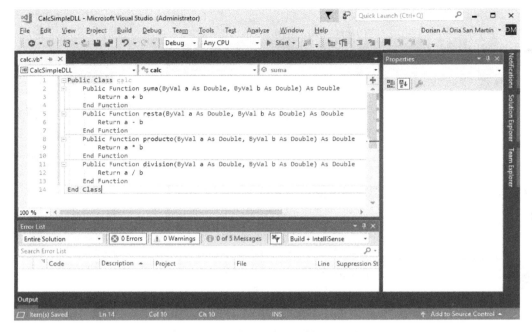

Figure 14.6. CalcSimpleDLL library code.

Let's go now to the project properties window. To go there we must select Project -> CalcSimpleDLL Properties, as shown in figure 14.7. Once this is done, the window will look as shown in figure 14.8. In this window we will select *Application* (on the left side of the window) and on the right side we will press the button that says *Assembly Information...* When doing so, the window shown in figure 14.9 will appear. In this window we must verify that the *Make assembly COM-Visible* box is selected as can be seen in figure 14.10. This step is necessary for the library to be used by COM clients. COM (Component Object Model) is a method to share binary code between different applications and languages.

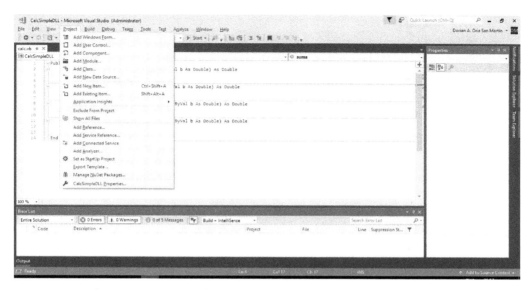

Figure 14.7. Access to the property editing window of the CalcSimpleDLL library.

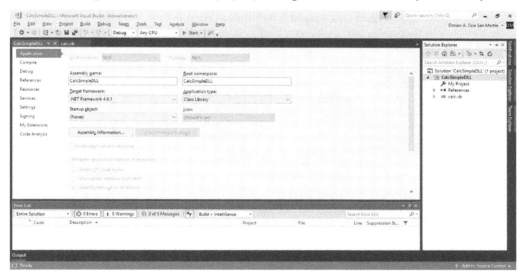

Figure 14.8. Editing properties of the CalcSimpleDLL library.

Now, returning to figure 14.8, select the *Compile* option (left side of the window, below *Application*). We must go to the end of the window that is displayed on the right side, until we find a box that says Register for COM interop. Once this option is selected, we will change the option of *Debug* to *Release* in *Solutions Configuration* (combo box enclosed in rectangle in figure 14.11).

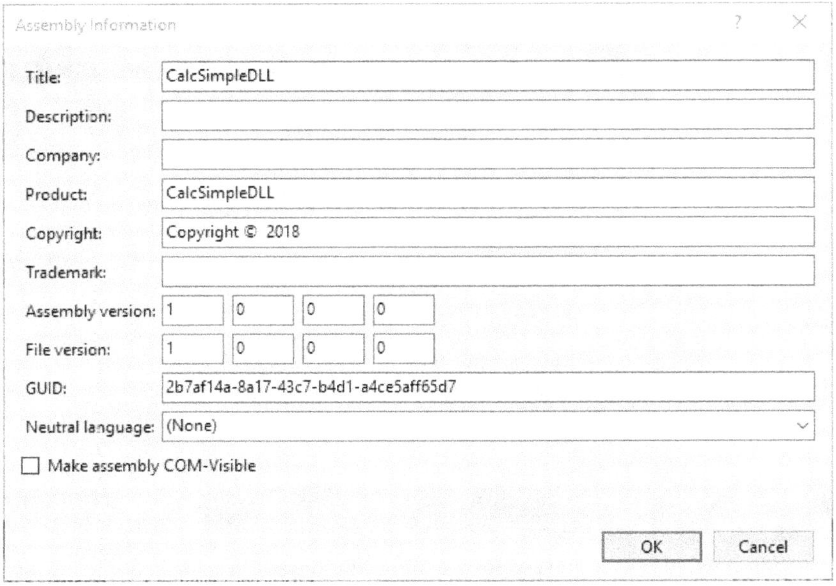

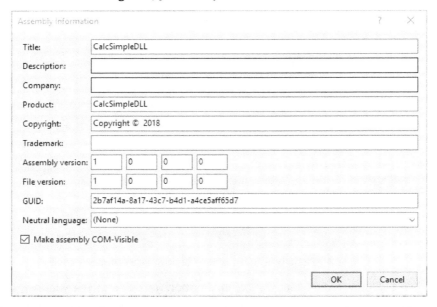

Figure 14.9. Assembly Information Window.

Figura 14.10. Assembly Information window with the option Make assembly COM-Visible selected.

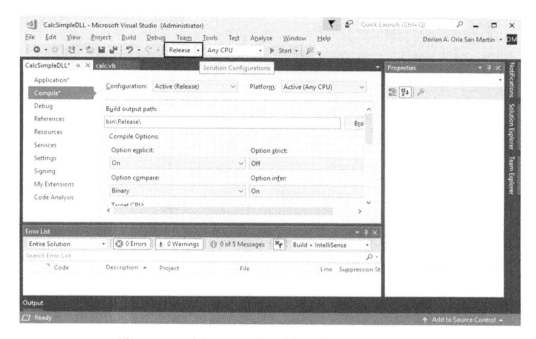

Figure 14.11. Editing properties of the CalcSimpleDLL library.

Save the project and now build the solution. To do this we go to Build -> Build Solution, as shown in figure 14.12.

If the process finishes successfully, the window of your application will look as shown in figure 14.13.

The library is now ready to be used in VBA-Excel. The next step is to create an Excel file enabled for macros. Once this is done, we go to the Visual Basic environment and there we select from the menu the option Tools -> References, as shown in figure 14.14. Once done, the window shown in figure 14.15 will appear. In this window we will search the library file (with the Browse button). Remember that, as described in figure 14.11, the Release mode was chosen for the elaboration of our library. Figure 14.16 shows the navigation through the Windows directories to find our library. The search path is the one that was established at the beginning of the creation of the solution in the Location text box (figure 14.3). The file that we are going to select is the one with extension .tlb, as shown in figure 14.16. The file with extension **.tlb** (type library) is a binary file that contains information about the properties and methods of a COM object (in our case of the created library) in a form that can be accessible for other applications at run time.

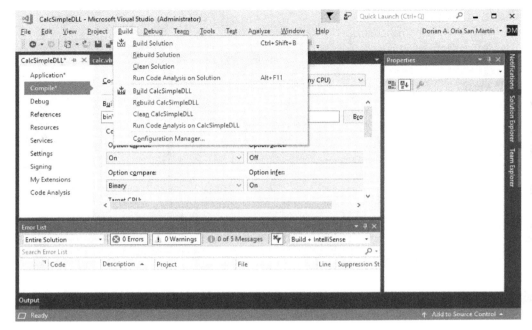

Figure 14.12. Building Solution.

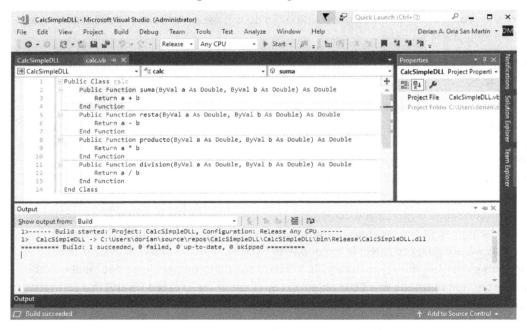

Figure 14.13. Successful completion of the application building process.

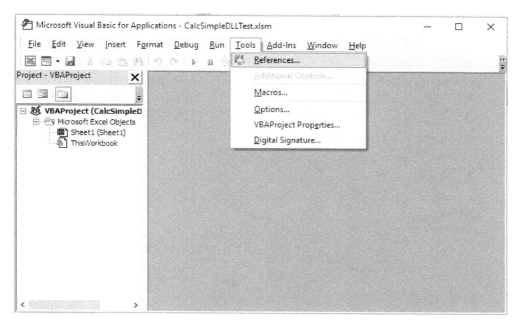

Figure 14.14. Steps to open the References window.

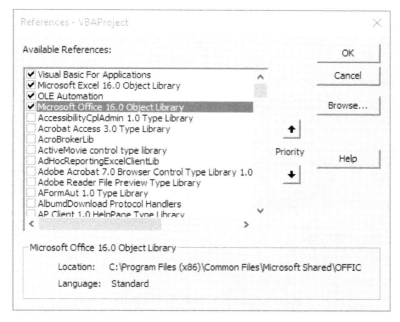

Figure 14.15. References window.

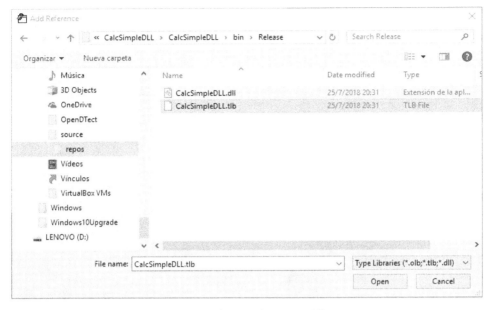

Figure 14.16. Selecting the created library.

By selecting the .tlb file and opening it, the window shown in figure 14.15 will now look as shown in figure 14.17, reflecting the selected library.

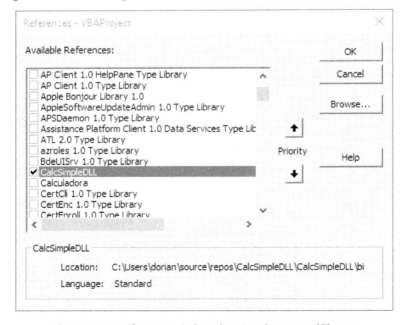

Figure 14.17. Reference window showing the created library.

Now comes the most anticipated moment: the moment to use the library created. To do this, insert a module and then copy and paste the code shown below.

Subroutine 14.1.

1	Sub TestDll()
2	Dim s As CalcSimpleDLL.calc
3	Dim x, y As Double
4	Set s = New CalcSimpleDLL.calc
5	x = 4.3
6	y = 5.2
7	MsgBox "The sum of " & x & " + " & y & " = " & s.suma(x, y) _
8	& vbNewLine & "The subtraction of " & x & " - " & y & " = " & s.resta(x, y) _
9	& vbNewLine & "The multiplication of " & x & " * " & y & " = " & s.producto(x, y) _
10	& vbNewLine & "The division of " & x & " / " & y & " = " & _
11	Format(s.division(x, y), "0.00")
12	End Sub

As the code is written, you will see that Intellisense recognizes the library that you want to use, as shown in figure 14.18.

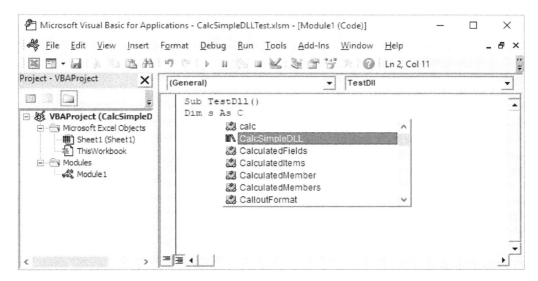

Figure 14.18. Introduction of the sample subroutine code in VBA-Excel.

Let's now analyze the code of the subroutine. In line 2 the declaration of a variable is made so that it will refer to the library that we have created. Notice that next to the name of the library it is necessary to add the name of the class (in our case calc) where the functions we want to use are (suma, resta, producto and division, as shown in the code 4.1).

The library is an object for VBA. That's why the **Set** instruction in line 3 is used to create a reference to the library.

Now let's see how it works. If I want to add two numbers, the instruction s.suma(x, y) is used (the rest of the functions can be seen in figure 14.13). Note that the order is important, since the order in which the values (or variables) are placed when the invocation is made, in the same order the values are passed to the function that will perform the operation. That is, in our example we are adding "x" and "y". When we pass those values to the suma function of our library, "x" becomes "a" in our function and "y" becomes "b".

When executing subroutine 14.1, the window shown in figure 14.19 appears.

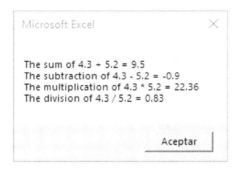

Figure 14.19. Result of the execution of subroutine 14.1.

Now, we are going to use some small changes in the 14.1 code so that it can be used as an add-in. For this, we repeat all the steps that were explained until figure 14.6. To differentiate it from the dynamic library project, we have called this project **CalcSimpleAddOn**. In the first line of code 14.1, let's change the word Class to Module. We add a number 2 at the end to the names of the functions. The new code will be as shown below.

Code 14.2.

```
1   Public Module calc
2       Public Function suma2(ByVal a As Double, ByVal b As Double) As Double
3           Return a + b
4       End Function
5       Public Function resta2(ByVal a As Double, ByVal b As Double) As Double
6           Return a - b
7       End Function
8       Public Function producto2(ByVal a As Double, ByVal b As Double) As Double
9           Return a * b
```

10	End Function
11	Public Function division2(ByVal a As Double, ByVal b As Double) As Double
12	Return a / b
13	End Function
14	End Module

After these changes, repeat the steps explained between figures 14.7 and 14.10.

Because we are working with the Community version of Visual Studio, we must add a library so that the library we develop can be used as an add-on in Excel. This library is called **Excel-DNA** and to install it you must do the following: follow the path from the Tools menu -> NuGet Package Manager -> Package Manager Console, as shown in figure 14.20.

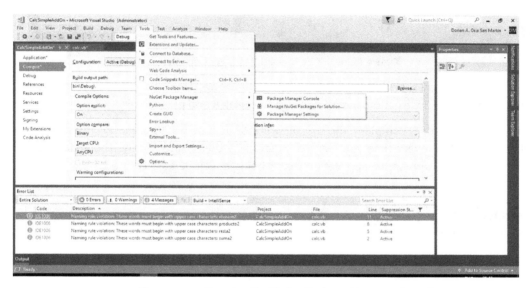

Figure 14.20. Opening the NuGet Package Manager Console.

After this step is completed, the Visual Studio development interface looks as shown in figure 14.21.

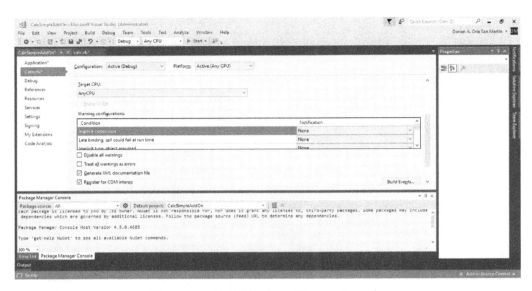

Figure 14.21. NuGet Package Manager Console.

The console is shown enclosed in a rectangle in figure 14.21. In this window, where the cursor is, write the instruction: **Install-Package Excel-DNA** and press *Enter*.

Once the installation is complete, the console will look as shown in figure 14.22. This process must be repeated every time you want to create an Add-In, since during the installation other files related only to the application that is being developed are created.

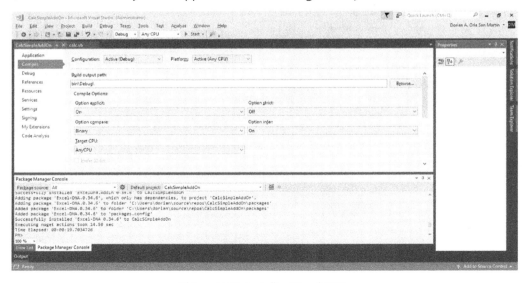

Figure 14.22. Installing Excel-DNA.

We are ready to build the application (from the step described in figure 14.11). Once this step is completed, we go to Excel to use our add-on. Let's create an Excel file like the one shown in figure 14.23.

In the DEVELOPER tab, we click on the Excel Add-ins button and this makes the window shown in figure 14.24 appear. With the Browse button we look for the control that we want to add.

In the search window, we select the Add-In, as shown in figure 14.25. Once this is done, the window shown in figure 14.24 will look as shown in figure 14.26, showing the newly added Add-In. Our Add-In is ready to be used.

To prove it, in cell D4 of the created spreadsheet, write suma2 (which is one of the functions that our Add-In has). By doing this, *IntelliSense* will display the available function as shown in figure 14.27. Test the function by inputting the values that are in cells D1 and D2. The function will be seen as shown in figure 14.28. If you test all the functions, the spreadsheet will look as shown in figure 14.29.

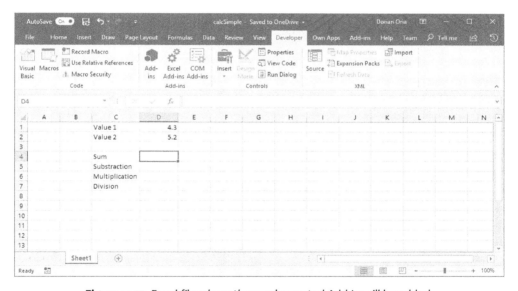

Figure 14.23. Excel file where the newly created Add-In will be added.

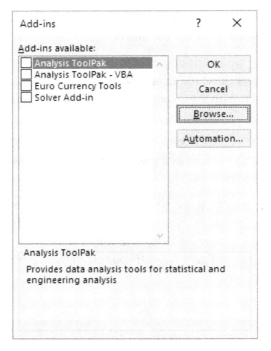

Figure 14.24. Add-ins window.

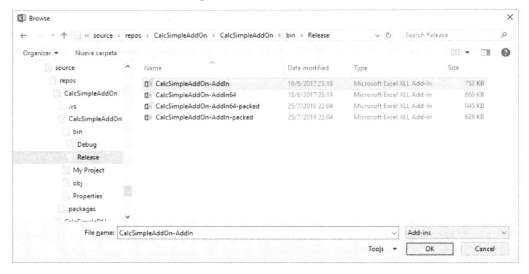

Figure 14.25. Selecting the Add-In.

Figure 14.26. Added Add-In.

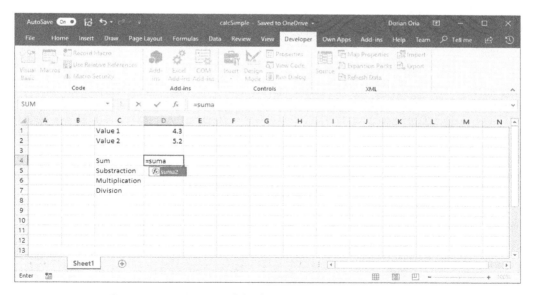

Figure 14.27. Using one of the functions contained in the Add-In.

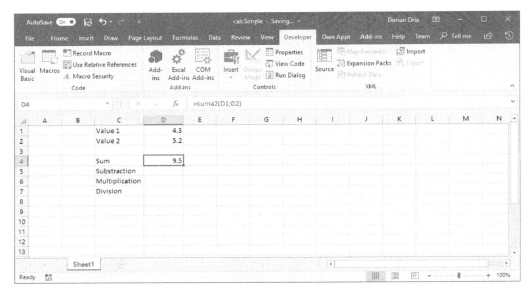

Figure 14.28. Using the Add-In with added parameters.

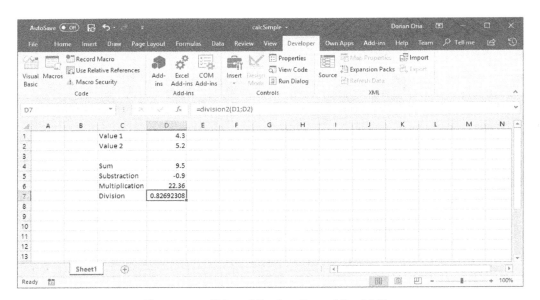

Figure 14.29. Using all the functions of the Add-In.

References

1. **DeMarco, Jim (2008).** Pro Excel 2007 VBA. Apress Publisher.

2. https://brainwavelaboratories.com/las-ondas-cerebrales-vision-general/

3. **Nakamura, Shoichiro (1998).** Métodos Numéricos Aplicados con Software. Prentice Hall.

4. **Roman, Steven (2002).** Writing Excel Macros with VBA. 2nd edition. O'Reilly Publisher.

5. **Walkenbach, John (2013).** Microsoft Excel VBA Programming for Dummies. 3rd edition. John Wiley & Sons, Inc.

www.ingramcontent.com/pod-product-compliance
Lightning Source LLC
Chambersburg PA
CBHW080622060326
40690CB00021B/4787